The Sacred Bombshell Handbook of Self-Love

The 11 Forbidden Secrets of Feminine Power

Abiola Abrams

Love University Press, New York NY

El Dorado Publishing/Love University Press
The Sacred Bombshell Handbook of Self-Love
Abiola Abrams

Copyeditor: Alissa McGowan
Cover Design: Lan Gao
Interior Design: Richard A. Dueñez

Abiola Abrams
244 Fifth Avenue #A268
New York, NY 10001
www.AbiolaTV.com

Sacred Bombshell Handbook/Abiola Abrams——1st ed.
ISBN 978-0-9660707-8-1

The Sacred Bombshell Handbook of Self-Love

Namaste.
The divine bombshell in me
sees the divine bombshell in you

"Does it come as a surprise /
That I dance like I've got diamonds /
At the meeting of my thighs?"
—Dr. Maya Angelou, *"Still I Rise"*

Table of Contents

Bombshell Invocation   ix

Foreword   xi

Introduction   1

The Secret of Creation   23

The Secret of Radical Self-Being   55

The Secret of Receptivity   87

The Secret of Emotions   125

The Secret of Self-Devotion   157

The Secret of Fullness   201

The Secret of Authenticity   241

The Secret of Nizhoni   271

The Secret of Releasing   301

The Secret of Abundance   339

The Secret of Ubuntu   367

Afterword   383

Interview Index   393

Sacred Bombshell Invocation

Release and surrender.
Breathe fully, deeply, and with great intention.
Light your candle or incense.

Gently close your eyes and enjoy the moment of silence.
Release negative thoughts as they impede your flow.

Invite a connection to your spirit.
Ask for anything that your heart and spirit desire.
Proclaim your intention out loud with an open, pure heart.

How else will the goddesses hear you and grant you favor?

Be still as your intention soars through the ether.

Express your gratitude and say quietly, "It is done."

—Donna D'Cruz, Rasa Living Expert in Meditation and Rituals

Foreword

Abiola Abrams and I have a history. I loved her from the moment I met her. We're on the same journey and I love that. You must love, cherish, and honor yourself. That's what *The Sacred Bombshell Handbook of Self-Love* will teach you.

I think what makes me a bombshell is that I have come full circle. Ask yourself: "Am I in the same place, doing the same things over and over again?" If the answer is yes, ask yourself why. When you step out and try something different, you will see things in a different light. Don't be afraid of change. It's the only way.

When I first met Abiola I was on the path of acting and writing in New York City and I was trying to make ends meet. I was really good at bartending and every year I got a bigger and bigger following. One of my clients said, "Why don't you open a restaurant? Instead of working for someone else, work for yourself. I will back you."

So I went on the journey of finding my restaurant and then I got diagnosed with breast cancer at the age of 33. I was so ashamed. At that point, I owned a restaurant called Haven and I just didn't know how to deal with it. I pushed the whole thing under the rug.

Two years later I got breast cancer again, diagnosed at Stage Four. It was two weeks before my wedding. This rocked my world. I didn't even want to talk about it because I was so embarrassed. I didn't want people to say, "Oh gosh, she has cancer. She's about to die." You don't want to scare other people. You don't know what to tell them.

They gave me three months to live. My doctor told me, "If you believe in miracles, maybe a miracle can happen."

I walked out and I said, "I believe in God and I believe in miracles."

My faith got stronger. I just got on my knees and I prayed, "God, if it's my time, then it's my time. But if it's not, I'm a fighter. Give me the tools to fight because I want to fight to live."

I started doing the work. Doing the work is soul searching,

meditating, praying, and reading. Little by little, I changed the way I thought. I changed who I was. I started getting into myself. I became a vegan. I got into juicing. I had a regimen. I started exercising every day. I changed my whole belief system and declared, "I am a warrior. I'm going to beat this."

Every year, my doctor would say, "Wow, Bershan! The tests are looking good."

I'm now considered "no evidence of disease."

This experience changed me for the better because now my life is about giving back. Before, maybe I was selfish; I was thinking only about me. Now it's not about me. Life is bigger than me. I know my purpose. I want to help people who are stuck or lost because when you're near death and someone tells you that you have three months to live, you don't know what to do. When you come out of that you say, "I have a purpose in my life."

My purpose is to show you that you don't have to live in fear. My journey is to help facilitate positive change in people's lives. I now help others heal through human connection. I do that as a motivational speaker, certified life coach, and CEO of my inspirational community, URAWarrior.com, where I share my stories and yours.

Don't suffer in silence. You don't have to stay stuck. As Abiola also teaches, step into your greatness. If your default setting right now is set to self-hate, fear, confusion, and drama, then it's time to reset yourself to self-love, abundance, prosperity, and self-confidence.

I am a bombshell because I do the work on myself. I am a bombshell because I don't live in fear. I am a bombshell because I try to be the best person that I can be. Looks fade. Pretty hair and strong bodies fade, but character lives forever. I try to get better and better each day.

Bombshell Bershan is making a stamp on life because I am a bombshell warrior. You picked up this book because it's your bombshell time, too. Own your bombshell power and step into your greatness.

—Bershan Shaw, Star of *Love in the City*,
Oprah Winfrey Network

Introduction: Own Your Bombshell

This book is not for everybody. I wrote it just for you.

The Sacred Bombshell Handbook of Self-Love is for my superwomen who do too much, my ladies-still-in-waiting, the diva who fears that she is not yet the woman she was born to be. *The Sacred Bombshell Handbook of Self-Love* is for the woman who looks around one day and says, "Oh crap. What if my whole life has been wrong?" I wrote this guide for the woman who wakes up and wonders who the stranger in bed is, even though she is you.

Come closer, gorgeous. Slip off your heels. Consider yourself at home. Please, leave the door open.

If you are looking for a perfect guru, then kindly cross the street. If you came to the party to judge, well — this is not that kind of party. If you feel uneasy implementing modern magic, then this book may not for you … yet. No matter what, it's okay. Be where you are. There is no race. This is a judgment-free zone where we welcome, accept, acknowledge, and co-create miracles. This book is not about female superiority of any kind. We celebrate the sacred feminine and the sacred masculine equally. You must only be willing (just *willing*) to imagine that you can love yourself without conditions, that your life can be more, and that you are in fact already complete. This is a book for women who want to be *for* themselves rather than *against* something or someone else.

If you're looking for a sign, this is it. There's a Feminine Evolution taking place around us and within us. *The Sacred Bombshell Handbook of Self-Love* is your invitation and initiation to become the woman you were born to be and to finally live the life you were born to live. Welcome. By reading past this point, you are agreeing to go on a journey. Consider this a vision quest to the center of yourself. Your bombshell self is that most empowered part of you, the part of you that knows your true worth. When I say "own your bombshell," I mean own what you believe about yourself, own your story, own loving yourself without apology, and own how you move in the world.

Did you feel that? Every time a woman makes a decision to stop hating herself, there's a seismic shift in the universe. The very tectonic plates just shifted because of YOU.

How to Know if This Is Your Journey

- Are you tired of feeling stuck?
- With "everything you have going for you" is something still missing?
- Are you capable of far more than your current situation?
- Do you feel like you're running out of time?
- Most importantly, are you still waiting to step into your greatness?

This book is for Jeanette from Facebook, Lexi from YouTube, and Mia from Twitter. This book is for Toni, 38, an incest survivor who tracked down my number and called me one night crying after seeing me give advice on a talk show. For Vicky, 31, who begged me to help her stop overeating and leave her boyfriend. For Nita, 42, who left her native country, came here to sing, received a standing ovation, and is too terrified to perform again. This book is all yours.

Melanie added me to her team to help heal her ideas about love when, at 36, she was in line to make junior partner. She was beautiful, rich, and desperately lonely. As the only brown woman at her law firm, Melanie felt that she had no right to want more. The problem was that she wanted much more than the one night stands that were her only connection. Melanie wanted a full life with friends, freedom, and the perfect husband that she was promised if she followed "their" rules. This book is for Melanie.

I met Circe when I was in graduate school. She was an affluent Southern belle in her 50s trying to reclaim the free-spirited artist she once had been. When she whispered, "This is not who I really am," I didn't know what she meant. She confided that although she looked like an uptight Daughters of the Confederacy housewife, she did not feel comfortable in that world. Inside she was a wild, edgy, non-conformist. I wrote this book for Circe.

I met Manny when he organized a bookstore reading for my debut novel **Dare**. He rightly called **Dare** a self-help book disguised as fiction and chanted its affirmations daily. Manny saw himself as a Diana Ross's little sister. He wanted to sing, dance, and rock life in a purple skirt. I leave the door to this feminine power guide open for Manny.

A shocking study called "The Paradox of Declining Female Happiness" published in the **American Economic Journal** revealed that although we women are more educated, healthier, and richer than ever before, there is greater unhappiness. It's time for us to get filled up with the sacred power of self-love rather than all the empty goods we fill our lives with. When a woman is in love with herself, she empowers her partners, children, family, and friends. If she chooses to have no partner or children, then she is a spark for her community.

The Tao of Bombshell: The Four Core Bombshell Beliefs

1. I am only in a relationship with myself. My life reflects the love I feel for me. I must see myself as the Universe sees me.

2. There is nothing more important than feeling good, being with goodness, and accepting my highest good. This is my birthright.

3. I am fully responsible for myself, my life, and my personal power. Anything else is just a story.

4. Being willing to welcome feminine energy – femergy – is the pathway to my Self.

About Your Bombshell Breakthrough Coach

Greetings, Bombshell! I'm Abiola, your coach, sister traveler, and love-body-spirit guide on this journey. As a teacher and student, I am honored and humbled that you chose me as your sacred partner in activating the deluxe bundle of love, consciousness, and soul power that is you. Welcome to your inner bombshell r/evolution!

I am a fourth generation conjure woman. My great-grandmother was a midwife and women's fertility healer in Guyana, South America. Great-Aunt Irene's home was an unofficial bed-and-breakfast-style sanctuary. My mother was a teacher and remains the family advice-giver. My father is a journalist and a minister. He was also a freedom fighter.

When I first felt called to do this sacred work, I fought it with every inch of my knowing. I balked and flat-out refused. I figured that I could take a more hands-off and artistic approach. I spent the last 15 years using written, broadcast, and theatrical media to teach, coach, and empower women, and tell our stories.

The lessons in this book have been transformative not only for my coaching clients but for me personally. I have used the tools here to overcome many of my personal demons. I have battled disordered eating and body image issues, social anxiety, being bullied, workaholism, and trust and abandonment issues. I have pushed karma to the edge and reveled in the hot buttered mess – and I am still a sacred work-in-progress. I come to you not from on high, but heart-to-heart. You and I are one in the same.

Whereas my great-grandmother helped women give birth to babies, I help women give birth to themselves. So cheers to you! You have decided to birth yourself. Congratulations on taking this step toward becoming the woman that you were born to be.

Sign your Bombshell Manifesta contract at SacredBombshell. com.

What Is a Sacred Bombshell? Reframed and Redefined

Traditionally, the word "bombshell" has been used to mean a woman oozing with sex appeal. It is no accident that to "drop a bombshell" means to drop a surprise bomb, good or bad, into someone's life. A woman who knows her power is a force ignited.

Some women merely wear the label of bombshell. These Surface Bombshells tend to frequent music videos, men's magazines, and sometimes Instagram. That's okay. We never hate on another woman for the choices she makes. We have made some of these choices ourselves, haven't we? Still, that's not what this book is about.

Bombshell, for our purposes, is not a look. Bombshell is a way of being. Our objective is to bomb the shell of who you have been in favor of who you are becoming. It's a journey for a bombed-out shell to remember that she's a Sacred Bombshell.

Let us decree that a Sacred Bombshell is a woman who unconditionally loves, honors, and accepts herself – a woman in full ownership of herself and her divinely ordained feminine power. She is flesh and blood and sacred all at the same time. A bombshell adores her womanly self. Yes, a bombshell is force to be reckoned with. We're talking about women like Dr. Maya Angelou, Eve Ensler, Oprah Winfrey, and Gloria Steinem. We also include traditional bombshells like Dorothy Dandridge, Marilyn Monroe, Halle Berry, Sofia Vergara, Beyoncé Knowles, and Sophia Loren. First ladies like Eleanor Roosevelt and Michelle Obama are also Sacred Bombshells. The beautiful Venus and Serena Williams are bombshells, as is Jennifer Lopez.

Yes, a true bombshell is skilled in the fine art of seducing life, but she is firstly head-over-heels in love with herself – mind, body, and spirit. A Sacred Bombshell knows how to use the power of her emotions to manifest joy that others only dream of. If naysayers think that she is a witch or a bitch, it doesn't matter because a true bombshell doesn't care what "they" think.

This is a book about how to be your own bombshell. You weren't born to live a puny, cowardly, love-starved life. That's what we call a Dry Life Crisis. You deserve to live and thrive without being crippled by fear. Bid a fond farewell to your ready-to-wear, one-size-fits-all method of half-living. When you tap into your fullness, you will manifest more blessings than you ever thought possible.

How do you own your bombshell? As a prophet once wrote, "Let the weak say I am strong." Claim it. Call your power into existence, and then welcome it into your life.

What Is Femergy?

"The masculine side of love is 'I love you.'
Love's feminine quality is 'I am waiting for you. I
am longing for you.'"
—Llewellyn Vaughan-Lee

Femergy is my term for feminine energy. Before you dismiss energy, have you ever felt someone's eyes on you or thought of someone and there they were? That's because we're all energetic beings. Each of us have both yin (divine feminine energy) and yang (divine masculine energy) within us. As a daughter of the feminist movement, I fought these concepts for a long time. After all, any kind of essentialism – the idea that one gender might have something "native" to its biological members – has been used to keep women small in the past. As an African-American womanist, the idea was especially dangerous to me.

We are taught to never acknowledge any differences between men and women – that men and women are exactly the same. This is simply not true, and I wouldn't want it to be. Feminine energy makes us feel self-loving, in tune, brilliant, powerful, and full. Because I am in my femergy, I find masculine energy attractive, powerful, heat-giving, and equally brilliant. Why would we want to be the same? This womb-anly journey is not politically correct.

Rather, we all have both the divine feminine and the awakened masculine within us, and we are all either more masculine energy or more feminine energy individuals. Regardless of your gender or sexual orientation, your sexual essence can be either masculine or feminine, or more rarely, neutral. Feminine energy is intuitive, receptive, process-oriented, creatively unstructured, and attracting, like a negatively charged magnet. Masculine energy is assertive, directed, focused, and goal-oriented, like a positively charged magnet.

The feminine yin wants to be filled up. The masculine yang wants to be emptied. It is this polarity that we all seek. The feminine desires to be loved and the masculine desires to love. So when we feminine energy women are yang-heavy, we are out of balance. A woman centered in her divine feminine power, in contrast, is radiant, vibrant, and attracting. This is irresistible to masculine energy.

This is not about stereotypes, but rather about magnetism and duality. We're not talking about if you're a male-bodied person or a female-bodied person. If you are a woman standing more in your masculine energy and that's healthy for you, that's great. I'm speaking only to those who feel like things aren't working, regardless of biological gender. If you feel a personal deficit, you may be craving feminine energy. And no matter what your own ideal energy balance, we each need a complimentary opposite-energy partner to have a balanced relationship and steamy intimate life.

So why don't we already know this?

Our mothers couldn't teach us the lost power of femergy – truly embracing and loving ourselves – if they didn't know it themselves. So instead they taught us that in order to survive and get ahead, we had to out-man anyone else – and rightfully so. The world we live in values yang energy traits such as achievement, competitive spirit, and linear thinking. Whether they used the word feminism or not, we often saw these strong women playing both mother and father even when there was a father figure in the household. Many of us were taught to despise our "cursed" bodies and to be suspicious of other women.

You may be thinking, "I thought feminism made us all equal.

What's all of this masculine/feminine crap?" Pithy ads that reduce our feminine essence to a body part, or comical representations like the horny "inner goddess" of *50 Shades of Grey* leave us giggling or angry but still lost. It's enough to make the average woman say there is no such thing as the sacred feminine. After all, it can sound like a load of bull when we haven't been taught to value our bodies or ourselves.

This has nothing to do with traditionally marketed patriarchal ideas of femininity or masculinity. We see masculinity depicted as kicking back brews, watching sports, or yelling "you're fired" at adversaries. Femininity is portrayed as sipping sugary cocktails with girlfriends, crying into ice cream when feeling hormonal, and cartwheeling through pansies via "feminine protection" ads. We are taught that masculine "doing" energy is superior to feminine "feeling" energy; that competition trumps cooperation.

We wouldn't be so confused if we knew that the answer begins right within the bodies we spend so much time hating. Divine feminine power is the mojo that creates life. However, (for those who choose to procreate) we don't give birth alone. The female's egg has to be fertilized by the male's sperm – even in a test tube. We forget this fact of nature when we're burned out and screaming, "I don't need anybody!"

So how do we access our sacred feminine power? Of course, that's what this book is all about.

My Big Fat Bombshell Diary: The Starter Husband

"I don't want to be a wife; I only want to be a bride!"

I cracked this joke with my virtual bridal buddies on TheKnot. com, at the Brooklyn bridal shower given by his family, at my bridal tea party in Bronxville, during my traditional Guyanese Queh-Queh pre-wedding celebration, after my bachelorette party, and during my rehearsal dinner in Montego Bay.

The only time I didn't tell this stupid joke was three months after we were married when my new husband's phone butt-dialed me by accident from his jacket pocket. Because both of my names start with "Ab," I'm the first person in everyone's phone. People's phones accidentally dial me all day. "I don't want to be a wife; I only want to be a bride!" May you get what you wish for.

On the morning of December 4, 2004, we removed my beloved Aunt Silvy from life support. She was one of the few people on the planet who I knew believed in me with her very soul. Aunt Silvy, who had given me a loving "support the bride" foot massage only three months earlier on the day of my dream wedding. Aunt Silvy, who found out the evening that we returned from our honeymoon that she had cancer.

On that day in December, my Dear Husband made his apologies that he couldn't be there with me for the tragic, life-ending event. Henry had to be in Washington, D.C. for business. Of course I understood. So when Henry's number popped up on my phone, I assumed he was calling to check in on me. You know, share in my grief and give his condolences. I answered in tears.

"Teddybear," I said, using my nickname for him. Instead of "Hey baby," I heard lots of laughing. First Henry's voice, and then a woman's voice that I did not recognize. Then, glasses clinking and banter with a waitress.

"Thank you for coming to Caroline's!"

Caroline's? Henry was apparently at a comedy club. He was also on a date. My new husband was on a date with another woman in New York City – our city – just three months after our wedding. On the same day we removed my aunt from life support. For the next four hours, I sat motionless in my craptastic beige living room cradling the phone to my wet face while the air slowly seeped out of the room.

I listened to my husband and the fun mystery woman leave the club for drinks and then leave drinks for her apartment. I was eavesdropping on an insane reality show: *The Bachelor* meets *Cheaters*. I heard them yucking it up while he quizzed her about her adventures with Ecstasy. Ecstasy? Who was this man?

Did she know he was married? Was he was wearing his ring? Was this really happening? When they pulled up in front of her apartment and he said, "So this is where you live," I hung up. To hear any more would have been too much.

I never had a chance to be a wife, only a bride. I thought I had found my prince, but the ugly-ass glass slippers hurt like hell when he turned into a toad.

My marriage was over before it started. Before our photographer finished the gilded-silver wedding albums. Before I could get my carefully chosen ecru – not ivory, not white, not crème, not pearl – Cinderella-style wedding gown to the cleaners. Before we made our Jamaican nuptials that were legal worldwide complete in the States. Before the ridiculous "Our Story" documentary wedding video was complete. My marriage was over before my Aunt Silvy – the second sister my mother had lost in six months – was buried. And I had just sent out the thank you notes. Damn.

I didn't make it to our huge, four-poster Victorian bed that night. I fell asleep curled into a tight ball on the cold, shiny hardwood floor. I couldn't even gather the brain cells to remember to turn up the thermostat. The idiot who runs the picture show in my dreams kept replaying our wedding and then the phone call. My Inner Bully taunted me with funny little details like how in Henry's vows, he'd promised to love me forever. *Forever.* How he had dramatically refused to sign the ceremonial Ketubah-style contract at the reception. I thought about how we'd had my aunt's leg amputated to save her but it was too late. I was at the hospital – alone – that night, too.

Henry came striding in the next morning, jaunty and energetic. I was shocked that he was still handsome. You'd think that dirty deeds would stamp themselves on the face of the perpetrator to warn off others.

"Hey babe, how are you feeling?" he asked, barely looking over.

I was still in the living room, freshly showered now and wearing beige pajamas that blended completely into the couch. I had been crying so hard for so long that I no longer had a headache. The dull hammering just seemed like my natural state of mind.

"As you would expect, I guess," I almost whispered. "How was your business trip?"

Henry shook his head and in a burst of delirium I thought he would explain that I was mistaken. Yes! Somehow wires had gotten crossed and I had heard the wrong radio play.

Instead he said, "You know DC. Crazy with egos and everybody wants to be king. Gotta watch who you hook up with." Then my husband started to spin a colorful tale about his idiot business partners.

"Were any of them at Caroline's last night with that woman?" I blurted out.

I didn't get married intending to be divorced; but that's everyone's story, right? And when my marriage ended, there was no one to confide in. My mother and my entire family were dealing with intense grief and I felt like too much of a loser to tell even my closest friends what had happened. After my big, fabulous, flashy wedding for 75 of our closest loved ones at the Ritz Carlton in Montego Bay, Jamaica, I was the lucky one. The charmed one who had gotten her man to put a ring on it. The actual chick posing with her fiancé for an annoying story in **Modern Bride**. We were living in Westchester County for goddess's sake! There is no divorce in Westchester.

Game. Set. Match. But the match wasn't over because after the lovely wedding I had to go home and start a life with him. Even before the cheating, there were clear issues. And neither Nicola, the persnickety wedding planner, nor the snow white doves were there to help. I had sentenced myself to a man who brought dinner home only for himself and labeled it with his name in our fridge. He padlocked his den because I cleaned the attached private bathroom, shooting meaner and meaner insults at every turn. One day while I made lunch for him to take to work, he informed me that I no longer had to do so as his secretary would be bringing him food from home.

Dr. Maya Angelou calls this being "pecked to death by ducks."

She says that some people don't have the nerve to just grab your throat so they snatch little pieces of you instead. Henry didn't have the courage to say, "I love you but I don't want to marry you," so instead he picked at me a little more each day. And for my part, I didn't have the courage to honor his feelings. He was reacting like a creature caged against his will. I take full responsibility because I taught him that this was an acceptable way to treat me.

When someone shows you who they are, trust it the first time. Henry had cheated on me before. I had caught him having an emotional affair with the clear intent to make it physical a few months before the wedding. "He just has cold feet," I told myself. I even consoled the other woman when she called me crying! But at least I wasn't single, right?

Whoa. I used to get *pissed off* at myself looking at that rundown. Yeah, sure, it looks hella obvious all listed out like that, but like in any situation there were tons of good times in the nine happy years before we got married. The hard truth is that I was angrier at myself than I could ever be at him because I never should have married him in the first place. In my heart of hearts, I knew better. But my actions show that I thought that any man was better than no man. Henry had expressed his fear of commitment numerous times but I felt that if I could just get him down the aisle then we could work through everything else.

What was my problem? I was no weeping willow. I was a proud, card-carrying feminist. I gave talks and workshops on empowerment. I directed festival award-winning art movies about personal power.

Still, even before the cheating, I made excuses about how Henry hadn't received enough love. *I* would show him unconditional love. *I* would save him. *I* would rescue him from himself. What a pompous crock of self-righteous excrement.

After he was busted, my DH begged for forgiveness. He threw himself on the mercy of the "court" and bought my parents' favor by remodeling my mother's kitchen as a "thanks for the wedding" gift. He was just "going through a quarter-life crisis," he explained. He needed me to give him a year to sort himself out. Dummy that I saw myself as at the time, I thought, *What's one year over the next 50 plus that we'll be married?*

I was ashamed that my marriage – my life – had fallen apart so quickly. I had to give us a chance to fix it. Surely it was somehow my fault. I was traveling too often for work. I was back in LA about a month after our wedding. Plus, it couldn't have been easy for him having a spouse who was broke all the time. I was in grad school, working as a teaching artist to make ends meet. I had to give him a chance to make amends.

We made a farce of appearing at events like everything was okay. "The newlyweds are here," friends and family would shout. We sat together awkwardly at my cousin's wedding and then at Henry's best man's nuptials. As the loving couples stood on the brink of their new lives, I wanted to object, to stand up and scream, "This is not worth it. You'll see! RUN!"

So many people are there for the commencement of a marriage. For the good cheer. But when it was all over who was there? No one. Just me in one corner and him in another. With breakup grief bearing witness between us.

Healing My Body with Femergy

"You, yourself, as much as anybody else in the entire universe, deserve your love and affection."
—Buddha

One of the ways that I coped with the aftermath of being suddenly single was with emotional eating. Food became my intimate friend and I pushed my body into a state of ill health and well-styled, still-cute fatness. Eating until I couldn't feel anything became an almost daily practice.

The metaphysicians always say that we teach what we need to learn ourselves. Working as a self-love coach, I find this to be true. It is one thing to know intellectually that you should love yourself. It is another altogether to make self-love, self-care, and self-adoration your "default setting."

A couple of years ago, I participated in a PBS-funded web series called **Black Folk Don't**. The thought-provoking series takes on stereotypical ideas that people of all backgrounds -- including African-Americans -- have about what it means to be black. I joined other talking heads such as Melissa Harris Perry and Touré to laugh, cry, and pontificate on race, gender, the danger of assumptions, and finding healing. Some of my episodes included "Black Folk Don't ... Camp," "Black Folk Don't ... Get Married," and "Black Folk Don't ... Have Eating Disorders."

The idea that black folks or black women don't have eating disorders is a particularly insidious one. The idea persists because studies show that black women are more comfortable in their bodies than white women and because African-derived cultures tend to appreciate curvy women. Our interventions based on body image issues more often focus on hair texture and skin color self-hatred.

When I look around at the beautiful people in my extended family, I see a microcosm of the health statistics that plague the black community at large. Hypertension, diabetes, cancer, and other such illnesses have ravaged the bodies of the people I love. The Centers for Disease Control reports that people of African descent are diagnosed later and as a result are more likely to die from some of these preventable maladies. Hypertension, obesity, and diabetes specifically are linked with the ways we eat.

In my Caribbean family, our "soul food" includes roti, bake (fried bread) and saltfish, fried plantains, fattening peas and rice, pepper pot, and a host of heavy, meat-laden stews and dishes. Like other formerly enslaved peoples, my Guyanese family inherited the tradition of making appetizing food from the slave master's leftovers. Yes, the food is yummy, but as I heard a Rastafarian say once, "People are losing their lives over taste buds." In addition, there is a clear pattern of emotional eating that is laughed off, dismissed, or ignored by the intelligent and hard-working people I share genes with. Food is used to celebrate but also as a drug to numb, comfort, and soothe.

This, my friends, is disordered eating. Eating disorders may not always look like the "popular" models of anorexia and bulimia, but emotional eating and compulsive eating are eating disorders, too. There is a category called Eating Disorder Not Otherwise Specified (EDNOS) that serves as a clearinghouse for "other" eating disorders. The idea that black people don't have eating disorders is a damaging one because if something is not acknowledged and diagnosed, it will not be addressed, treated, or healed.

When I made the decision to face my own disordered eating head-on, the feminine power tools I now share with you were an invaluable resource. I had tried to fix the symptom of the problem – and had temporarily released excess weight before with weight loss plans – but never had I addressed my real underlying emotional challenges. I had even worked with an exceptional nutrition and fitness coach, but I didn't know what to do about the fact that after a hard day, salvation came in the form of French fries and nachos. I didn't understand why I would promise the coach that I would exercise and then lie to her after I once again did nothing. I tried attending a food addicts meeting with a friend but found the structure intimidating.

Here's the thing: My immediate family – father, sister, and brother – are primarily vegetarian. Sugar cereals were not allowed in my house growing up. Although my extended family ate a Guyanese-slanted version of the Standard American Diet, my father lectured often about the importance of eating right and treating one's body as a temple. I didn't have the excuse of living in a food desert or food insecurity from going hungry. I just knew that I was powerless over a box of Oreos, my drug of choice. My family was aware of my weird eating habits, but they didn't know that when I ate the cream inside the cookies and left the rest it was because I was terrified of the extra calories.

My body was not the accepted standard of beauty   not in prep school as a teen and not as an adult working in TV. I felt like a failure because I just couldn't let go of the weight. I adapted cultural stories such as being "big boned." I assumed a posture of loving myself just the way I was, but "just the way I am" was taking my body on crazy pre-diabetic blood sugar rides and leaving me ravaged by food allergies and sensitivities.

It took a multi-layered shift in perception to allow my body to release the unhealthy pounds. This is why I prefer the term "release weight" rather than "lose weight." There is more power in releasing than losing. I would like to say that I received one wake-up call, but I received many. The "get healthy" alarm clock was beeping out of control by the time I started to take my own advice. The choice to wake up from my donut fog has not been without controversy, largely due to my cultural background. I had to write my own father a heartfelt letter when he told me that I looked "too skinny."

Women's bodies are always up for conversation and everyone thinks they get a vote. Just recently someone on my Facebook page left an all caps message — "THE NEW YOU IS KINDA SHOCKING. I LOVE THE OLD YOU. ALWAYS DID AND ALWAYS WILL" — as if he had been asked. He went on to say, "No harm intended. I was just used to seeing you nice and thick in the right places. The slender you is just a shock to me." Well, who asked you?

The only way that I was able to make a change was to challenge my own Belief System, or BS, as I call it. I've always been "girly" or feminine in the way that our patriarchal culture defines femininity. With my ultra-femme mom, my sister and I had almost no choice in the matter. However, tapping into your femergy and womanly power has nothing to do with skirts, frills, or the color pink. Although I only started wearing pants and flat shoes a couple of years ago (true story) and pink is my favorite color, I was not in balance with my femergy at all.

I started to research my body and brain and interview other women about what we felt to be deficient in our lives. This gap for me was filled when I delved deeper into the philosophy of sacred feminine and masculine energy. I am a New York City girl, the first person in my family born in America, an entrepreneur who has always worked freelance. As a result, my energy was aggressive, cutthroat, competitive, and goal-focused; I was operating under the belief that there was only so much to go around. Take or be taken.

That is rampant go-go-go, do-do-do masculine energy.

To say that I was an extreme workaholic and perfectionist is putting it mildly. Putting in 12-hour days and not coming up for air was routine for me and I demanded the same of anyone who worked with me. Sure, I may have been doing it wearing a cute skirt and lip gloss, but I was not in alignment at all with my femergy. Taking time to care for my mental, physical, and spiritual person seemed frivolous.

People always ask how I let go of the unhealthy weight. We all know how to release excess weight: Eat less and move more. However, accessing the feminine principles in this book – like receptivity, radical self-being, Nizhoni, blisspower, and blissipline – and using them in every aspect of my life is what helped me get to that. Yang energy action steps such as working out with kettlebells, changing the way I eat completely, and keeping a food log were life-changing too, but they were secondary.

When I say that the Sacred Bombshell Secrets of Self-Love saved me, I mean this on every level.

How to Use This Book

The Sacred Bombshell Handbook of Self-Love is actually 11 secrets to activating your personal power. You have undoubtedly heard pieces of these "secrets." You will recognize some of these timeless truths in your bones, for you carry them in your genetic memory. The real question is: Are you using them?

Why do I call these sacred principles "forbidden secrets"? These are the gems of women's wisdom and power that we are starved for in our "just do it, bring home the bacon, never let them see you sweat, must be fierce, must be fabulous, social media-obsessed, you can be anything" lives. We are permitted to relish in competition, goals, going for the burn, and outshining the Joneses, but tuning into the femergetic powers of creation, feelings, self-devotion, and fullness gets the side-eye.

This self-love handbook features empowering life lessons, helpful tools, inspiring dialogues, healing modalities, and life-changing exercises with detailed steps on how to connect to your real strength and activate your most fulfilled life. You learn to "own your bombshell" when you tune into your feminine power.

Each chapter will teach you how to implement a Sacred Bombshell Secret for your healing, growth, evolution, and pleasure. Each begins with a Sacred Feminine Law, a Historical Bombshell Mentor who lived the secret's principals, and a sumptuous Bombshell Declaration that illustrates the secret in action and what it means for you. These affirmative statements can be read in the mirror or carried in your bag for reinforcement. Each chapter closes with two Bombshell Dialogues and takeaways from successful women who live the principles of each secret today, plus resources and affirmations.

The introductory section of each chapter is followed by the lessons of each secret. The lessons can be reflective, intense, and provocative. I urge you to go deeper with the Bombshell Tools, which give you concrete methods to apply this knowledge daily. The Bombshell Explorations and Bombshell Playbook Exercises are your opportunity for soul searching and soul growing.

Don't gloss over the Bombshell Dialogues. They are 21 sacred self-love classes disguised as conversations with powerful real-life goddesses who have much to teach. This list of women includes: spiritual gurus, a Grammy winner, a therapist, an Oscar nominee, a minister, a lawyer, reality TV stars, successful entrepreneurs, social media sensations, a burlesque dancer, *New York Times* best-selling authors, and a pole activist. You may recognize most of their names, but they've earned a place in your lesson plan because they live these secrets and you can, too.

I recommend that you add a Bombshell Power Hour (BPH) to your day to do this play/work. That's an hour every day to regenerate. If it's easier, try a half hour in the morning and a half hour before bed. I use my BPH in the evening to meditate, complete my food and gratitude journals, and replenish myself with healing tools and inspirational books like this one. Use your BPH to practice the Bombshell Tools and do your Bombshell Explorations and Playbook Exercises. You are advised to buy a loose-leaf notebook for your Bombshell Playbook, which you will use to complete assignments. Decorate it and move in. Light a luscious candle or incense and have some aromatic tea or hot water with lemon. This is how you respect your own journey. This is blissipline and blisspower.

The most powerful approach to this sacred journey is to read this book chronologically, taking the time to complete all exercises as you go. Alternately, you may prefer to read from beginning to end first, then go back and do the exercises. Some women will find value in going straight to the sections they need most. You may take a couple of days with some sections and a month with others. This is your book and the journey isn't linear.

Ideally, read with a Sacred Bombshell Sister as your accountability partner. If you don't have a book club or reading group, start your own Bomb Squad, Bombshell Club, or Bombshell Playgroup. Join me on my Facebook page and in the Sacred Bombshell Club online, where I can guide you through the lessons and answer your questions. You can also find more support — including a free course, additional dialogues, guided meditations, and visualizations in audio and video — at SacredBombshell.com. Please note that the interviews in this book are edited for clarity. You can find full versions on the site.

All beliefs and orientations are welcome at our non-discriminatory party. You may see references to God, the Source, the Creator, the Universe, and Most High. If that makes you uncomfortable, just focus on the God of your understanding, Divine Mind, Great Spirit, or the highest part of your Self.

Approach this journey with the nurturing energy of blisspower and blissipline rather than the punishing energy of willpower and discipline. This means evolving by leaning toward bliss. We seem to have decided jointly as a society that change and personal development should be grueling. Is it any wonder that people avoid change like the plague and lessons don't stick? Some of us are self-helped out. So let's take a different approach. Passion, pleasure, joy, fun, play, and happiness are not forbidden on this journey. Neither is pain. Giving birth involves contractions.

Bombshell Tool: Self-Love Matrix

Light your candle and prepare your tea. It's time for something delicious: your very first Bombshell Tool! You may be familiar with SWOT analysis, an assessment tool used in business to evaluate a company's Strengths, Weaknesses, Opportunities, and Threats. We're going to use our own version of this tool to see where you are emotionally, mentally, spiritually, and physically.

1. Divide a page in your Bombshell Playbook into quadrants and label them:

Self-Love Strengths	Self-Love Gaps
Self-Love Opportunities	Self-Love Threats

   Under "Self-Love Strengths" list all of the things you love about who you are and that you enjoy about the life you've created. What do you do well? Where do you feel passion, pleasure, happiness, joy, and fun?

2. Under "Self-Love Gaps" list the areas where you feel you fall short – places where there is room for improvement. How do you abuse yourself? What are you unhappy about?

3. Use the "Self-Love Opportunities" section to explore ways you can love yourself more. What opportunities exist currently for you to jump into your power?

4. Use the "Self-Love Threats" section to list things that you see as threats to your happiness. You'll learn as you do this work that nothing real can actually be threatened, but for now, what do you avoid or tolerate? Where might you be in denial?

You'll notice that the items in the left column register as positive and coming from a place of love in your life, while the items in the right column come from a place of fear and may register as negative. In addition, the top row is about right now and is interior in origin, whereas the bottom row is about your future vision and may feel more exterior. It's all up to you.

Because the top row is present tense, these are the things you can control right now. Your objective is to build and enhance your Self-Love Strengths and reduce and resolve your Self-Love Gaps. Of course, you also want to expand your Self-Love Opportunities and thwart your Self-Love Threats, although we will realize that the latter are mostly just illusions.

Using the information in the different quadrants, ask yourself:

- How can I use my Self-Love Strengths to maximize my Self-Love Opportunities?

- How can I use my Self-Love Strengths to avoid my Self-Love Threats?

- How can I avoid my Self-Love Threats by reducing my Self-Love Gaps?

- How can I overcome my Self-Love Gaps by maximizing my Self-Love Opportunities?

At the end of each chapter, you may find it helpful to do a Self-Love Matrix check-in. Remember: You are not in competition with anyone. This is only for your personal evolution.

Bombshell Playbook Exercise

Answer these questions in your Bombshell Playbook. Take five deep, cleansing breaths to get centered and begin.

1. Why am I ready for this journey now?

2. What do I hope to learn in this process?

3. What is the difference between knowing who I want to be vs. what I want to have?

4. What do I believe is possible for me?

Sacred Bombshell Sisterhood Permission Slip

Consider this a soul-binding agreement. When you are truly ready to embark on this journey, please read out loud, sign, make a copy or rip it out, and keep it. Take in these sacred lessons. Give yourself permission to have a Big Bombshell Breakthrough Life – to embrace pleasure, passion, positivity, play, and possibility.

I, _Anniek Verholt_ , now give myself full permission to rise into my shine. It is my time to own my bombshell. I am ready to stop playing small.

I am allowed to love myself.

I am allowed to claim my feminine power.

I am allowed to be unapologetically me.

I am allowed to express my feelings.

I am allowed to be a force of love.

I am allowed abundant joy.

As a Sacred Bombshell Sister, I claim my right to pleasure. I embrace my right to passion. I welcome positivity. I drink in my right to play. I revel in my inner wild woman. I am open to a regret-free journey of possibilities.

Signed: _____

Dated: _26/1/15_

One

The Secret of Creation; Giving Birth to Yourself

The Sacred Feminine Law of Creation

The Sacred Bombshell knows that her creative feminine energy is a catalyst. She remembers her womb wisdom and she is born again as her true Self. She knows that she is a conjurer, an alchemist, and a fierce creator. She is a woman who can rebirth herself at any time and create as she chooses. She accepts her creativeness as a gift. This is sacred self-love.

Historical Bombshell Mentor: Josephine Baker 1906-1975

Jazz Age icon Josephine Baker and her phenomenal feathers would be notorious even today. The press christened her as the Black Venus. Ernest Hemingway said that she was "the most sensational woman anyone ever saw." La Baker knew how to cause a scene, but beneath the flare was a humanitarian who fought racism and adopted a "rainbow tribe" of 12 children. The erotic chanteuse and comedienne was also a civil rights activist and decorated Word War II spy for the Allies. In 1963, Madame Baker spoke at the March on Washington and garnered praise from Dr. Martin Luther King, Jr., himself.

The Creation Declaration

I am a creator. Experience has spread desires under my feet and I have tread carelessly. I have asked the world for paltry results and that is what I have received. No more. My purpose is to create a delicious life. My life is a gift from my Creator and what I do with it is my gift in return. I am a new woman today and I am creating my best right now.

I have dream today, and it is coming true.

There is a goddess, a Sacred Bombshell in me whom I have hidden in shame, guilt, and doubt. Because I was afraid of her life-creating power, I tiptoed through my existence. This ends now.

I have a dream, a want, a need, a desire to give birth to my life.

I am extraordinary. Previously I suspected this fact, but I know it now to be the unmistakable truth: *I am extraordinary*. Out of millions of sperm, only one was able to fertilize the egg that nested me. I am a winner, successful before I was born, the product of a miracle. I exist for a reason. Before today I lived selfishly – keeping my gifts a secret – but now I am a woman with a passionate mission.

Would I be given desires without the power to bring them into fruition? I am reborn. I cast off the dress of victimhood and walk forward into a blindingly bright future of fulfilled promise. Kindred souls may join in creating this journey. Let us now co-create.

With every step that I take, every word that I speak, I am here to be of service. For this I am so grateful.

And so it is.

Creativity and Your Birth Voice

*"If you don't love yourself how in the hell are
you going to love somebody else?"*
—*RuPaul*

We all start out as beautiful and happy babies. Children want to laugh and play and cry and ponder and think and feel. When you're a child having a good time, you revel in it. When things suck, you boohoo and move on. You feel like the world revolves around you, and so it does. You love being … *you*! As well you should. You are frigging loveable; even when you're not.

Then one day you realize that something about you is different. Maybe your family background, skin color, or freckles set you apart. That's okay, because nothing is inherently wrong with difference. In fact, difference rocks. Some of us revel in the velvety delight of rose petals and others dismiss roses as too common. Some of us melt for billowy dandelions mislabeled as weeds. Both roses and dandelions have a purpose in the ecosystem and can be enjoyed aesthetically or used medicinally. They are different and individual for a reason. The same is true of us.

Maybe one day someone rejects you, abuses you, bullies you, or treats you in a way that says that you are less than. Maybe you begin to let other people change your beliefs about yourself. Initially you are confused. You? The beautiful rose, dandelion, sunflower? How can you be less than? How can anyone not see the magical creature that you are?

You approach adolescence and "the curse" is upon you. The goal is to become a woman. Now there are all sorts of ways you have to alter yourself to even be presentable. Presentable is code for loveable. You never stop to ask who created the "suffer for beauty" standards that you hold yourself to. Even if you see through "the matrix," it doesn't matter. You just want to be accepted for who you really are. You want them to like you. You want to be loved.

Your rollercoaster emotions are dismissed as drama. Your natural body smells need to be deodorized. Your body size needs to be uniform. Your yoni needs to be douched. The hair sprouting on your body needs to be shaved. Your face is missing something. Let's not even get into the inappropriate mess that is the hair on your head. Your breasts are the wrong size and so is your ass.

By the time you are 18 you have been told in 1,001+ ways that you are inadequate. Everything about you, you are told by commercials, magazines, and people you know, is just wrong, wrong, wrong. In other words, the force that created you got it wrong. Your reflection is a mistake. But take heart! You can buy enough stuff to alter yourself into a reasonable facsimile of what you are supposed to look like. After all, you're supposed to look like everyone else, right? So you hate yourself into submission, unless you are lucky enough to look like whatever society currently says is "in."

Sadly, none of this makes you love yourself more. Instead, you loathe yourself for how much you still miss the mark even after all the effort.

Exhale.

The residue of women hating ourselves is all around us. Self-harm is an epidemic. Cutting, bullying other girls, judgment, eating disorders, dieting, promiscuity, and addiction are all forms of self-mutilation. Given all the ways we are taught that self-hatred is normal for female people, we shouldn't be surprised when we despise who we are. It's downright shocking and countercultural when we don't.

Unconditional self-love is a revolutionary act. This revolutionary act begins with claiming your powers of creation. We all have the power to create life. I'm not talking about giving birth to a child, which is without question a miraculous blessing. I am talking about giving birth to ourselves. Our bodies mature, but the decision to grow, expand, and evolve into a self-actualized woman is yours alone.

A self-actualized woman is one who is making a difference in her family, community, or corner of the planet because she feels comfortable expressing her voice. This is what I mean when I say own your bombshell. A true bombshell is a woman who owns herself.

A Sacred Bombshell or self-actualized woman is not stymied by the puny visions of others. She accepts and celebrates herself. She is open to the magnificence of life and the delicious grandeur of possibilities. She trusts herself and is in tune with her intuition and her creative power. In psychology, self-actualization is at the peak of the hierarchy of human needs. Self-actualized women are in full acceptance of themselves and others.

Bombshell Exploration: Recreate Your Personal Story

It's time you became the author of your own story instead of the inheritor of patched-together interpretations you assigned to your experiences as a child. Choose five experiences from your personal history that negatively affect your opinion of yourself. Be clear about what you made each story mean about yourself. For each one, write down 10 alternate interpretations of the experience.

The Sacred Feminine Power of Creativity

Although creation in nature requires masculine and feminine energy, creativity is often viewed as a yin energy trait. The reason is that no matter the discipline, creativity requires a trust in fluidity and the spontaneity of the muse. Creation is taking an idea from the formless, gestating it, and giving birth to it. For most of us, thriving as creative beings requires welcoming a balance of masculine and feminine energy. Intuition plus inspired action is a powerful force.

What are you passionate about? The true answer to that question is your voice and your purpose, or what you are here to create. Your voice is your means of expressing your life on this planet. When I talk about this in groups some women say: "But what if my passion is dolls?" "What if I get excited about peanut butter?" "What if baseball cards make me giddy?" To which I say: "Aren't there people who are making a living or have thriving hobbies related to these things?"

The scope is not the priority; your well-directed and passionate creative expression is. My favorite prayer from *A Course in Miracles* is "What would You have me do? Where would You have me go? What would You have me say, and to whom?"

People say they're not creative because they don't have the talents of a painter, sculptor, or writer. This comes up often when women are trying to find out what their purpose is. My sister Damali Abrams is a professional visual artist. Her voice and creativity is obvious in her thought-provoking collages, handmade books, and video art.

My childhood best friend Ginger is flawless on the outside with a singing voice that sounds like a voicemail from angels. She used to say that she was unsure of her purpose, but there it is – right there. Her creative purpose is to sing. Does that mean she should be somewhere tearing up the stage like Alicia Keys? Possibly. But there are also so many other ways that a voice like that can spread joy.

My mom has always lamented the fact that she can't draw. Yet she is one of the most creative people I know. Like my father, she is a poet and storyteller. My mother's garden is also an artistic masterpiece. I didn't realize this fully until I read an essay by Alice Walker called "In Search of Our Mothers' Gardens: The Creativity of Black Women in the South." Walker speaks of poet Jean Toomer finding the art of unsung women living before the civil rights era in the beauty of their gardens.

When I was a kid, the seemingly chaotic wildness of my mother's garden intimidated and embarrassed me. I thought it was messy-looking and unkempt because it was not the same dull, flat lawn with flowers on the perimeter that every other house in the block association had. As I matured, I found that my mother knew every plant. Every seedling was carefully selected. She had placed every sapling exactly where she wanted it. My mother's suburban mini-jungle is an unabashed treasure. It is breathtakingly alluring. In my youth, I was too blind and ignorant to appreciate its lush splendor. I once hated this unsung, wild, goddess garden because it made me stand out even more as weird and different. These are things I welcome as an adult.

The ability to create something from seemingly nothing is magic. Aunt Silvy was a masterful cook. It has been 10 years since she made her transition and people are *still* talking about her homemade Guyanese dishes and sauces.

What is *your* passionate purpose? Where do you need to express your voice? How do you give birth to you? Are you a politician or a deacon who uses the art of charisma to lead, share, and govern? Are you the family storyteller, historian, or scrapbooker? The pie genie? The jokester? The one who makes everyone smile by expressing her talents on the barbecue grill?

Bombshell Challenge: Remember when you were a child and could find pleasure in anything? Invite creativity back into your life. Buy crayons, Play-Doh, blocks, dolls, and scraps of cloth for yourself. Turn off the TV for 24 hours and make time for creativity and play. It is self-loving to express your creativity. This raises your energy vibration and taps directly into your feminine power.

Bombshell Exploration: Create an Altar or Sacred Space

To my greatest childhood embarrassment, I grew up with altars in my house. My father's altar was grand, beautiful, and in the dining room where any of my childhood guests could see it. Among other sacred items, my father's altars always contained a lit candle, holy incense, fresh water, and an open Bible on a white tablecloth. Now, when I move in somewhere or am staying in a hotel, my personal altar is one of the first things I set up. This reinforces my spiritual intentions to invite peace, beauty, and blessings into my life.

An altar is simply a dedicated place charged with your most positive energy and highest intentions to be connected to the Divine. It may be tied to a specific religion or not. It could be on a table, on a shelf, or on the floor.

Your altar could feature family talismans, precious stones, items of remembrance, or photographs. Mine currently includes wood from my ancestral home, family funereal cards, a crystal gifted by a friend, amethyst, and a small cross. At times I have included feathers, leaves, soil, or shells from my travels.

There is no right or wrong way to make an altar. As a Catholic, for example, my mom may have different associations with an altar. Altars can have themes, like gratitude or family. Be creative and even playful. Maybe you include fresh flowers and chocolate. Dedicating a wall in your home to your familial ancestors might be your sacred altar space. This is a place for your spiritual practice, whatever that includes. Pray, meditate, chant, or just breathe. Keep the space physically clean. Clear the energy with white sage. Let your altar reflect the inner life that you are creating.

My Big Fat Bombshell Diary: Ain't I a Woman?

A few years ago, I attended a family reunion in Maryland. On the drive down, I planned my reply for any mean remarks that anyone might make. Some older members of my paternal extended family can be cold and cutting under the guise of "speaking it plain." I am a highly sensitive person, plus I don't know them well enough to feel comfortable with rudeness positioned as teasing. This is a bad combination.

For me, stepping into these reunions is about as warm and cuddly as stepping into a mosquito nest. I told my sister Damali that no matter what mean thing any family member said to me, I was going to reply with, "Thank you for sharing your opinion. I'm sure you don't mean to be as rude as you're coming across."

I arrived at the reunion and lifted another family member's sweet new son into the air. As I turned to greet one of my aunts she accosted me with, "So you're holding her baby now? Where's your baby?" Just in case I had any doubt about her line of questioning, she topped it off with, "Are you not a woman?" I had been there less than four minutes.

Ah, the tyranny of OPE – Other People's Expectations. To her, being a woman meant giving birth. I had no children so I was not a woman. She has no idea whether I can have kids or if I even want them. I handed the baby to a cousin and went to the bathroom to cry in private. As the water whisked away my fresh summer makeup, I thought about all the projects I have given birth to, in full alignment with my life's purpose of empowering women. How fertile I felt. Still, my womanhood – my personhood – was in question.

In the 1940s, my maternal grandmother Evadney, whom I call Eve, had her womanhood questioned as well. When she married my grandfather, the people in his village saw her as an outsider and usurper. They thought her uppity because she insisted on wearing stockings in a time and place where many people didn't even wear shoes. Then she went three years without bearing children. This was unheard of back then.

The townsfolk mocked Granny for being barren. When she did start bearing children, she gave birth to four girls in a row. One baby died and three survived, but the villagers didn't care about that. First this woman was barren and now she couldn't have boys?! It was a scandal. Clearly she was not woman enough. Luckily for her, she then started giving birth to sons.

All women may not make the same choices but we all have access to the same stream of power. Think of the mysteries of the planet. It is no accident that the moon reveals herself on a 28-day cycle, as do we; we all know that the ovulation cycle is in sync with the moon and the tides. We – women – are the stuff that magic is made of.

When a baby girl is born, her body holds all of the eggs she will have in her entire lifetime. This means that when my great-grandmother was born in 1880, she held the eggs that birthed my grandmother, who birthed my mother, who birthed me. When discussing the cellular intelligence of our bodies, and how connected we are to Mother Earth, Deepak Chopra says that our "biological rhythms are actually the symphony of the cosmos."

Translation: You are an absolute freaking miracle capable of creating miracles! This has nothing to do with who you love, how you look, how many babies you have, or what equipment you were born with. Can you imagine if you were raised celebrating all of the blessings of your body rather than being told you were cursed?

Bombshell Exploration: What Is Womanhood to You?

The original subtitle of *The Sacred Bombshell Handbook of Self-Love* was "The 11 Sacred Secrets of Womanly Wisdom." To my surprise, when I asked for feedback from my Bombshell Ambassadors (the women on my Love-Body-Spirit mailing list), many reacted strongly to the word "womanly." They either found it too intimidating or too old. I understood that coming from those in their late 20s, but women in their late 40s felt the same way! I am as girlish now at 41 as I was at 31 or 11. After all, I am a girl's girl and as girly as they come. Still, I revel in being a *woman*.

What does being a woman mean to you? Is womanhood about

voting a certain way or looking a certain way? Then how do you explain our rainbow of opinions and wide-ranging beauty types? Is womanly wisdom about having ovaries or a uterus? Then what about when we have hysterectomies? Do "real women have curves"? Some of us have bombshell curves and some are bombshell "bean poles." Can we be more or less womanly? Is our femaleness the makeup and high heels that we are told is sexy by someone else? Does being born a "cis" female de facto dictate being a woman? Does our sacred feminine energy have anything to do with the "sugar and spice and everything nice" that little girls are supposed to be made of? Journal in your Bombshell Playbook about what womanhood means to you.

The Creative Wisdom of Menstruation

The popular current mythology says that women are crazy and irrational during puberty, menstruation, childbirth, and menopause. But according to board-certified OB/GYN Dr. Christiane Northrup, our menstrual cycles govern information, intuition, and creativity. There is a season for everything else in nature. Why wouldn't there be seasons for us? For menstruating women, this means where we are in the current cycle as well as in our life cycles. For example, studies show that our levels of attraction and who we're attracted to change during ovulation.

In some cultures a woman on her period is regarded as unclean, and in others a menstruating woman is thought of as having the power of lightning. CryoCell.com had the first menstrual blood bank because research shows that the stem cells from menstrual blood have similar regenerative capabilities to stem cells from umbilical cords and bone marrow. Unfortunately their site now reads, "Due to consumer inhibition, this service has been suspended."

What if women were initially banned from participating in certain religious ceremonies because our strength was feared, not because we were considered dirty?

Menstruating Khoisan women of the South African Kalahari Desert are viewed as omnipotent, and a girl's first period among some groups of Hindus in India is seen as a time of celebration. Madhu Kishwar, founding editor of Indian magazine **Manushi: A Journal About Women and Society** writes about a woman's party to announce that her "daughter's happiness has come" that would rival any wedding.

According to the site SouthAsianParent.com, spiritual leader Swami Chinmayananda believes that his culture's taboo forbidding menstruating women from sharing utensils, worshipping, and other daily life events was created because it was the only way women could get the prescribed three days of rest needed while menstruating!

My mother only knew that I had my first period because I had wadded up so much toilet tissue in my pants. She had never spoken to me about my period, so I didn't feel comfortable enough to tell her that it had come. I learned about menstruation through pamphlets, the stories of friends, and books including Judy Blume's **Are You There God? It's Me Margaret**. I was excited to finally get my period, since all of my friends already had, yet I felt ashamed about the changes in my body in my own home.

My great-grandmother – who delivered babies and healed women's wombs – helped raise my mother. But despite this history, with her religious and societal conditioning, my mom just didn't feel comfortable enough to share the natural facts of life with her daughters. I don't blame my mother or anyone else, but now it's time for us to create a new celebratory paradigm around our womanhood and the energy of creation.

Just as our bodies have cycles, the cycles of Mother Nature are also important. Certain times may work better than others for creating new ventures. Trying to plant summer fruit in snow won't yield a harvest no matter how badly we want it to. For some, trying to birth something new while the planet Mercury is in retrograde leads to confusion. Being able to read the best time to move forward based on where we are in our cycles is a gift. This is how to go with the flow – literally.

Bombshell Exploration: Period Tales

About 10 years ago, my friend Zelma Davis and I wrote a series of stories called "The Gift" about the menarche, or first period. Our tales bestowed power and positive energy on the rite of passage of a girl coming into womanhood. One of the reasons we weren't able to publish the novellas is due to the taboo nature of menstruation. Look for "The Gift" as resource on my site in the future. Write your own period-positive tale and share it with your Bomb Squad or Bombshell Playgroup!

Bombshell Tool: Period Power Calendar

These period lessons come from Dr. Christiane Northrup, MD. You can read more about the creative wisdom of menstruation in her book ***Women's Bodies, Women's Wisdom***. Count the first day of your period as the first day of your cycle, and use this tool to align yourself with nature's cycles and the natural cycles of your body for peak manifesting power.

- From the onset of our cycles through ovulation, we are our most shining star selves. This is when we feel most like supporting others and are brimming with enthusiasm. Here's when we are most outwardly expressive.

- When our periods start, we experience a biological and psychological cleansing and we may feel an urge to organize and clean up our physical lives as well.

- At mid-cycle, during ovulation, we are fertile with new ideas and receptive to others. This is when our libidos are on full blast and we are more sexually attractive to others.

- Between ovulation and the start of menses is considered premenstrual time, when we want to retreat from outward activity, turn our bedrooms or homes into huts, and be more reflective. Society judges us as emotional and unpleasant during this time but any tears are there to tell us something. Pay attention to signs and guidance about what is not working for you. This is a time of inner knowing.

● Intuitive "lunar" information comes right before or during our periods. Northrup says that the info comes "in our dreams, our emotions, and our hungers." If we block the information that comes in the second half of our menstrual cycles, it will rage back as PMS or menopausal craziness – so pay attention!

Wo-Manifesting: Creating on Purpose

Most of the time we are creating our lives by default. Wo-manifesting is creation on purpose. Being creative – or giving birth to your Self – also means the ability to manifest or create what you want in life. This book, your favorite TV show, the shirt on your back – all started as visions that were manifested and created.

Wo-manifesting, or creating circumstances as you desire them to be, is an art form – and a science. You would probably be hard-pressed to find a successful person who doesn't believe that our thoughts are powerful. The Law of Attraction mantra "ask, believe and receive" from the documentary *The Secret* sounds simple enough. For the Biblical folks it's right there in the Book of Matthew, "And all things, whatsoever you shall ask in prayer, believing, you shall receive." Every religion has similar lessons. Right now you're probably asking: "So where are all of the riches I've been praying for?"

Wo-manifesting is a science because there is a prescribed order to co-creating with the Creator of all things. Wo-manifesting is an art because we can never understand all of the mysteries and timing of life. Leaving room for mystery is part of the magic of creation. Taking action is the fusion of masculine and feminine energy needed to give birth to your vision.

Your Big Brave Bombshell Bliss Board

This is a wo-manifesting tool for creating on purpose. A Big Brave Bombshell Bliss Board (B5) is an evolved vision board that will help you take your bombshell energy to the fifth power. Viewers or readers of the inspirational movie and book **The Secret** are familiar with the idea of a vision board. In the past I've also called this process a life map, treasure map, or Goddess Dream Book. Alternately, I've made other kinds of inspiration boards and advised coaching clients to do the same. I have a self-celebration board in tribute to who I am and the things I am proud of, while my gratitude board celebrates what I am grateful for.

What Exactly Is a Vision Board?

A vision board is a life creation and manifesting tool that I've made since I was a little girl, even though I didn't know to call it that at the time. You use a collage of images to create a picture of events, things, people, feelings, career choices, or whatever it is that you would like to materialize in your life. If you're a visual artist (or want to be), you can do this with some chalk, crayons, charcoal, paints, or whatever other medium you choose to create something magnificent. I use magazines, printouts, pencils, and pens.

Why Vision Boards Don't Work

I developed this process because for most people a vision board is not going to work. Yep, I said it. The reason is that most people just create glorified catalogues or "want boards." That kind of board is rooted in self-image rather than self-love, and that exercise is perfectly fine – and fun – but completely different from creating a vision where you assume the feelings of your wishes fulfilled, as Dr. Wayne Dyer would say.

For this to work, you must do the work before you make the board to figure out what you really desire and why. This exercise is useless if you're not aligned with your vision. It's worthless if you glue together a bunch of cool images that are about what society says you should want rather than who you are. Let's make this about *who you want to be* not what you want to have. Got that?

The Bombshell Board Upgrade

The power is in feeling the energy of each vision. And the corollary to vision is action. That's masculine/yang energy and feminine/yin energy together. The feminine is visualizing and feeling.

The masculine is taking action. We need both.

One of the questions to ask yourself – after "what do I desire?" – is "what am I willing to exchange for this vision?" What are you willing to give? Are you willing to exchange mindfulness, time, service, money, information, attention, or transformation for your vision? For every action there's an equal and opposite reaction. If you have a vision of becoming president and you're not willing to get off your sofa, then you're not willing to exchange your time and energy for it. So under those conditions, is it going to happen? Probably not.

B5 Preparation

I've driven across the United States twice with the trip itself as the main destination. Once on the northern route and again on the southern route, I started out in New York City and then flew back when I reached the west coast. One of my goals is to visit every state, and I think I'm at 46 states so far. Before each trip, I gathered paper maps and made note of the towns I wanted to visit, experiences I wanted to have, places that were culturally significant for me, hotels I wanted to stay in, and people I wanted to meet. I enjoy traveling abroad too, but it's important for me as the daughter of immigrants to have grounding in the country of my birth.

Think of this B5 process in the same way. You are creating a collage that is a beautiful map of where you're going made stronger by acknowledgement of where you've been and gratitude for where you are. Spend a week or two beforehand just collecting significant images, personal photos, and inspiring words and statements. Include your Historical Bombshell Mentors. Claim these great women as a part of your own ancestral heritage. Incorporate your own handwriting. Write out your affirmations and copy your Bombshell Laws and Declarations.

Use a big piece of cardboard or construction paper, or a sturdy photo album if you prefer. I've used this same method to create a Goddess Dream Book rather than a board. Each page had a different area that I wanted to shine in, stop playing small in, and manifest goals in. For example, there were pages for finances, for relationships, for the body, and for my career. You can make this board or album for one specific area of your life or to represent your life in general.

Do this work with reverence, ritual, fun, and ceremony. Nurture yourself and involve all of your senses. Take an Epsom salt bath before you begin for cleansing and detoxification. Indulge in aromatherapy and clear the space with femergetic sweetgrass incense. This practice is also called "smudging" and it's a ceremonial tradition popular in Native American and other cultures for clearing negative or unwanted energies. Light a green candle, the color that represents the energy of your heart chakra. Set the tone with jazz, classical music, or reggae rhythms. These all stimulate our pleasure center and leave us feeling "irie," as our Jamaican sistren say.

B5 Sections

The Big Brave Bombshell Bliss Board has three parts. Write at the top "I am," or if it's a notebook or album, write it in the beginning. The space to your far left represents your past. The space to the far right is for your present. And your future area is the center. You may be asking, "Abiola, why would I put the past there when you told me to stop looking at the past?" That past area is your self-celebration section. The area on the right – the present – is your gratitude section. The area in the middle is your vision section. Visually, this looks like:

I AM

My Past/	My Future/	My Present/
Self-Celebration	Vision	Gratitude

Mix the time that you spend working on this board with taking action. Do this project with your Bombshell Playgroup, reading group, or Bomb Squad. There is strength in having others hold your vision for you. Join my joint Pinterest B5 board where we can hold the energy of vision intentions for each other.

Your Self-Celebration (Past) Section

What are you proud of? The self-celebration section can include things like: your business card from that big promotion, your graduation picture, a card from your daughter, a photo of the glorious spread from last Thanksgiving, your honeymoon plane tickets, that fit and healthy body you enjoyed living in, your grandmother who adored you, or a picture of you winning that award in fifth grade. Include words like "love," "success," and "it feels good." You can also include images of people who look like you and the situations you're celebrating or images that in some other way symbolize these feel-good memories.

Your Gratitude (Present) Section

What are you grateful for? Your present gratitude section may include things like: you with your BFFs in Mexico, that vegan meal symbolizing how you've decided to eat better, a screenshot of an email acceptance letter, your fluffy puppy, the weights you're finally working out with, a mic to represent you speaking up, or a photo of a woman meditating to echo your own budding practice. Also include words: "I am grateful for the feeling that I am going to meet my perfect partner," or "I am grateful that this will be the year I step up and get that new job."

Your Vision (Future) Section

To create your vision, ask yourself:

- Who do I want to be?
- How do I want to feel?
- What do I want to experience?
- What do I desire to have?

In your vision section you should have photos of yourself pasted with the things you are celebrating in advance. It is always today. The future never comes, so celebrate it as though this vision is real right now. This process infuses your vision with joy and meaning. You want to mix the dreams with the "reality" that has happened.

Your board should have pictures of you on it because you want to see yourself there in your vision. If you are studying to become a doctor, for example, take a picture of your face and find a picture of a doctor's uniform and cut it out and put those together. See yourself that way. If you are writing a book, create the cover. Put a photo of your family in your dream home. See it. See it as if it is already true and your brain will start to work on it. Your mind will say, "Okay, I've got to figure this out because this is what's happening. It is inevitable. There is the picture."

Own Your Bombshell Bliss

This board process is a flexible, fluid, and ongoing because our desires, visions, and goals are never finished. While you are creating your vision, don't just recite flat affirmations over it. Infuse your bombshell life with the joyous feelings you will have when you are "there." Visualize; see yourself celebrating and victorious in every scenario. This is visioning plus.

Feel free to rewrite yourself in your past section. Use your imagination. Quantum physics posits that all time is happening simultaneously. So go back and revise your past. That day when those bullies pushed you down and you decided that you were a pushover? Tell yourself a different story. "No, I didn't just lie there and cry. I spoke my mind. This sassy little girl represents that moment. I love who I was then and I love the way I see myself now." Rewrite yourself into your glorious future.

Allow the sections to overlap. This is you creating a vision for who you are becoming. This is you looking back and celebrating. This is you feeling grateful for right now.

Bombshell Exploration: Five Ways to Flex Your Creative Muscles

1. **Notice and acknowledge creativity.** Take note of creative people and expressions wherever you find them. Unsung art can range from masterful hair braiding to colorful street performances. Acknowledge your own expressions of creativity as well. If you are a professional artist or have aspirations to write, draw, paint, or sing, lose the word "aspiring" and dare to jump in.

2. **Create a mural.** Do you have an empty play space that you can paint? Maybe it's a garage wall or somewhere in the attic where you can feel more free to play artist. In my old

apartment, I painted a series of bold 3D goddess murals. This helped me express emotions differently from journaling or being in a support group. Besides, it was fun!

3. **Redesign a room in your home.** Even if it's just a corner or foyer, designate a space to reflect the evolving you. Use colors and design ideas that would usually make you clutch your pearls. Stretch beyond who you have been to see who you can become. This is not a space for your partner or kids. It is your "room of one's own."

4. **Funk up your clothing style.** There are all kinds of ways to embolden your artistic side. Do you have clashing prints that are just not you? Maybe there's a T-shirt you can paint or cut up for a new look.

5. **Create a new holiday.** This day can be just for you and your family or your whole community. Maybe it's Great-Aunt Matilda's Sweet Potato Festival in celebration of your auntie who made masterful pies. It could be a holiday welcoming a daughter or niece into womanhood. Whatever it is, make it bold and fun. Plan a party with related invitations, decorations, and games. Use your creativity to come up with the special date, meals, clothing, and new traditions.

Bombshell Dialogue with Viola Davis: How to Step into Your Creative Power

Creative supernova Viola Davis is the perfect study of a woman who has found her voice and given birth to herself. Many of her fans first discovered her in the film *Doubt* with Meryl Streep and then supported her in *The Help*. Viola faced controversy in the African-American community head-on for her choice to play a maid in the racist south during the civil rights movement. Since then, she appears to be everywhere. Loving wife to actor Julius Tennon and mom to daughter Genesis, the Juilliard-trained star is blazing a trail all her own. Ms. Davis is set to star in Shonda Rhimes's series *How to Get Away with Murder*. Her multiethnic production company, co-founded by her husband, is named JuVee Productions.

I visited Ms. Davis on the set of the film *Beautiful Creatures* in New Orleans for a press junket interview. Viola plays Amma, a seer who communicates with her ancestors, "the Greats." Clearly this is a character who is in tune with her feminine intuition. At the time, people were buzzing about Viola's Oscar night bombshell moment when her natural textured hair made a stunning red carpet debut. The Tony award-winning, Oscar-nominated actress was thrilled about her life in present tense.

Abiola: Thank you for coming down to do this.

Viola: Oh, you're welcome. At nine-thirty at night? (laughs)

Abiola: How did you prepare for the role of channeler Amarie "Amma" Treadeau?

Viola: I'd like to tell an interesting story, but I didn't have any channelers that I could just call: 1-800-channeler. So I had to do a lot of work on the Internet. It's not a really big role so I just felt like I had to make it as authentic as possible without looking too cartoony with it.

At one point [my character] had to channel a spirit and I did some research on Yoruba religion. I felt like that was one of the ancestors she channeled. I learned some Yoruba for it. Hopefully anyone who speaks Yoruba is not going to go, "What is she doing? That wasn't Yoruba. That was 'your something' but not Yoruba." (laughs) I just thought the script was fabulous. I'm a sucker for a great love story.

Abiola: The character Amma is a force of nature, a seer. I hear that in the script she's even larger than she was in the book. Originally she was a maid, right?

Viola: Well, in the book Amma is an older woman who is a housekeeper. Then there's Marian who is the librarian, who has a Ph.D. They combined those two characters. I said, "I don't want to be seen in an apron. I don't want to clean anything. I don't want to cook anything. I'm just a friend."

After coming off of *The Help* (and even if I didn't come off *The Help*), I didn't want to see the pieces of the [film] puzzle put together and for my piece to be one of servitude. I want to be in it. I'm a friend of the [character] Ethan's mother. I said, "I want to look like the friend after the mother's gone. Every time I'm coming in I'll come in with some food but if we're eating we're going to eat together."

Amma's interesting because she's not what she appears to be at first. You're introduced to her and you think, "Okay, who's the black woman in the town? Who is she in Gaitlin, South Carolina?" In the book it says that she doesn't even belong there. I love that they put [that] in the book because I was thinking the same thing when I read the script. What the hell is she doing there? When you see that she has all these abilities, I love the mystery about it. It's a mystery that is smart and it's put together in a way that is so well thought out. I love her because I think she has room to grow.

Abiola: You had an incredible style moment at the Oscars in 2012 with revealing your natural hair. I see that you're rocking your hair for the Amma character. Did you realize that you were making such a statement when you decided to de-wig?

Viola: Any sister who takes her wig off knows she's making a statement whether wanting to make a statement or not. You know what? I wish I had a better story to make me sound more heroic .... Tomorrow is my anniversary so my husband and I will be married nine years. He kept saying, "V, you got to take your wig off. I'm tired of the rags on the head at night." So I finally took the wig off and did it for him. I happened to go to the [*LA Times*] magazine shoot and they said, "I love the hair." Once people saw the magazine, they thought I looked cute in it. Whenever someone says you look cute you're like, okay I'll go further with it.

I did feel that it was liberating for me. I thought it was the perfect time to do it with *The Help* because through *The Help* I found my voice because I felt so much that I had to defend my choice for doing that. Through it I either had to sink, and fold, and cave into myself, or I had to just step into my voice as an artist and as a black woman.

Then the Oscars came; which was kind of the tail end of everything that happened. I felt like it was just fitting for me to take the wig off. It felt great. I never questioned it. I have to tell you some white people said, "You look good," but all black people felt that it was such a powerful statement. They were so thankful and grateful for it, and it made me feel good. It made me feel like I was more than just an actress.

Abiola: Any hair care tips to share now that you're wearing your own hair?

Viola: Yes... At first I was like, "God, it doesn't do anything. My gray is coming in and I have to pick it and all that." I realized with my wigs I was always doing the same thing. I was having to work it or whatever. But working my natural hair, I feel like me. Marianne Jean-Baptiste, the actress from **Secrets and Lies** who I love, she's a friend of mine. She's like, "I feel like me, Viola." And I do. I feel like me. So I have all kinds of products. There are times when I look into the mirror and I think to myself, "Why didn't I do this before?" Wet it, do everything in the shower, and it comes out looking fabulous. You know; and Moroccan oil.

Abiola: Moroccan oil, I was going to tell you!

Viola: Yes!

Abiola: How do you pick your roles?

Viola: It's like a loaded question. It's not a loaded question but it's a complicated question. You don't pick – at least I don't pick. Some actresses probably have a set of scripts and they go, "Eeny, meeny, miny moe. I want to do a light comedy next," or "I want to rock and be sexy," or whatever. I don't get those kinds of choices. There aren't those kind of choices for me being 46, being African-American, being of a certain look. I don't have as much control. My thing right now is if I can work with the script, if I know that I can humanize the person. If I feel like I'm just going to come in and I'm going to facilitate something, and I don't know how to problem-solve enough to make it into a person that anyone would even recognize, I can't do it. I've got to recognize who that person is on the page. I've got to do it for myself as an actress and as an actress of color.

When I was growing up I was a theater geek and I didn't see a lot of people [who] looked like me on screen. When I did, I never knew what the hell they were doing. Isabel Sanford is a fantastic actress of the stage and I remember her in **Guess Who's Coming to Dinner**. If you blinked you would have missed her. And Beah Richards. They came and went and I don't want to do that anymore. So, I do choose in that sense. But there's lots of things that I would like to do.

Abiola: Like what? What would your dream role be?

Viola: I just want to be fun. I want to be sexy. I want to be light. I want to be complicated! That's why I started my production company. I have so many projects that I'm developing. I feel like I'm more in control with what goes on with everything else. The hair, the production company, the baby. I feel like this is the time to just bust out and into who I am instead of kind of shrinking into the background and letting other people dictate who I am.

I love working with mythology. It gives you a sense of play that you don't get when you're playing someone who's completely realistic. It gives you a sense of being larger than life. There's a sense of theatrics to it which I really appreciate. I love it. I love working on a role that's different. That's why I would love to do sci-fi.

Abiola: Like Octavia Butler!

Viola: I love Octavia Butler. I'd love to see myself in space.

Bombshell Takeaways:

- 🌢 You can reinvent yourself at any time by revealing more of you.
- 🌢 There are many different sides to who you are.
- 🌢 Every woman's journey is unique.

Bombshell Dialogue with Rha Goddess:
How to be a Creative Change Agent

A change agent is a champion who swoops in as a catalyst for change. Envision a lithe, lovely, and majestic woman. Now hear her mighty voice as she holds her crown high, sits across the table from other CEOs, leans in, and says, "My name is Rha Goddess."

Ancient Egyptians believed that the sun deity Ra called each form of life into existence by speaking its secret name. Rha Goddess called herself into existence and helps others give birth to their passions by speaking the language of love, abundance, and belief. Rha's coaching academy Move the Crowd is an entrepreneurial training company dedicated to helping creative and cultural entrepreneurs to "stay true, get paid and do good." Rha proudly announced on her Facebook page that spiritual teacher Gabrielle Bernstein is Move the Crowd's first official millionaire! I am honored to be part of the Move the Crowd tribe. Rha Goddess is an artist, activist, coach, transformational speaker, and creative entrepreneur.

Abiola: Rha, you beautifully hold a sacred space for change. When I first met you I was doing my stage show *Goddess City*. We are both featured in director Daniel Banks's anthology *Say Word: Voices from Hip Hop Theater*. You created magical theatrical work.

Rha: For over two and a half decades, I've had the privilege to work as a creative change agent. At first I was a reluctant artist but when I finally did surrender I knew that I wanted to use my art to make a difference. The disciplines that I worked in were writing, performing, music, poetry, and theater, but the commitment was to move the needle on some of the most pressing social, political, and economic issues that face our society.

I remember a conversation I had with Danny Glover not too long ago where he talked about being a citizen first. I really do resonate with that. I'm a citizen who happens to be an artist. I'm an artist who is committed to being a citizen. My history has really been all about working at the intersection of arts and social justice – and social change – and using those mediums to raise awareness and to encourage and ignite action around the issues that I'm most passionate about.

Abiola: Well, thank you for your contributions as a citizen and an artist. One of the wonderful things you teach is that there's no discord between being creative or spiritual and financial prosperity. How did you know how to monetize creativity?

Rha: I had to learn. This is at the heart of what we teach at Move the Crowd. It's the disconnect and the divide that we are working to heal every day. You can be about your creativity and you can eat. I, like many of us, was conditioned to believe that that was not the case. That in order to be a creative soul you had to take an oath to starvation and insanity. I had to undo that mental noise and heal and transform those messages in order to be able to be empowered around monetizing my craft.

Abiola: I encounter women who say, "I don't know what my passion is." They have the feeling of wanting and needing to birth something but they don't know what.

Rha: Sometimes people come to us and they say, "I don't know what my passion is." They know what it is but they're scared. And fear is common, as you know, Abiola, because of all of the amazing work that you do and all of the ways that you also hold sacred space. We deal with a lot of fear. We get glimpses of how powerful, amazing, talented, and off the chain we are and we want to run for the hills.

Abiola: When it comes to fear, what do you do for your personal self-care when you feel less than your Rha Goddess magical self?

Rha: I've learned to make peace with my fear. I've learned how to work with my fear and ultimately through my fear. It isn't that I don't get afraid because I totally do; especially anytime I'm starting something new or embarking on something that's really near and dear to my spirit. What I've learned to do is acknowledge it. Embrace it. Sometimes [it's] that part of my "little girl" needs to be reassured that we're not going to get her into anything dangerous or crazy. Sometimes there's that part of me that needs to know that being in my truth is more important than getting so-and-so's approval. Sometimes it's that part of me that needs to stand for what I feel really strongly about. Sometimes that may fly in opposition to what is the status quo and it's just about calling on my courage and being willing to go for it.

One of the things that I do as part of my self-care is I talk to myself. I ask myself, "Which part of me is activated here?" Is it my historical trauma? Is it my people pleaser? Or is it the activist in me, the part of me that is about shaking things up, that is about wanting to usher in a new paradigm?

Abiola: Beautiful, Rha. How did you learn to love yourself?

Rha: Spending time with myself, getting to know who I really am. Being willing to own my unique talents and gifts, the things that I do provide [for others]. Sometimes we do it so unconsciously [that] we don't even realize all of the ways that we make a difference for people every day. So taking that time and that space to acknowledge that what I was doing mattered was part of that self-love journey. And then teaching others how to value me, dare I say. And I know that may sound really arrogant, Abiola...

Abiola: Not in the goddess bombshell universe! We are all about that. Please go ahead.

Rha: Teaching people how to value you is really important; and that's everything from how to acknowledge you to having them respect your time, energy, and support when you do provide it. This is about how we deal in multiple currencies.

Abiola: Yes. Those are all feminine power healing principles. You say, "First we must stop apologizing for being women and we must stop trying to conform to structures that are not made to honor and support the truth of who we are." What does it mean to be a woman, Rha? How do you define feminine power?

Rha: The first word that comes up for me is embodiment, the commitment to be fully embodied, which is really about owning every facet of who we are. One of the entrepreneurs that we have the privilege to work with has an amazing venture called "Receive Everything." A big shout out to Emily Tepper. Emily and I talk about this a lot. This is about how you own your yeses and your nos; and what is it really means to stand up in the fullness of who you are.

So this idea and opportunity is also in our femininity – to own our softness as well as our warrior-ness. Because we have both. We engage and express along a continuum. So we want to own that part of us that will kiss you on your mouth and we also want to own that part of us that will kick your ass. Sometimes we do need to be a little tougher and sometimes we do need to be more nurturing, more conscious, and more gentle in our approach. The more we're fully embodied in the wholeness of who we are, the more we have access to all these different facets of ourselves.

Abiola: What makes you a bombshell, Rha?

Rha: I say this humbly because I'm not tripping, y'all. This is God moving through me – when I can get out of the way enough to allow it. As I know that when you come into your talents and gifts it is God moving through you, right? None of us got the monopoly on that one. But I would say my love; I lead with love. It takes a constant effort but my commitment to lead with love, my commitment to choose love no matter what is going on, I think might earn me some bombshell status. Then, my generosity in spirit. I was raised to believe that if you get any advantage you have an obligation and a responsibility to make a way for others. It is something that I admire deeply in other people and it's something I try to model. Wallace Wattles in *The Science of Getting Rich* calls it being "an advanced man" or "an advanced woman." Part of the anatomy of a conscious entrepreneur is that it's about being "advancing." That you're always looking at not only making it better for you but how to make it better for everybody else. Then I would say the embodiment; the commitment to walk my talk; to really be a living, breathing example of what I teach.

Bombshell Takeaways:

🔥 Living in your creativity and financial prosperity are not mutually exclusive.

🔥 Make peace with your fear; you're human.

🔥 Tap into your creative power by leading with love.

Secret of Creation Resources

1. *Tapping the Power Within* by Iyanla Vanzant

2. *The Artist's Way* by Julia Cameron

3. *Sacred Woman* by Queen Afua

4. *Resurrecting Venus* by Cynthia Occelli

5. *The Red Book* by Sera J. Beak

Creation Affirmations

1. I have more power than I ever thought possible.

2. I own my divine feminine magic.

3. The Universe co-creates my desires with me.

4. I can go where I want, be who I want, have what I want, and experience what I want.

5. My success is only limited by my imagination.

Two

The Secret of Radical Self-Being: Living This Moment

The Sacred Feminine Law of Self-Being

The Sacred Bombshell knows that there is power in just being, in self-being, in nowness. Thus, she gets out of her own way and beholds the present moment. She accepts what is and allows the flow. When she does not have access to self-love, she begins with mindful self-being. She appreciates where she is in this very minute. This is sacred self-love.

Historical Bombshell Mentor: Tina Turner, born 1939

"Just give me my name," Tina Turner reportedly told the judge when she walked away from her abusive husband. She not only had the courage to leave but also did many other women a service by writing and talking about the abuse she experienced when she was already a famous performer. The Buddhist mantra and prayer "Nam Myoho Renge Kyo" helped change her perspective, raise her vibration, and save her life. As she told Larry King, "My reality is that God has given us the faith, but we have to work on finding it, finding the God within us."

The Self-Being Declaration

Faith, trust, and instinct are my sisters in this present moment. This, the simplest of all lessons, is the most important. I have complete faith that my intuition is clear. I have no need to do. I need only be. The light is in self-being.

The answers are always within me. I only need to listen for guidance. I stop, breathe, listen, and trust. My eternity is this moment right now.

When I am at my lowest, I realize that seeming opportunities that fly in the face of what I know will present themselves. These false leads and temptations are just that. I will shut them down with a NO that can sink mountains. I trust that there are greater opportunities in my path.

I stop, breathe, and listen to my inner wisdom. My life is full of tremendous possibilities. I have faith that I am only a thought away from the life I deserve. The unseen guides me as I stand at the edge of my future. Yet I delight in right now, in this very minute, for I will never be here again.

This is more than mere positive thinking or masking. Mindfulness is being. Being is positive knowing. Faith is positive knowing with absolute conviction. This, self-being, the simplest of all lessons, is the most important. I have complete faith in myself. I only need to stop, breathe, listen, and trust. Now. For this I am so grateful.

And so it is.

My Big Fat Bombshell Diary: When I Couldn't Get to Self-Love

I jumped the broom in August 2004. I finally waved the white flag in January 2006 when I found another woman's menstrual products in my private bathroom. We remained platonically close and I finally finished moving my stuff out in June 2008.

That first night, I grabbed all that I could carry – physically and mentally. One of the first things I did, before even buying furniture, was to type and print my favorite affirmations and inspirational thoughts: "I am enough." "I may bend but I will not break." "I have more power than I ever thought possible." "I am a survivor." "This too shall pass." And my favorite: "No weapon formed against me can prosper."

I hung these words in hot pink print everywhere. These womantras were vitamins in those terrible days; even though I didn't – couldn't – fully believe them. Loving me again was too big a leap to make. I had wrapped my identity so much into being half of this perfect couple that I didn't know who I was uncoupled. Eventually I began to recover the pieces of my broken spirit.

"Dream bigger and love yourself." That was the signoff for my

Planet Abiola online show in 2007. "If no one has told you today, I love you." That was the signoff for my *Goddess Factory* podcast in 2005. I abandoned both of these lessons when I found myself embroiled in a relationship with an unavailable man.

It was my first relationship after the death of my marriage. I hired Samuel as a lead team member on one of my productions and we became friends. He lived out of town and was often abroad but traveled into my city frequently for work. We started dating; spending time with this African prince gave me life! Then he confessed that he lived with the mother of his children. He said that they lived in separate quarters, and presented photos to "prove it." Of course, he "didn't love her and was only there for the kids." He explained that it was important to him not to perpetuate the stereotype of his kids growing up in a black family with an absent father.

My own childhood abandonment issues triggered, I convinced Samuel that the only right thing for him to do was to marry the mother of his children, who still apparently loved him. Before going through with the marriage, he proposed to me and I declined – citing his untrustworthiness. I ended it so that he could create the picture-perfect African-American family. Then we kept seeing each other for another couple of months while he claimed that he was not intimate with his wife. Obviously this was an epic disaster and not my finest hour.

I had decided that all men were liars and cheaters. My father, who loves me unconditionally, is the best man I know and in the past he had betrayed my mother. My ex-husband was a community pillar and he seemed to be a serial liar. I felt like at least now I was on the inside rather than the one being betrayed. I reasoned that I didn't make a commitment to her; he did. I stupidly believed that there was no risk but karma. The truth is that I was doing to another woman what other women had done to me, and to my mother.

During this cowardly rebound drama, I settled for a cheap facsimile rather than the risk of a real relationship. I was acting out in a profoundly unloving way toward myself and everyone involved. Being with "somebody else's guy," no matter the circumstances, is an act of violence against another woman and yourself.

By encouraging Samuel to marry a woman he did not love, I added mayhem to chaos. The most self-loving choice I could have made would have been to opt out of the friendship and the relationship as soon as I found out about his living situation. However, I didn't have access to the self-love it would have taken to do that. I had moved from bad to worse. Luckily, I was able to eventually take my own advice and slam the door on this chapter.

I immersed myself in my own healing and started to really deal with my core issues. I made amends with a personal pledge to be in service. I actively focused my studies on mind-body-spirit healing practices, coaching, psychology, and spiritual excavation. I pulled tools based in sociology, art and drama therapy, and personal development from my educational background. I researched yin and yang energy and living with passion. My experiences led me to help other women find healing and personal power in matters of love, dating, sex, and relationships. Naturally, this work always comes back to self-worth, self-acceptance, and self-love.

The Sacred Feminine Power of Self-Being

Sometimes we just can't get to self-love. At those times, I say reach for self-being. Self-being is leaning into the essence of who you really are, versus the persona that you have created to be accepted by those around you. Where are you judging and rejecting yourself? How are you being mean and unkind to you?

Intellectually, I knew the importance of self-love and rebuilding my self-worth, but I felt like I didn't have access to either at the time. I was too splintered. My heart was still on the bottom of my ex's shoe. My vibrational energy was dirt low.

Eventually I no longer felt self-loathing, but I still couldn't align myself with self-love. Then it hit me all at the same time: nowness, enoughness, and acceptance. I realized that "where I am is where I am." I embraced the state of self-being. I stopped trying to get attention and started paying attention.

Because I couldn't find my source of self-esteem, I had to reach for what I did have access to: the present moment. In times of trouble and pain, we realize that this moment – right here and now – is all we have. Yesterday is gone and tomorrow is just an idea. Right now is it.

Being is the crux of femergy. When you can't do, just be. For me it was about starting from where I was. You can't start anywhere else, really. I had to rebuild a grown woman from scratch.

When I speak to women's groups where everyone is coming from different experiences, the idea of self-love and self-worth can seem far away. That's when I talk about the importance of self-being. Self-being is appreciating and milking the moment, being present and grateful for who you are at this very minute.

The Pathway to Self-Being: The A-List

I learned as I progressed in my personal development studies that the masters Ellen Langer, Ram Dass, Eckhart Tolle, and Barbara Carrellas were all teaching sister lessons to self-being as mindfulness, nowness, stillness, Zen, and Barbara's "gasms" of ecstasy. Find my Bombshell Dialogue with Barbara at SacredBombshell. com.

Choose Authenticity

Radical self-being is living authentically. It's so easy to get caught up in the trappings: the right car, the right man, the right look. Shoes are fun, but they have nothing to do with who you truly are. Interlocking Cs on your bag won't help you live authentically, although the two are not mutually exclusive.

Choose Allowing

Radical self-being is allowing. We are fierce get-em-girls and wonder women who make things happen. The world at this present moment feels like it's all about the hustle. And action is important, but so is allowing.

When I started weight training with kettlebells, I loved them so much that I wanted to work out every day. I wanted to hurry up and burn calories and turn fat into muscle. Unfortunately, the body doesn't work that way. You have to take days off in between lifting weights to allow muscles to form. Life is like that too. We have to learn how to be, how to allow things to flow.

Choose Awareness

Radical self-being is awareness. Surrender. Be where you are. Be *who* you are. Let go of who you think you should be for who you truly are. Let go of what you think should be happening for what actually is. The great thing about self-being is that you don't have to work at it. You're already there. Just acknowledge, honor, and appreciate it. You are worthy. You are loved. You are self-love.

Choose Appreciation

Radical self-being is appreciation. No matter where you are, be grateful. Have gratitude that you are still here, alive. Appreciate the moment. Appreciate yourself. Appreciation is self-honoring. It's not about trying, just being. Our lives are a reflection of how we feel about ourselves, so honor yourself. You will not find your bliss until you honor who you are right now. How would you treat yourself if you honored you?

Choose Acceptance

Radical self-being is acceptance. "And so it is." That is the mantra of acceptance. Radical self-being is accepting who you are right this moment. Not you after a few more months of self-improvement, not the future you who has more money, not the you who has lost that 10 pounds. Radical self-being is accepting who you are without conditions. This is the foundation of self-love and self-worth.

It doesn't mean that you don't try to better yourself. However, if you don't accept yourself today, you won't be able to do so simply because you have more trinkets. Self-acceptance is giving yourself permission to be who you are. Remove the blinders and victim-colored glasses. Turn a light on the blind spots. Stop the blame and take full responsibility. It is a privilege to be you.

Choose Attention

Radical self-being is attention. Give your full attention to everything you do, and to every moment of your life. Being fully present is the way.

Bombshell Tool: Chocolate Meditation

All you need for this self-being exercise is a Hershey's Kiss and your mind. Mindful and intuitive eating have been key for me in releasing disordered eating and unhealthy weight and in learning to love my body. The feminine energy practices of being mindful and intuitive are empowering for any gender. The Chocolate Meditation Tool is about bringing your awareness to the present. I strive to eat all of my meals this way. This prevents me from mindlessly bingeing or being caught up in other emotions while numbing myself with food. Here's how:

1. Engage all of your senses. Observe your breath and the silver, flat-bottomed dewdrop. Behold the tiny Kiss in its festive aluminum wrapping. Contemplate the narrow plume of paper emerging from the thin, twisted metal. Examine the distinctive-looking candy and consider its unique beauty. As you unwrap this mini-present, pay close attention to the crackling sound of the foil opening. Breathe in the rich scent.

2. Your full attention is on the teardrop-shaped, bite-sized candy. Follow your breath. You are not worrying about yesterday, today, or tomorrow. Your entire existence right now is focused on this rich chocolate. Turn it around in your fingers. Consider the color, shape, texture, and design.

3. Send positive thoughts to all that conceived of and prepared this magnificent gift just for you! No matter what is going on, be grateful for how wealthy you are to have the means, the time, and the wellbeing to experience this moment. Maybe even kiss the Kiss.

4. Take a deep breath. Inhale the bold aroma of the chocolate. Take another breath. Feel the texture with your fingers. Does it rub off in your hands or stay solid? What would you call this color? Notice every pore and nick on the cocoa surface.

5. Are you able to take a bite of the Kiss or can you only eat it

whole? Let that first taste roll around your tongue. Does it taste different with the tip of your tongue than on the back of your tongue? Savor it, nibble by nibble. Close your eyes and feel the chocolate move down your throat and esophagus. If there are melting remains on your fingers, lick them slowly and enjoy the pure pleasure of the experience.

6.   If your mind wanders at any point during this meditation, always come back to the Kiss. Remain aware. Connect with your senses. When you inhale and exhale, notice the gap between your breaths. Everything in this moment is perfectly okay.

7.   How do you feel? You are not in the future or past – you are with the chocolate. Close with a few deep breaths. You are exactly where you should be.

Am I There Yet?

If you're like many of the bombshells I meet, you may be asking: "When will I arrive?" It's a valid question for any journey: Are we there yet? You say to yourself: "When will I be finished, healed, or complete? I've done so much work already. When will I have my dream life? Where is he or she? When will I get there?"

The answer to that very valid question is this: You are there. This is there. The journey is the destination.

I said this to a coaching client and she said, "Well if this is there then that's depressing." But there's no reason to despair because this is where all of your power is – in the present moment. Your spark is not in the past that you can't do anything about. Your strength is not in the future that doesn't exist. All that you can affect is this very present moment.

You just have to start with radical self-being. Be where you are, living in present tense, realizing that the trip to "there" is also the destination. The next time you're asking yourself, "When will I finally be the woman that I want to be?" wake up and say, "I *am* the woman I want to be." You have that power right now. And from there you can continue to evolve.

Another client said, "Well if I loved myself now, then why would I try to lose the weight or do anything better?" The reason you would try to do better for yourself is *because* you love yourself. If I love my baby, I want to feed her well and I want her to be healthy. I want her to learn to crawl and then walk. I want to optimize her life in the long term, but it doesn't mean that I don't love who she is in this very minute. Get that?

You may love your family members, your spouse, your parents, your friends – but you still want them to evolve and be the best they can be. So yes, you can love yourself in this very minute. You can appreciate and show gratitude for right now, but it doesn't mean that you're stuck. It's actually the opposite.

Let's look at procrastination, for example. You beat yourself up, blame and shame yourself because you feel like you're not moving forward because of procrastination. You think you're procrastinating because you're lazy. Well, maybe you are. One way to stop beating yourself up is to accept it and say, "Okay, sometimes I am lazy. We're all lazy at times, and I accept that," and move forward.

Go deeper. Don't stop at the label of lazy. Don't stop at the blame or the shame. Go deeper. You're more than lazy. You're scared. Sometimes maybe we should be scared. Sometimes it's a path we shouldn't be going down or what we're fearing is a big change or decision. Maybe you've known in your bones for the past year that you need to leave your husband. Maybe you're scared of taking that new job because of the timing.

Be where you are. Maybe it's not your season to be doing "that." As the granddaughter of farmers on both sides I'm a big believer in seasons. Maybe it's your season for healing inwardly instead. As our Historical Bombshell Mentor Zora Neale Hurston says, "there are years that ask questions and years that answer."

Appreciate where you are. Maybe you have to heal that rift with your dad or your girlfriend before you can have the wisdom to do what you want to do. It may not seem like it, but you're a logical creature – if you're procrastinating, ask yourself why. Be curious about you.

Once you get still enough to realize that you're scared, then you can work on the fear instead of castigating yourself for being lazy. You can "be" enough to see, "Oh! I'm scared to make a speech because when I got up in front of the class in third grade the kids laughed at me." Once you get that, you can ask yourself, "Am I still in the third grade?" No. "Does Mrs. Schneider still have power over me?" No. You can then move forward. Start with being where you are and embracing baby steps. Set your GPS to where you want to be but don't curse it when you're halfway there. The vitality is in enjoying the journey.

Am I there yet? No, not when you give up on yourself. Am I there yet? No, not when you're ungrateful for the fact that you woke up. Am I there yet? No, not when you still can't forgive that guy who stood you up five years ago. Am I there yet? No, not when you're facing backward and trying to move forward and wondering why you're stuck and why you're procrastinating – it's because you're looking the wrong way!

I am in a state of peace and forgiveness toward my exes – ex-loves, ex-bosses, ex-friends, ex-enemies. This is life in the present tense. In the present, none of us are betraying or misleading each other. The misdeeds happened in the past.

For those of you insisting that you will be happy when you get "there": false. Be happy now or you will never be. I'm not saying put on a happy face and start tap dancing. You're not going to access exuberant joy if that's not where you are. But no matter where you are, you can feel a hair more joyful in the present moment – all you have to do is reach for it. Reach for a tiny feeling of happiness – just a little bit more than yesterday – and squeeze all the joy that you can out of every little victory.

"Wow, I did all of my Bombshell Explorations in that last chapter." "Cool, I read that dialogue between Abiola and Gabby Bernstein and I signed up for Gabby's newsletter." "Awesome, I asked my friends to form a Bombshell Playgroup with me." Superb! Baby steps. Throw a parade for yourself. That is the joy in the journey. A tiny bit more gratitude, a tiny bit more joy, a tiny bit more fun, pleasure, and self-care than you had yesterday.

Bombshell Tool: Sacred Pause Meditation Technique

Now that you know the concept of self-being, you can access the moment whenever things get too hectic or busy. You can always return to the center of yourself with Sacred Pause Meditation. The Sacred Pause is putting life on hold to focus on the breath.

1. Get comfortable. Close your eyes. Become aware of the sounds around you. Notice the smells. Feel the state of your body.

2. Imagine that you have an inner pause button, as on a remote control. Whenever you press pause, the illusions of past and future fall away and you are in this present moment where all is well. Your only job during this Sacred Pause is self-being, focusing on the breath.

3. Inhale through your nose and exhale through your mouth. Notice which nostril is dominant. Do you favor your left or right nostril? For balance, alternate breathing dominantly through either side.

4. Now take 100 breaths. Yes, 100. You can start by just counting and breathing: Inhale-One-Exhale, Inhale-Two-Exhale …. Eventually, you want to be able to inhale for four counts, hold for eight counts, and exhale for four counts.

After taking a Sacred Pause, you can go back to your life more acutely aware of the present moment. Pay attention, and look for moments where you can do the Sacred Pause in motion – where you can stop life, notice the breath, and come back to yourself.

The Marvelous, Mystical Art of Radical Self-Being: "Just Be It"

When I came to this work, the last thing that I wanted to do was surrender to anything or anybody. What? Give up control? Me? Control in all its various forms – from workaholism to physical perfectionism – was second nature to me. That changed when my life fell apart – again and again. I felt as though I had lost control, but the greatest realization of self-being was that I was never in control to begin with! None of us are. Yes, we are co-creators, consciously or unconsciously, in our own experiences. However, we are not in control. The hardest thing for a superwoman to do is to relinquish the reigns. Let go. Surrender to your life. Practice by being flexible. Just be it.

So the breakthrough is that this is "there," this is it, this is the journey *and* the destination. You're never "done" because you're meant to desire growth and change. You're always led to want more. Look at Oprah Winfrey: 25 years hosting the top show and she wanted more. She took a risk that her haters said would fail – but she had to challenge herself because she's still alive. So when you get "there," wherever you think there is – the promotion, the marriage, the baby – it is only natural that you will desire something else.

How many times have you experienced a dream-come-true event? You went on a dream vacation or married your soul mate, and you thought, "Good, I've arrived" – only to realize that it was the beginning of another journey. You found that perfect person and then you wanted to start a family, or you landed that dream job and then wanted to move up. There is always room to evolve.

Don't think of "being there" as an exhausting consequence. On the contrary, it is empowering when you're aware of it and say, "I may be in the muck right now, but I am meant to desire more. I am meant to evolve." If none of us desired anything, we wouldn't move forward as a species.

I remember a conversation with a friend over 10 years ago about being happy "ultimately" – when I get that done or get this thing accomplished. Write this down in your Bombshell Playbook: There is no happiness on a layaway plan. You will not be happy "one day."

This is why a practice of gratitude is so important. This is why in the Bombshell Dialogue with therapist Meg Batterson, she advises us to drop down into our bodies in order to heal from trauma. That means to get present in your body. This is why meditation or yoga is a crucial part of this journey because those are two ways of becoming present. You can't balance on one leg while thinking about tomorrow. You've got to be right there, in that balancing point.

My Sacred Bombshell Sister, this is why you feel drained. Our yang, masculine energy society is all about doing, right? We need that active energy, but the other part that we're missing is equally important: being. Instead of "Just do it," from now on I'm saying "Just be it."

You've got to milk this present moment. When you're looking at your sibling and loving him or her. When you're having a moment because your boss just said well done. When your partner gives you a kiss on the forehead and it feels so good and reminds you why you are in love. When your heart is broken or you've lost someone precious to you. Milk those moments. Stay in that present. Do not run from it, good or bad. Just be it.

We all get scared. We have fears about how much anything we can stand. Feeling your feelings, finding your gratitude, and forgiveness is how you realize that this is there. Otherwise, when you get the dream house and you realize that it, like everything in life, is imperfect, you'll be miserable again. You will never be happy if you're waiting for exterior circumstances to *make* you happy.

When we are stuck in either the past or the future, it manifests in all kinds of ways. For example, I used to be known for being clumsy. I stopped saying the word clumsy for a long time because I was using it to bully myself. Now I get a laugh out of it. It's a personal shadow that I'm spatially disadvantaged at times and it is a blessing because it forces me to remember to focus on the present. I've got to stay grounded in the now because the reason I was knocking things over and running into stuff is that my brain was never in the present moment.

My thoughts were always on where I was going and what I need to get done. Instead of thinking about the next thing, be present.

Otherwise you might spill hot lemon water on your laptop. (Yes, I did that – January 2014.)

Be here with your present because otherwise you are missing out on your own life. If you are filling in the blanks while your partner is talking, thinking, "he's going to say this; he always says that," then you're not in the present. The power is in the present moment. If you have ever said, "Oh my God, where did that year go? I can't believe that we're already in this month," it's because you're missing the present moment.

Being sad, feeling guilty, dwelling in blame or shame about the past or anxiety about the future eats up time. If you're grieving, grieve. It's the healthiest thing for you. But if you are stuck in "what if?" "why not?" "why didn't I?" or could have, should have, would have – you're missing your life.

Those of us who are emotional eaters know that it's all too easy to scarf down something and ask, "Where did the meal go?" Be in your present moment, in every single morsel of whatever you are eating. Make a great wonderful meal that loves you back. Be there on your plate. As in the Chocolate Meditation, engage all of your senses.

Even be present in the things that you think suck. This is blisspower, blissipline. Light candles and incense to do your taxes. Get some $14 caviar (or whatever works for your income level) and have a bill paying session. During my workouts I used turn up the music loud enough to distract myself, but then I started thinking, *be present*. Affirmations help me do that. Now I'm present with the workout instead of barreling through it. Victory!

Life doesn't begin when you lose the weight or get the job or find love. Enjoy the cycles. If you are waiting until you "arrive" to start living, you're MIA in your own life, Missing in Affirmation.

Surrender. Go with the flow. Yes, it sounds much easier than it is. However, when we acknowledge how much more difficult not going with the flow is, then we can surrender to the femergy of fluidity. After all, feminine cycles and flow are the natural way of our bodies. Your life does not have a linear path. There are wiggles.

curves, trails, and veer-offs with roundabouts and repeats.

Take a breath. Just be it.

Bombshell Challenge: Vow to keep your word to yourself for 24 hours. If you can't do it for 24 hours, start with one. Show up for yourself for that hour. Own your bombshell for that hour. Be present. That is self-being.

Bombshell Explorations: Ten Ways to Nurture the Self in the Present Moment

1. **Watch what you eat.** If your great-grandparents wouldn't recognize it, don't eat it. Instead, eat the rainbow of foods that grow from the ground. We claim that we can't afford healthy food and then we spend exorbitant amounts on clothes or gadgets. Put your money into the one thing that will still be with you at the end of your life – your precious body. You buy your car the best fuel you can; do the same for your sacred vessel.

2. **Move your body daily.** Whoever said move it or lose it is right. If you can't run, walk. If you can't dance, sway. If you can't jump, wave your arms. No matter how your body is abled, celebrate her and keep your heart healthy. Take the stairs. Get off of the subway a stop early. Leave your car at home and get moving.

3. **Baths are more than an indulgence.** Bubble baths might seem easily dismissible, but they are an act of self-compassion. Think of every bath as a baptism. I'm a shower person, but I employ the same principles. Later we will examine the self-healing tool of spiritual baths.

4. **Give back.** What do you believe in? Volunteer. Give your time. Give your money. Earn your right to complain. It's not enough to grumble online. Change something. Start a petition. Join a campaign. Write a letter. Take on a pro bono client.

5. **Learn something new.** Seeking knowledge is an investment in yourself. Take a cooking class if you want to feed yourself,

a pole fitness class if you feel uptight, or a boxing class if you feel physically unsafe. Learning something new can raise your self-esteem. New knowledge is a great beginning to re-parenting yourself and learning to take care of your own needs.

6. **Develop bedtime and waking rituals.** The time before we go to bed and when we first wake up is sacred. The time right before I go to sleep is my Bombshell Power Hour. I use this time to record in my food diary what I have eaten along with the emotions I felt at the time. I light a candle and incense. I listen to spiritual recordings or meditative music. I read. I journal and make a gratitude list. In the morning, I have started a practice of always making my bed, meditating, and having my protein shake. Sometimes I do Emotional Freedom Technique (more on that later), affirmations, or self-reiki. I work out and clean my apartment on alternate days. Then I hop into the shower, which holds its own rituals, and begin my day. This has made a world of difference. As hokey as it sounds, start and end each day looking into your own eyes in a mirror and saying, "I love you, beautiful. I am here for you and you are safe."

7. **Build a support team.** No woman is an island. Check out my "Thanks Giving" acknowledgements section to see how many people were essential for this single book by one author! You don't need to bring home the bacon, fry it up in the pan, have marathon sex, and make partner all by yourself. You need support. It is fine to call a babysitter so that you can go for a solo picnic in the park. If you can afford a housekeeper, nanny, personal trainer, or personal assistant, please hire one immediately. I could look at my grandmothers and say, "They each raised seven to ten children alone. Why do I need help?" If I look closer, they had help. They had neighbors who would tell them if their kids were running astray. They had family members who brought support when something was wrong. They put the kids to work doing chores. Their community fed each other when pickings were slim. Most of all, neither one of my grandmas would want me to live lean because they did. They would want my life to be greater.

8. **Forgive yourself.** Do you think that your Creator looks at
    you and thinks: She's ugly, stupid, or a mistake? Absolutely
    not. It's practically an act of blasphemy to see yourself as
    anything other than the living, breathing miracle that you are.
    Sure, you might be a little rough around the edges, but here's
    the big secret: We all are! You can stop beating yourself up
    now. Forgiving yourself is the best thing you can do for you.
    Be woman enough to say "I made an error in judgment" and
    move forward. Love all of your Selves. Love the you in prog-
    ress. Love the you of your past. Love you.

9. **Engage in healing modalities.** We all have triggers. Most of
    us spend our time in a state of trigger management rather than
    getting to the root of the issue and dissolving our triggers.
    Healing practices like yoga and qi gong can help change your
    default state to one of self-care. Who cares if you are "not the
    kind of person who does these things?"

10. **Turn the noise off.** You can't honor your voice if you can't
    hear it. Between work, bills, family, and trying to have a so-
    cial life, our brains are packed. Add to that TV, radio, and the
    Internet, and it can feel like life never stops. Consider unplug-
    ging from the noise. There should be no TV in your bedroom.
    Our phones are mini entertainment and work centers so they
    shouldn't be there either. In the past I've turned off TV news
    for a year or two. People said, "But how will you know what's
    going on?" You'd be surprised how little local fear-based
    news has to do with your everyday life.

Bombshell Dialogue with Gabrielle Bernstein: How to Create Miracles

I was struck by the glorious light in Gabrielle Bernstein's home, from the front door all the way up to her "Zen Den," as she called her attic play space. Light, airy, and formerly owned by a rocker, her home reflected the intense welcoming that I felt upon meeting her. Gabby is leading the charge for us to move past our egos and into the light. Gabby's newest book is *Miracles Now: 108 Life-Changing Tools for Less Stress, More Flow, and Finding Your True Purpose*. The yogini has spoken openly about her recovery from several addictions. Those seeking better lives can connect in her online community, HerFuture.com.

Gabby: Hello, welcome to my home!

Abiola: The energy beaming off of you, lovely woman, is incredible. Let's get into your work.

Gabby: *Add More Ing to Your Life* was my first book and "ing" stands for inner guidance. And so this book is all about really activating your inspiration and your intuition and connecting to that loving voice within you. My book *Spirit Junkie* is my memoir but it's also a guidebook. It gives amazing metaphysical principles that you can apply to your day-to-day life.

MediDating is meditations for fearless romance. We all get tripped up in romantic relationships, right? Everyone has their own romantic mini-dramas in some form. Whether it be fear of finding a partner, fear of not having a partner, or not enjoying the relationships that you do have – fear really runs the show in the romantic arena often. So I created this album to help listeners really clear that negativity, release their resentments, and clear space to become a magnet for a really powerful relationship.

Abiola: Yes, that's where the power is. Clearing the space and becoming a magnet. Allowing all of the magic that's in the universe to come to you.

Gabby: That's pretty much what all of my work is about. It's really about releasing the blocks to the presence of your inner power – the presence of love within you, the presence of that magnetic energy. We all have it. We just block it, and fear is just the primary way we block that energy, and all of these products – particularly this meditation album, the first seven meditations – are all about releasing the blocks, letting go of your resentments, and clearing that space. And the last one is about calling in the romance.

Abiola: How did you get started?

Gabby: I was looking for my happiness in all the wrong places and I was really just trying to fill myself up with these outside sources. Whether it be my credentials or my romantic relationships or access to some nightclub and all of the silly things we get caught up in. So by the time I was 25, I hit a "quarter-life crisis." I hit a big, big bottom and had no other choice but to shift my energy and my perspective. And that was a great gift.

Abiola: So many people contact me and say, "I've hit a personal crisis" and they don't know what to do. How did you rise up from that?

Gabby: The first step for any of us that hits a bottom is to first and foremost really accept that we have to change, to become willing to change. That slight willingness was all that I needed to really take that next step forward and really receive all the guidance that came [after]. But if you are unwilling to change, you block the guidance. So that first step is really about having the willingness and accepting, "If things are not working, I am not happy and there has to be a better way."

Abiola: Then you started living in your truth and developing your "ing."

Gabby: Yes, "ing," which typically is a gerund for most of us – skiing, running, whatever – became more of an acronym. It became another part this of spiritual lexicon. It's called inner guidance in my vocabulary. Many people might call it "God" or "Holy Spirit" or "Christ mind," or whatever comes forth. The Universe, right? That connectedness, that intuition, I call it "ing."

Abiola: Ah, so your title *Add More Ing* is like getting more spirit, more Universe, more of what fills us up rather than those ego things that are superficial or feel temporarily good; the quick hits. What will we learn about you in your memoir?

Gabby: It's really telling my story from adolescence to the present of how I've had spiritual interventions throughout my life and then had many moments of really recognizing there's much more beyond what we can see with our eyes, and how I deepened that connection and really strengthened that relationship to spirit and through that relationship overcame many, many, many fears. And [I] continue to practice these principles every single day to stay connected and centered and today live far beyond my wildest dreams as a result of living the *Spirit Junkie* way.

Abiola: What I love about you sharing your personal experience is that many people feel like, "Wow, look at this woman. She's beautiful, she's got on pink, she's vivacious, she's exciting," and they think you just lived the last 30-something years of your life this way, and that you didn't have to overcome anything.

Gabby: That's right. I felt like it was my duty to tell my readers more of my story in my first book and be extremely transparent and forthcoming about what it took to get to the place that I'm at today. And be a power of example for them because if I'm not honest about my path and all of the dark corners, then how can I expect my readers to resonate and follow?

Abiola: Is *MediDating* the first time you've directly addressed relationship issues?

Gabby: Yes. I am a recovering co-dependent so this is really beautiful work that is dear to my heart and my own personal recovery. I've recovered from lots of addictions: drug addiction, love addiction, work addiction, food addiction — but the romantic addiction was really the [deepest] one for me and I understand how crippling that can be for women in particular and how we can get so hooked into that false belief system that "without a romantic partner, I am incomplete."

Abiola: Especially because our society feeds that belief system and tells you that you need to be fixed if you're not in a relationship.

Gabby: In *Spirit Junkie* I have a chapter called "Spirit Became My Boyfriend" and it talks about how through the practice of meditation and mindfulness, and really clearing my own fears, how I awakened a relationship to a spiritual connection that fills me up. And at the point that I became full through my spiritual connection I was then not only in a place of really being very attractive to other partners – because you're beginning to vibrate this frequency of "I love my life" – but I also was in a place where I could hold and be in a container that was really a very holy relationship. And it wasn't a place of needing that partner to fill me up. I was finally full. I could just be there and enjoy. I can be here today and enjoy the connectedness of two whole people coming together. That's the ultimate goal of this work; to help you clean up your stuff, your fears, your lack feelings, your feelings of inadequacy...

Abiola: Your junk!

Gabrielle: Your junk — and then as a result of clearing that space, the final meditations are really about becoming a magnet to call in what it is you desire, and more importantly get clear about what you want. Because many women are running around thinking, "I want this," "I want that" but there is not a clear vision. Without a clear vision, you're going to be calling in some funky stuff!

Abiola: I'm thrilled about this project, Gabby! Please lead us through a *MediDating* meditation.

Gabby: Because we are in this time of seasonal change, it's a time when people really want to call in a romantic partner. We can do a manifesting meditation.

Let's shut our eyes. Just put your palms facing upward because this is when we can really call in all of the vibrational energy around us. Take a deep breath in your nose, and breathe out of your mouth, and just identify any area in your body where you might be holding on to any discomfort.

Take a deep, deep breath in and just feel the energy of the room around you. And keep breathing deeply in your nose and out of your mouth and just think for a moment of the feelings that come over you when you think about romantic love. What is the feeling of romance for you? Is it a feeling of freedom? Is it a heart-palpitating experience?

Think your way into that experience of romantic love and hold the vision in your mind of yourself holding hands with that romantic partner. You don't need to give [him or her] a body or a form. Just see yourself with this being of beautiful energy holding hands, walking through park.

Feel the feelings coming over you with the awesome emotional breakthrough. Allow yourself to be fully present [in the feeling of] a romantic relationship. Allow yourself to experience those feelings and breathe them in and then exhale, release. See yourself walking through the city, hand in hand, or through your neighborhood celebrating the holidays, in this beautiful, divine union. Continue thinking your way into this romantic bliss without having to put face or body to this partner, just knowing that there is [an] energy of romance around you.

[Feel] that experience of romance, and [know] that when you feel that experience of romance, you are activating an energy of romance, and that energy is what is calling that partner toward you. Take one last deep breathe in and release. When you're ready, open your eyes.

Bombshell Takeaways:

- You can access your "ing," your inner guidance, at any time.
- Facing your addictions and issues happens in the present moment.
- There is power in being transparent.

Bombshell Dialogue with Donna D'Cruz: How to Tune in to Your Bliss

This is a time for vulnerability, strength, and claiming our wisdom. Next on this wondrous life-changing adventure called today: Meet Donna D'Cruz, magical goddess of rituals and kindred spirit. Donna, who gives the blessing at the beginning of this book, is a DJ, yogini, and entrepreneur. I attended her "Music and Meditation" class at Jivamukti Yoga School in Manhattan and I am still vibrating joy from the experience. In addition to her musical talents, Donna is also well-versed in the womanly arts of "spirituality, senses, and style." The "Sensualista" brought her exquisite homemade tea to our chat. She teaches rhythmic yoga and meditation at Phoenix House, one of America's largest drug and alcohol rehab organizations. Donna's company Rasa Living sells soulful products such as chakra-balancing gemstone necklaces, pure single-note soy candles, and her CD, ***Meditation 101***.

With love, gratitude, and intention, enter into our sacred conversation...

Donna: I'm so happy to be here, very excited.

Abiola: I am, too. One of dynamic things about your work is the way you bring together different healing modalities. What's your background, Donna?

Donna: I heard a beautiful quote once by Hazrat Inayat Khan and he says that where we are ends up dictating to some extent the vibration that we have on a spiritual level. And I'm always grateful for having been born in Southern India. That's where Ayurveda comes from. Thanks to my parents I was brought up to ask, "How can I serve?" That question really changed my life. When you put your ear to the ground and your hand on your heart and you learn what the wisdom traditions offer us, there's great wisdom, great strength, great femininity, and great power.

Abiola: What does meditation and mindfulness mean to you?

Donna: It's a way to create space. To me, meditation is a beautiful opportunity to sit in stillness. The greatest irony is that we think we're too busy to meditate. We think our lives are too full; we're too harried and hurried.

Abiola: But it's the opposite, isn't it?

Donna: Absolutely. When you make the space and you come into that space of meditation you actually become more productive. Ideas flow to you. Love flows to you differently. And in truth, there is life before meditation and there is life after meditation. Just like great love. It's like seeing the world in black and white and then seeing [it] in full blown color. That's what meditation did for me.

Meditation is not only for those times when things go swimmingly, but for those times when they don't. It's most useful for those times when you may not feel like meditating. As part of my meditation practice I play music that I created and produced. It acts as a sonic balm. When I play it, it immediately brings me back to me, back to my center, back to my breath. Music provides the "express-lane" ability to calm, soothe, and relax me. Music is said to be our first sense when we come into the earthly realm and also our last, as we depart it.

Abiola: Donna, will you please guide us through one of your famous minute meditations? We're drinking tea, so let's do a "tea meditation."

Donna: Absolutely. In truth, everything about your life can turn into a meditation and into a moment of repose. I've just come up with my own way of taking what's ordinary, ritualizing it, and making it extraordinary because our lives are extraordinary. To me, this is a great, simple meditation. Of course, I'd like to light the candle first. (Donna lights a candle.)

Abiola: When I do workshops, I sometimes do a "chocolate meditation" because emotional eating was a challenge that I had to conquer. Mindfulness, self-being, and mindful eating and making every meal a meditation have been very healing.

Donna: Taking your word "mindfulness" – if we were in a hurry and not really aware, we would just take the cup and saucer, pour it, and start slurping away. But in a mindful way our opportunity here is to inhale, pick up our cup and saucer, reach for the teapot, exhale and pour. Then I inhale again.

In a lot of Asian traditions, offerings are made like this. (Donna holds the full tea cup and saucer forward in the palm of her left hand. The left side of the body represents feminine energy. Her right hand is under the left, facing up.) And we just say, "Give thanks." It can be done silently. Just expressing a second of gratitude shifts things. It's all about awareness.

Take an inhale. Take an exhale. And maybe just for two to three seconds just close your eyes and try it again. And in gratitude for this few seconds of peace, take a deep breath in and gently place your cup and saucer down. All of which took us maybe thirty to forty-five seconds. In that little space of time we've come back to our body, come back to our breath, and come back to that real capital "S" Self. When we come back with awareness of the Self, we have the power to change everything.

Abiola: That was lovely. As you know, prayer is our speaking to the Creator. Meditation gives us the opportunity to listen. Please tell us about your company, Rasa Living.

Donna: The word "rasa" is a Sanskrit word and it means the essence or the flavor of living. It can literally mean the sap from a tree but it also describes vibration, sound. Love is a rasa and so is anger. I am having the best time. I feel like this is that shift, that divine feminine opening. It's here. My game is just to shift it. If I'm going to walk into something, nothing about it is going to be usual because when we lay it down for the last time and take that last breath, it's a series of memories and moments that we're left with. A moment of lighting a candle, kissing a loved one, knowing just when to inhale and exhale and being present.

Abiola: Magical moments. Can you please share two yoga moves that someone could work with for healing and releasing emotional pain?

Donna: There's a very simple one and it's actually a release yoga. We call it a stress buster but this is actually very specific for the release of emotions. This is for all of us that are holding on to something that maybe we're ready to let go of or that we know doesn't serve us.

Put your elbows up and put your hands close to your ears. Your wrists can be loose. You don't want them to be stiff. It's almost like you're doing a tambourine dance. You want your hands to be closed but not tight. And you start doing this (twisting wrists) as quickly as you can.

Close your eyes. You can do this for about two to three sets, ninety seconds a time. You'll start noticing one wrist might get a little tired. Just keep going as fast as you can. Keep that wrist soft and when you're ready, bring it down.

The second is called the sipping breath. The sipping breath is to cool the emotions so you do this almost like you're sipping through a straw. Take a deep breath in. Let go and take another quick one. You do three or four of these when you're really stressed and you're going to lash out. This will immediately drop you down into a place where you can be a little bit more informed and make a smarter decision.

Abiola: Thank you, Donna. What makes you a bombshell – and a goddess?

Donna: Whew! What a large and expansive question, Abiola. It's time our sisterhood reclaimed many things for ourselves, beginning with definitions and there's no better place to start than with two such visceral words – bombshell and goddess.

Etymology has always fascinated me and I was intrigued to learn that the word bombshell originated around 1710 and was, of course, military in origin and meant an object designed to explode on impact. I like turning this on its head and seeing the positivism of that impact, not the collateral damage. I like to define bombshell as living in [a] state of surprising unexpectedness and high-impact changes that lift one up, propelling us forward with speed, decision, and a target in mind.

As for goddess, being born in India, a country with literally thousands of goddesses to choose from, it wasn't hard to realize what the Universal female spirit meant. I seek out the goddess in every woman, no matter how prosaic she imagines herself to be or how society may view her. We are all a reflection of the Eternal Feminine, the eternal goddess.

Our goddess, our inner bombshell, our outer and internal beauty are all gifts to be used not to seek and destroy but rather to uplift, inspire, and to replace light where there might be shadow. "By God, when you see your own beauty, you will be the idol of your Self." That's a Rumi quote.

Bombshell Takeaways:

- Begin by asking, "How can I serve?"
- Meditation and focusing on the breath creates space in our lives.
- Ritual and ceremony are life-enhancing.

Secret of Self-Being Resources

1. ***Getting in the Gap*** by Dr. Wayne W. Dyer (book/audio)

2. ***The Magical Path of Intuition*** by Florence Scovel Shinn

3. ***Be Here Now*** by Ram Dass

4. ***The Power of Now*** by Eckhart Tolle

5. ***Conscious Breathing*** by Gay Hendricks

Self-Being Affirmations

1. This moment is my delicious eternity.

2. It feels good to be here now.

3. I am present.

4. I embrace my best life right this very minute.

5. My life is a constant stream of miracles.

Three

The Secret of Receptivity: Receiving Your Good

The Sacred Feminine Law of Receptivity

The Sacred Bombshell knows that she deserves to receive the finest that life has to offer. She is open to receiving positively charged energy, sacred relationships, enchanting experiences, and every blessing because she is worth it. The more she loves herself, the more love she receives. The more she receives, the more she is able to give. This is sacred self-love.

Historical Bombshell Mentor: Diana Ross, born 1944

Diana Ross was once named "Female Entertainer of the Century." Call her Miss Ross. Many of her performance photos feature the divine diva standing arms wide open – fully receiving the adoration of her audience. The bombshell energy of this captivating singer-actress caused a smitten former husband to buy her an island. This loving mother also managed to raise five well-adjusted children under the glare of the spotlight. According to the actress who played her in Broadway's **Motown: The Musical**, the legendary Diana is also a lover of Psalm 23, which features the receptive words. "my cup runneth over."

The Receptivity Declaration

Today I remember my birthright and I am open to receiving. As I stand fully in my feminine power, I know that I have the strength of my ancestors within me. I feel them rooting for me. The actions of many who came before – many I will never know – have caused me to prosper. I welcome the rich blessings they created for me. I allow the sun to shine on me. I wear the crown they bought for me. I receive and I am outrageously grateful.

I welcome my desires, like a dying woman welcomes air. Previously I buried my desires in the deepest part of my soul. Now I set them free. I emerge and shout my desires from on high; so that they echo in the rafters of my being, changing my very biology and

by proxy changing the makeup of the world around me.

It feels good to receive. I open my arms and my heart. I shall not want. My ego may feel discontent but my soul knows that I am fully provided for, always and in all ways. I have complete faith that everything I desire is accessible to me fully. I need only allow my blessings in. I need only receive all that I am worth.

I receive now with grace, with wonder, with exuberance and humility. I receive all good things. I lean into my perfect blessings. I embrace my enchantment. How wondrous my life is. How wonder-filled it is to receive. I am receptive to the blessings of the Universe. For this I am so grateful.

And so it is.

Superwomen: Too Strong to Receive

As I write this, my brother and his beautiful wife are expecting a precious little bambino. (Yay!) I am proud, excited, and looking forward to meeting the sure-to-be magnificent person that Ovid Jr. and Tammi create. My brother is intelligent, fun, and kind – as is Tammi – so I already know that my niece will be a great person.

Yesterday, Tammi was offered a seat on the subway for the first time. It was the first acknowledgement from a stranger that she's "showing." The woman obviously felt compassion upon noticing a pregnant woman standing on a crowded train during rush hour.

So did Tammi, a strong career woman who plans to work almost until delivery, take a load off of her stylish feet and sit down? No, she refused. Feeling slightly taken aback at the newness of the situation and also not wanting to seem somehow weak, Tammi continued to stand on the long ride.

Of course, the days are long gone when pregnancy was thought of as a condition of sickness. On the day we found out she was pregnant, Tammi warned us that she doesn't want to be treated like an invalid. Women can and should live their lives full-out while incubating a tiny person in their wombs. So what's the problem? A tiny, mad idea.

Many of us have issues with receiving. First of all, receiving requires vulnerability. Then, receiving also feels like surrender, which we've been taught is weakness. In addition, when someone gives us something and we accept it, we then feel like we've signed a social contract and we owe them. We fear that there are strings attached, and who wants another debt? The ego tells us that if we receive something from someone else, we are acknowledging that we are less than the giver. We don't feel worthy of whatever we're being given. We fear that we haven't earned it. Lil ole small, tiny, insignificant me? We think we haven't earned the right to have what we want. We're taught that a woman who desires something may be viewed as selfish.

The Sacred Feminine Power of Receiving

It's time that we change the way we look at the femergetic practice of receiving. Some of us don't want anyone holding doors for us or offering to carry our bags. Some of us take public kindness from men as a throwback to the chivalrous belief that we are the weaker sex. So we politely say, "No, it's okay. I can do it myself."

Guess what? There is power in receiving. My sister told me about a magnificent coach (also mentioned by Rha Goddess) named Emily Tepper whose website is ReceiveEverything.com. Yes! Receive everything. Being receptive – open to receive – is a spiritual practice. It's necessary for our evolution. Being receptive is not weak. Receptivity is part of creation.

If you are given something, you then have to receive it for it to be yours. How can blessings enter your life if you don't allow them in? Do you really want to keep sending the message to the Universe that you don't need anything? You may be thinking, "Abiola, this makes no sense. I have no issues with receiving anything. Give me something and I'll take it!"

Really? Go deeper.

Maybe you'd accept a seat from a stranger, but what about love? Do you freely receive love? How about compliments? Do you easily receive kind words? What about prosperity and abundance?

Do you effortlessly receive money and other good things? Do you readily accept gifts? Are you comfortable with receiving guidance and trusting your intuition? Is receiving passion, pleasure, joy, fun, and happiness easy for you? Here's a big one: How easy is it for you to accept help? Do you ask for assistance when you need it? Or do you feel like it's easier to just take care of things yourself? Are you burdened with the belief that no one can do things like you, so you might as well take care of everything? Even do-it-all superwomen need help.

I hear from women often that they feel lonely. Well, how open are you to receiving new friendships? Working in media, I have had offers of budding friendship from stratospherically powerful women, but these relationships never went anywhere because I was unable to receive them. Deep down, I felt inadequate and less than these outwardly prosperous and often famous women. Some offered mentorship and I was unable to receive that also. What I couldn't accept at the time is that they were giving me their numbers and planning playdates because we felt a genuine heart and soul connection that had nothing to do with outward gain.

So what did I do, from my non-receptive "playing small" vantage point? Without being consciously aware of it, I would sabotage these prospective friendships – usually before they took flight. We'll explore Impostor Syndrome in depth in Chapter 7, but on a subconscious level I feared that if these women could see the loser I really was they would reject me. So I rejected myself first by rejecting the friendships. I wouldn't follow up or call back and would pass on their invitations. Like any relationship, friendships have to be nurtured. Mine died on the vine.

To every woman who avoids vulnerability for fear of looking imperfect, you're off the hook! No one thinks you're perfect anyway. In fact, they're probably not thinking about you or your issues at all. We're all preoccupied with our own stuff. Phew.

Thankfully, I now know that I am worthy, deserving, and equal to any other human being. The coolest moment was when I was filming an interview with a megastar who helped to build American music. I accidentally overheard the interviewee using the toilet and it hit me – yeah, we're all human beings. Whether it's your intimidating boss, your father-in-law, or the popular chick from sixth grade, we all use the toilet. No one is any more special than anyone else.

Bombshell Exploration: Receive Your Blessings

For a while I hosted a #ThankfulThursday chat on Twitter. I invited tweople to share their #IAmGrateful thoughts for the week. We worked ourselves into a frenzy of joy just by acknowledging the good in our lives and the world! I used to call it #GratOrgy because it is an orgy of gratitude. We realized that things are more wonder-filled than we think when we choose to receive the blessings that surround us.

Gratitude helps you choose to live as if everything is a miracle. You can raise yourself to a receptive state of ecstasy by acknowledging every little wondrous thing you encounter. So what do you have to be grateful for right now? Whether it be the birth of a new family member or new nail polish (and the fact that you can afford to pamper yourself in such a way), accept all blessings and be grateful for them. This is how you harness the power of receptivity.

Your Heart Ceiling

In Chapter 10 we'll explore challenges with being receptive to prosperity. For now, let's examine being receptive to love. Picture this: The romantic film opens and the loving couple is incredibly happy. We could almost write what comes next. Despair? Tragedy? Raise your hand if absolute bliss leaves you waiting for the other shoe to drop instead of open to receiving more happiness. It's the way we approach every aspect of our lives. We close ourselves off from receiving our blessings because we are afraid. The ego says that receiving love or any other blessing is risky and therefore not safe.

In *The How of Happiness*, researcher Sonja Lyubomirsky

declares that we're each born with a genetically predetermined happiness set-point. The good news is that from there it's a matter of nurture, life choices, and circumstances. This means that no matter where you begin, your joy is still in your hands. Woohoo! The genetic set-point for joy can be raised.

Psychologist Gay Hendricks sees staying stuck in non-receiving mode as an "Upper Limit Problem." When our happiness exceeds the upper limit of what we feel is possible for us, we sabotage ourselves back to our comfort level. In matters of love, from familial to romantic, I call this the Heart Ceiling. If any experience or person tries to penetrate our self-created Heart Ceiling, we generally create an act of love sabotage. What's love sabotage? Starting a fight, pushing his or her buttons, creating an issue where there was none before, cheating, or shutting the other person out. Maybe you fear they will leave anyway so you push them away.

The key to growth is first recognizing where your Heart Ceiling is set. Fish don't know that they're swimming in water just like we don't always recognize the patterns we're swimming in. When you realize that you have low expectations for a relationships of any kind, and that you keep meeting those low expectations, then you can do something about it.

Of course this is all happening at a subconscious level. If someone asked whether we would purposefully try to blow a good thing, the answer would obviously be no. Your subconscious mind wants to keep you "safe," however. Anything different is scary and threatening. I had one potential love ask me often with confusion in his eyes, "Could we really be this lucky?" He was used to things being difficult and our happiness was just too easy so he felt like something was wrong. Sabotage kicked in. Have you ever tried to love someone who feels like he doesn't deserve it? It's exhausting.

You may have a low Heart Ceiling, or level of love that you feel comfortable receiving. You just don't feel that you deserve to be loved. Anything more than low level surface love and you subconsciously reject it. Ideally, you want to blow the ceiling completely off your heart so that you can receive everything. Be vigilant about acts of love espionage that you wage on yourself. You are worth loving.

It sounds so simple but just feeling comfortable enough to receive – love, abundance, blessings, friendship, good things – is a revolutionary act in a world that tells you that you are not inherently worthy. You have to feel deserving of love and blessings in order to receive and keep them. Otherwise, you will find a way to reject them. Practice receiving love and acts of generosity. Life itself is a gift that you didn't have to do anything to earn. Receiving and giving are the cycle of life.

"Just open your heart" sounds cliché, but this is the path to becoming receptive and living your fullness. If we expect shrunken, puny, and conditional love, that's exactly what we will attract. Sure, no one wants to be hurt. Heartache is among the worst kinds of pain we experience. However, we owe it to ourselves and our partners to practice loving like we've never been hurt. This is the path to the big, fat, juicy love that we all deserve.

You don't guard your heart by shutting it down. You guard your heart with self-love and self-trust. This is the path to receiving. The more comfortable you are with receiving, the more you will receive.

Bombshell Exploration: Expand Your Horizons

There are many ways to expand your horizons and receive knowledge, wealth, and wisdom from new sources. Listen to music that soothes the soul. Open yourself up to artists and genres that are unfamiliar. Read poetry. Poems are like the intersection between worlds. Study various religious and spiritual texts. Don't be afraid to reach beyond your own culture. You are a citizen and student of the world. Take a class. Join a club or recreational sports team. Step outside your comfort zone and push your own boundaries.

My Big Fat Bombshell Diary: Acts of Love Sabotage

There is one real friend that I particularly miss. She was my true goddess sister, beautiful inside and out. I stayed at her home and spent time with her family. She took me to Overeater's Anonymous with her when I needed guidance and introduced me to a big part of the work I do today. I can say without a doubt that I sabotaged our sisterhood. I was MIA, Missing in Affirmation, in our friendship. When I learned that she was adopting babies from another country, I callously and casually repeated a disgusting, racially insensitive "joke" that would taste like poison in my mouth now.

What had preceded the joke? She had made a large and much-needed contribution to my work. It didn't dawn on me until years later that this had exacerbated my issues with deservability and receiving. I was also going through the end of my marriage and wasn't able to be vulnerable enough to share my heartbreak. I was afraid of seeming flawed, broken, and less than perfect in the light of her seeming perfection. Because I was closed off, she could not feel comfortable enough to share her own marriage issues and money fears. Receiving requires openness. Sadly, the friendship fizzled after that.

I now see that the light I saw in her was my own light being reflected back. She nurtured our sisterhood not out of pity, but because there was value in what I brought to her as a friend before I sabotaged our relationship. We had been simultaneously learning from and teaching each other; giving and receiving. It just happened that her giving looked like plane tickets and cash while mine looked like creativity and hugs. I was the one making unfair value judgments.

Then there was my grad school brother, Tony Dattilo. Tony generously used his considerable artistic talents and personal resources to edit one of my art films. He even brought in a friend to assist at his own expense because he so believed in my work. Sinking in the simultaneous devastation of love lost and the shame of unconscious uncoupling, I had no ability to honor and receive Tony's gift of creative contributions so I shamefully *never even watched my own feature film that he edited*. I lacked the openness and courage to tell Tony about the depression I was experiencing and receive his help so I numbed out on "busyness" and let the project and friendship die.

Here's how the same receptivity issues played out for me in a romantic situation: For a change, I was the one being asked about my "availability."

"Are you ready for love?" he asked.

"Of course," I answered. This was after months of daily conversations. My long-distance friend and I spoke about everything but had never met in person. We'd connected because of work and he found little ways to stay in touch. Soon after, he began to lavish love and attention on me. Reflected in his eyes I was beautiful, smart, and perfect. We had a spiritual connection. His approach to love seemed whole-hearted.

Partnership with someone so loving and supportive held the possibility of all my romantic dreams coming true. Yet, the whole thing made me feel … suffocated. I started to avoid his calls and reject his attention. I noticed flaws and felt suspicious. He sent me presents and I laughed it off. The distance I felt was more than the fact that we lived in different states. His attempt to love me without conditions surpassed my puny expectations and low Heart Ceiling. This was not the shallow facsimile of love that I was used to receiving.

As I began to meditate on his question, I realized that I had no capacity to receive his love. It felt less risky to love someone who didn't have the capacity to love me back in the way I deserved. That was familiar. His kind of love was foreign. The half-cycle of me giving and not receiving was where the ceiling on my heart stopped.

So what behaviors *did* feel like home to me? At this point, my relationships and emotional life were just as toxic as my body. There was the "big sister" network exec that I introduced to my co-executive producer on a TV project. When I left them alone in a meeting I'd set up, my childhood "big sis" took the opportunity to say horrible things about me to my producer she'd just met. On another charming evening I was drinking in a bar with my girls and jokingly (and drunkenly) called one of them "ghetto." She didn't find it funny. Her hand made contact with my face and I fell from the bar stool to the floor. Cringe factor times twelve: my new lace-front wig flew off! Hit in a bar? Me? I'm a pacifist. I am deeply ashamed of that toxic "joke" and the resulting issue with my beautiful friend. I scrounged up my remaining shred of dignity and insisted on paying the bewildered bartender.

Then there was the BFF I invited to hang out with me and Mr. Super Crush that I was "totally in love with" – because I felt too shy to be alone with him. I left them in my living room to go make popcorn and came back to find them kissing. To my horror, disgust, and utter humiliation, they made out in my living room all night. She left the room in a shambles and never even said sorry – because she didn't have to. I wasn't vulnerable enough to say, "You hurt me deeply." I wasn't clear about the love I was worthy of receiving from her. I didn't teach her to treat me any better.

You are worth loving. Your relationships are a direct reflection of the love and respect you feel worthy of receiving. If you are in a bad relationship with anyone else, it is because you are in a bad relationship with yourself. What kind of love — and loved ones — do you truly feel you deserve?

Bombshell Playbook Exercise

Answer these questions in your Bombshell Playbook. Take five deep, cleansing breaths to get centered and begin.

1. How high does my Heart Ceiling go?

2. Are the people in my life capable of loving and respecting me?

3. How can I allow more love into my life?

4. Where can I be more vulnerable?

5. How can I become more comfortable with receiving?

Bombshell Challenge: Consciously receive and acknowledge your interdependence on others and your vulnerability as a part of your daily gratitude practice. Intentionally receive the love of your friends and family. Consider the assistance of all of the service providers that make your life run smoothly. Accept the ways that the unseen hands of those you'll never know improve your day-to-day life.

Getting Comfortable with Desire

We can't talk about receiving without talking about desiring. In Chapter 1, we tuned into the bombshell secret of creation. Creation begins with desire but it's not enough to just desire something and create it. Again, you have to also be able to receive it.

I was a participant in a Michael Baisden documentary called **Do Women Know What They Want?** The question annoys me because we all want different things. We're not a monolith. The thing all human beings, men and women, have in common is that we want to feel good. It's what gets us to that feeling that creates variety.

So, what do you desire? "Nice girls" don't really desire anything, right? "Good girls" just take what the world offers and make do. We live in a bucket list culture that says we only get to have what we want at the end of the game. We're taught that the party comes when you retire. Or worse, the reward is in heaven after you die.

Desire is defined as "a strong feeling of wanting to have something or wishing for something to happen." Like receiving, desire can be scary because it feels like need. We equate need with being needy and we equate being needy with being weak. Just meditate on the word "desire" for a moment. *Desire*. It sounds scandalous.

So, again, what do you desire? I have a coaching client who is terrified to want anything because she doesn't want to feel let down when she doesn't get it. We are afraid to desire because we've been hurt, let down, and had our hearts broken. So instead we bury our desires. We force our wants deep down inside. Instead of thinking about what we really want, we attempt to satiate the very human drive to desire with cheap thrills and quick fixes.

Ask yourself, "What do I really want?" We're afraid to ask the question because we fear that the answer will be "everything!" We're also scared of scarcity. "There just isn't enough to go around," you tell yourself. "Not enough money, not enough good men or women, not enough happiness."

We all fear disappointment, but disappointment is a teacher. The more you know what you don't want, the more you know what you do want. Life's negative experiences help you to refine your desires. As good retail salespeople know, every no brings you closer to a yes. Desire is not only healthy, but like receiving, it's also necessary for evolution because every great invention or idea starts with a desire.

So, what do you personally want, woman? Many of us don't even know. We just sign up for what society says we should want and then try to get as close to achieving that as we can. Stop *should*ing on yourself. We don't all want to be with Idris Elba or George Clooney. We don't all want marriage and kids. We don't all want BMWs or white picket fences. It's also okay if we do.

So how do you figure out what you really want? Pay attention to your feelings. Learn how to trust your intuition. Then be true to you. Be a conscious creator in your life and live on purpose. Learning how to desire is a skill, but it's only one half of a coin. The other half is receiving. Just like you have permission to desire, you have permission to receive. You are entitled to feel the joy and pleasure of living a big, brave, bombshell, breakthrough life.

Bombshell Exploration: Go On a Pleasure Diet

If you went on a "pleasure diet" of desiring, creating, and receiving yummy experiences, what would that look like? Are you allowing passion, pleasure, joy, and fun into your life? We all want to feel juicy, yet these pleasurable emotions are somehow forbidden except in tiny doses; and that's only if you really, really, really earn them. What a load of bull! What do you truly desire? A desire is a yearning from your soul, so if you ignore your desires, you are ignoring yourself. Allow your imagination to flow, and indulge yourself daily.

Receiving Your Intuition: "Be Still and Know"

How do I tap into my intuition? How do I know whether the voice I am hearing is my intuition or my own voice? Many of us were taught to respect outer authority and ignore our own inner authority. This is why we are the only animals that question whether we should listen to our intuition. When birds magnificently turn left together or elephants disappear right before a tsunami, they are following their intuition. Being intuitive requires being receptive.

One holiday season, my mom and her co-workers found the one place in town that had the hottest toys on sale. It was pretty far out so they planned to carpool after work. My brother, sister, and I knew to latchkey ourselves in, eat, and do homework until our parents got home. Still, at the end of that work day, my mom felt that she needed to get home to her kids immediately. Something didn't feel right. Her irate buddies said, "Fine, we're not shopping your list for you." Determined, my mom rushed home to find that a fire had started in our basement. We kids were two flights up watching **Little House on the Prairie** and had no idea that the boiler was going up in smoke.

It's helpful when trying to hear your intuition to get clear on what exactly intuition is. Intuition is guidance, or inner knowing. When we hear an inner voice, it is either coming from a place of love or fear. Your intuition or inner knowing (or "ing," as Gabby Bernstein calls it) will always speak from the highest vibrating energy of love for your well-being. Any voice that you hear telling you to do something negative or that creates anxiety within you is your own fear-based voice, not your intuition.

For example, let's say you're trying to decide whether to stay with someone, take a particular job, or move. Your intuition will point you toward what is best for you rather than focusing on worst case scenario outcomes. To hear your intuition, "be still and know." Once you hear that Sacred Bombshell whisper and receive that guidance, it is up to you to take action. If we don't catch our messages when they're whispered to us, eventually they start shouting. However, the Great GPS never punishes or chastises. You can reset your course at any time.

Guidance can come from anywhere: a song, a dream, a license plate, or a friend. Be in receiving mode, listen, and pay attention. Sometimes we need external cues. You can open your favorite sacred book to a "random" page for intuitive guidance. Some people talk to a clergy member, healer, or seer. Others read tarot cards. I used to read rune stones. For those who don't believe in or are uncomfortable with such things, you can also use my African Goddess Affirmation Cards as an intuition tool (available for purchase online). Focus on an issue and pick an inspirational card.

Bombshell Tool: Intuitive Guidance Techniques

If you need external confirmation that you are receiving inner guidance and not just hearing the voice of your Inner Bully, a quick trick is to flip a coin. Make heads one solution and tails the other. When you flip it, your heart will make a quick freedom wish just before it lands. Before you look at the coin, be clear on what you're hoping it will say from a place of love, expansion, and personal freedom. That quick wish is your intuitive choice.

I often ask my coaching clients – and myself – "If you knew the answer, what would it be?" We always know the answer when we get still enough to hear it.

Another intuition trick is to assign one color to one choice and another color to the opposing choice right before you go to bed. For example, pink is a yes and green is a no. Then, as soon as you wake up the next morning, write down a detailed and vivid description of your dreams. Those of us who are great dreamers can often receive clear guidance in this way. If your dream was green-inspired, there you have it!

A woman in touch with receiving her intuitive guidance can guide herself, her family, and her community. Intuition requires trusting yourself and having faith. Trusting yourself requires loving yourself. Loving yourself requires accepting yourself and the positive energy that comes your way.

Receptivity Blocker: Your Inner Bully

For many of us, the prospect of being vulnerable enough to receive anything is terrifying and our Inner Bully backs up that fear by saying, "No, don't risk it! You'll play yourself. You'll look stupid." The Inner Bully or inner critic is one of the blocks to us feeling comfortable enough to receive.

I was bullied as a kid and one of my coping mechanisms was to become a people pleaser. After all, our personalities are the characters we develop to survive the conditions of our childhoods. I am still bullied occasionally. However, none of my current bullies really exist. They're all in my head.

We each have a fear-based Inner Bully or gang of Inner Bullies that points out everything that's wrong with us. This inner critic rains down negative self-talk. There's one voice warning you that you're going to be a failure, another telling you that time is running out, and yet another shouting, "How dare you? You look stupid! Are you getting fat? Who do you think you are?" That nonstop gremlin voice says, "You are not good enough to receive. Don't surrender, stupid, it's not safe. Needing help is lazy. Don't take that from him – where's your pride?"

These ego-based bullies flare up in your mind, trying to keep you safe by blocking your moxie. These mind bullies try to squash creativity with judgment, quell intuition with fear, and repel manifesting with low-vibrating energy. This chatter matters.

Negative self-talk is the single most harmful thing you can do to yourself. That internal dialogue is a radio that is always going. Thought comes before action, so thoughts and words have real, physical power. You will never create a positive life from negative thoughts.

We're not even aware of most of the negative chatter running through our minds. Yet these thoughts are creating our opinions of ourselves, dictating how we move in the world and whether we feel courageous enough to receive love and live by our own design.

When we listen to the voices of these bullies they often don't even sound like us. Maybe they speak in the voice of a hurtful teacher, misguided parent, or real-life bully. Eavesdrop on yourself and find out what these Inner Bullies, these hurtful inner voices, are saying. Your mind may be replaying old hurts and keeping you in a state of suspended growth.

Bombshell Tool: Shine a Light on Real World Bullies

Outer bullies do exist in the world. I define a bully as someone who tries to block you from receiving joy because of their own insecurities. However, no one can block your blessings without your permission. When you encounter people whose energy clashes with yours, visualize them wrapped in white or pink light. You can shift negative energy with loving energy. Trust me – I have done it! When encountering a bully, silently thank him or her for the lesson to come and surround the person with the energy of love. Have compassion by considering the circumstances that led them to behave that way. Forgive yourself for your judgment of them or the situation. Then practice good self-care by having boundaries and not spending time around this low-vibrating energy.

My Big Fat Bombshell Diary: Overcoming My Inner Bully

My Inner Bully would always scold me for being half-assed. For a long time I had the belief that I was irresponsible. Anyone who knows me knows that I am completely the opposite. I revel in being early, am a detailed taskmaster to myself and others (sorry, team!), and am incredibly responsible. I may have lost things when I was a little kid, but I still carry the same key ring I had in high school! So why did I believe this lie about myself?

My childhood conclusions are what led to this belief. One instance that stands out is selling my school Christmas cards to my dad's co-workers. Overwhelmed by my own fifth grade dramas, I mixed up the orders. I couldn't figure out who had paid already or what anyone ordered. The cards were a huge debacle! When my father found out, he yelled that he was disappointed in me and that I was careless.

My father rarely yelled at me or disciplined me at all. That may sound great, but it means that the two or three times that he did made an epic impression in my childhood mind. When my father screamed that I was careless as I sat in a mess of cards and money, I believed him. When he said he was disappointed in me, I heard that I was a disappointment. This is how we form our core limiting beliefs. Our childhood minds asses a situation and we come up with the best conclusion we can.

So was my 10-year-old conclusion that I was a careless person accurate? Most importantly, is this still a valid story about myself 30 years later? No and hell no. It's the hardest thing to say that our parents might have been mistaken but this was my father's opinion of this incident. Opinion.

Another way to look at it is that my dad was under great pressure at that time. Maybe he was afraid of seeming careless to his co-workers as the only black person at his level. He would attend conferences all the time where colleagues he was dealing with over the phone were shocked to find he was black and stopped speaking to him. It could be that things were already tense at work. Perhaps he was low on funds and now would have to pay his executive buddies back out-of-pocket for missing cards. Who knows? Maybe he was just hungry and tired. It could have been anything.

It could also have been that maybe that day I *was* careless and it was a disappointing anomaly. All other evidence points to the fact that I was a highly responsible child. That's probably why he agreed to sell the cards for me to begin with and let me organize the money! So is this still a valid belief about myself to hold on to? No! Bully dismissed. I give love to that sweet 10-year-old girl for coming to the only wise conclusion that she could make at the time. My Inner Wise Woman is finally stronger than my Inner Bullies.

Bombshell Exploration: Five Steps to Making Peace with Your Inner Bully

1. **Eavesdrop on your mind.** Pay attention to the things you say to yourself. Your Inner Bully is speaking from the limiting belief system (BS) that you have about life. Write down all of the critical things you tell yourself, all the comments that your mind makes when it's left to run amuck.

2. **Uncover the source.** Being present with the Inner Bully voice helps us to realize that it is not our own. That belittling voice is a combination of negative voices we heard during our formative years. Go back as far back as you can and come up with three to five scenarios in your personal history that might have helped to create your limiting beliefs. For example, when I wanted to look into the belief that I was careless, I realized that one of the events in my personal history that helped create the belief was the greeting card fiasco.

3. **Don't believe everything you think.** Question your interpretation that led to the belief. Ask yourself for each belief, "Is what I think really the truth?" Come up with other interpretations of the situation as I did, realizing that maybe my dad was stressed and that even if I was careless at age 10 it didn't make sense to believe that it was still true.

4. **Address your Inner Bully directly.** Identify your bullies and subconscious critical voices. Change is scary, so they're trying to keep you safe. Thank them for their concern and invite them to move on. When these voices pop up during the day telling you what's wrong say, "Thanks for sharing" or "No thank you."

5. **Affirm the positive and find newer, more relevant evidence to back it up.** Combat the subconscious negative noise with

positive mental "music" of your own making. A good affirmation is usually the opposite of the self-bullying thought. If I was thinking "I am so disorganized," my affirmation would be the opposite. A new thought would be, "I am careful and reliable." I could back that up with the evidence that I take orders for my coaching programs all the time and never have any mix-ups. Use your self-being to listen to the negative self-talk and change the stories.

Bombshell Playbook Exercise

Answer these questions in your Bombshell Playbook. Take five deep, cleansing breaths to get centered and begin.

1. How do I block myself from receiving the blessings that I deserve?

2. Who, living or dead, do I owe an apology to?

3. When have I been a bully?

Clearing Your Chakras for Receiving Blessings

One of our definitions for bombshell is a woman who "owns it." What is owning it? It's you owning and receiving your greatness, owning and accepting your power. This is a seven-day treatment to open your energy to receiving blessings. What is a blessing? I define blessings simply as spiritual solutions, the highest good, and everyday miracles.

The concept of chakras is not as confusing as it may seem. Basically, just like we have arteries, veins, and nerves running throughout our bodies like superhighways, we also have chakras, or areas of energy. Our bodies have countless chakras or energy centers, but for this exercise we're going to work with the seven main ones. Each of the seven main chakras represents an area of our emotional, spiritual, mental, and physical lives.

If you have had challenges with receiving, this treatment will clear and open your chakra channels so that you can allow blessings to flow. Each chakra receives and expresses life force energy, also known as prana or chi in different traditions, into our bodies. When chakras are blocked or unbalanced, it's like being congested.

How do chakras become blocked or closed in the first place? Chakra blocks and imbalances can occur after fearful experiences, conflict, injury, emotional pain, trauma, or overindulging in one area of your life. Blockages can also be residue from beliefs that no longer serve you. For example, you may experience a betrayal that causes you to close your heart chakra so that you won't get hurt again.

This seven-day treatment will help open your receptive energy. Each day you will focus on clearing one chakra area and receiving positive and transformative energy. Repeat the day's mantra 11 times in the morning, 11 times at noon, and 11 times before bed to get it into your subconscious mind. Say the mantra to yourself, and if you feel comfortable enough, to other people as situations arise. The repetition is important because you're retraining your brain. Add color therapy: Wear the color that represents the day's chakra and eat foods of that color as well for extra focus. Close the day by meditating with your hands on the chakra area.

You will find my guided chakra-clearing visualization at SacredBombshell.com, but you can also do it yourself right now. The word "chakra" is Sanskrit for wheel, so you can picture a wheel or lotus flower spinning in each chakra area from the base of the spine to the top of the head. Breathe in through your nose and out through your mouth. Breathe in love and breathe out fear. Picture yourself standing on the ground with cleansing white light shooting up throughout your feet and hands. Pull it in, receive it, and allow it to spread throughout your body. As the light reaches each chakra area, it spins like a vortex, blowing out all that doesn't work and pulling in blessings in the color and energy of the chakra. See each beautiful chakra opening and expanding to let in an abundance of blessings. Imagine how it would feel to be completely open in each area.

Day 1: Root Chakra Opening for Receiving Security

Mantra: "I have the right to exist. I am open to feeling safe and secure."

Chakra location: base of the spine

Energy color: red

Healing ritual: Earthing or grounding is a simple process where we receive healing energy from walking barefoot outside. Go for a stress-reducing barefoot walk or skip.

When this chakra is in balance you feel secure and grounded. This day is all about your safety feelings. The root chakra represents security, survival issues like money and food, and stability. This chakra may be closed or out of balance if you feel anxious, distrustful, resistant to new ideas and life changes, materialistic, afraid often, or unstable.

Day 2: Sacral Chakra Opening for Receiving Pleasure

Mantra: "I have a right to feel. I receive pleasure easily."

Chakra location: below the belly button

Energy color: orange

Healing ritual: Play new, rhythmic music that inspires you and feel yourself as one with the notes. Dance yourself into a "feel-gasm." Allow every bodacious, undulating move to bring you more pleasure than the last.

When this chakra is in balance you feel comfortable with intimacy, you can express your emotions in a healthy way and allow others to do the same, and you readily accept pleasure. This day is all about your pleasure, creativity, and feeling good. The sacral chakra represents gratification, sexuality, abundance, passion, feelings, and delight. This chakra may be closed or out of balance if you are cold, unemotional, and seek to numb or avoid your own feelings, or if you find your emotions are out of control.

Day 3: Navel Chakra Opening for Receiving Power

Mantra: "I have the right to think. I allow myself to feel confident."

Chakra location: slightly above the belly button

Energy color: yellow

Healing ritual: Do one thing that you have been terrified to do for a long time.

When this chakra is in balance you love yourself unconditionally and have healthy self-esteem. This day is all about your confidence and standing in your personal power. The navel or belly button chakra represents self-esteem, self-worth, and desire. This chakra may be closed or out of balance if you are timid and never get what you want, or are overly aggressive and intimidating.

Day 4: Heart Chakra Opening for Receiving Love

Mantra: "I have the right to love. I receive love freely."

Chakra location: center of your chest

Energy color: green

Healing ritual: Do a Mettā (loving-kindness) visualization by picturing love, joy, and peace for yourself first, then for someone you highly respect, then for a loved one, then for a person you feel neutral about, and finally for a person you are having difficulties with.

When this chakra is in balance you easily give and receive love and your relationships are harmonious and balanced. This day is all about your love and compassion for others. The heart chakra represents joy, devotion, self-acceptance, healthy relationships, and inner peace. This chakra may be closed or out of balance if you are stuck in grief, distant and cold, or overbearing and suffocating.

Day 5: Throat Chakra Opening for Receiving Self-Expression

Mantra: "I have the right to speak. I am open to expressing my voice."

Chakra location: throat

Energy color: light blue

Healing ritual: Call someone and say what you have been too afraid to say in a way that is compassionate to both of you.

When this chakra is in balance you communicate easily. This day is all about having a voice and speaking your truth. The throat chakra represents self-expression, loyalty, trust, and communication. This chakra may be closed or out of balance if you feel unsure of yourself or are uneasy expressing yourself, or if you dominate conversations.

Day 6: Third-Eye Chakra Opening for Receiving Intuition

Mantra: "I have the right to 'see.' I readily accept my intuition."

Chakra location: forehead

Energy color: indigo

Healing ritual: Make a decision you have been holding off on and release it.

When this chakra is in balance you trust your intuition and insight. This day is all about your intuition. The third-eye chakra represents guidance, imagination, and the ability to make good decisions. This chakra may be closed or out of balance if you are unable to imagine, fantasize, or visualize, or if you need others to weigh in on your decisions.

Day 7: Crown Chakra Opening for Receiving Wisdom

Mantra: "I have the right to know. I am open to receiving wisdom and higher consciousness."

Chakra location: top of the head

Energy color: violet

Healing Ritual: Perform an act of selfless service, known as "seva" in the yogic traditions. Do something anonymously for others with no expectation of receiving in return.

When this chakra is in balance you are open-minded and aware of both the physical and spiritual world. This day is about your inspiration and bliss. The crown chakra represents divine intelligence, connection to your Source, beauty, empathy, and self-being or living nowness. This chakra may be closed if you have a lack of purpose, depression, nightmares, difficulty concentrating, or if you're prejudiced, negative, and judgmental.

Bombshell Dialogue with Cheryl Richardson: How to Create an Exceptional Life

Enter a woman who knows all about being receptive with grace. Self-care expert Cheryl Richardson first came to national attention on **The Oprah Winfrey Show** with her best-selling book **Take Time for Your Life**. Richardson currently hosts a weekly inspirational show on Hay House Radio. I interviewed her about her book **You Can Create an Exceptional Life,** which she co-authored with her mentor Louise Hay. Her latest project is **21 Days to Master Extreme Self-Care**. The life coach is happily married to her soul mate Michael Gerrish. They live with their sweet cat Poupon in Newburyport, Massachusetts.

Abiola: Cheryl, I often give talks to women who don't know how to honor who they are because perhaps they were raised by moms who didn't know how to honor themselves. What is your advice for the generation raised with quick fixes and instant gratification? On all of our favorite reality TV shows, negative behavior is rewarded.

Cheryl: You're right. Most of us – from women of my generation all the way to women I talk to in their early twenties – were raised by mothers who I'm fond of saying [hadn't] had the right to vote for very long, let alone the choice to live a life that reflects what their souls most want. So the next generation is interesting in that they've at least had some exposure to the concept of self-care.

In my generation self-care was a guilty pleasure. It was taboo to want to take care of yourself. "You should never put your needs before anyone else's." [Self-care has] been integrated more into women's lives now but we still have a long way to go. So what I would say to young women is to first recognize two things. Developing qualities like courage, like inner strength, the ability to trust oneself – the ability to trust your intuition, whether it's right or wrong – developing these inner qualities is critical.

As you invest in your own character, you're going to build such a strong inner core that it's going to be easier to make better choices. And the other thing is to develop impeccable communication skills. Practice taking risks and being rejected. Practice standing up for yourself. Practice saying to somebody, "I don't like the way you're treating this other person. It just doesn't make me feel good, and I don't want to be around it."

My mom used to say to me, "You know Cheryl, you are who you hang around with," and I can tell you now at 51, she was absolutely right. You really need to be mindful of the people you are spending your precious life with. If they are chronically negative, hurtful, sarcastic, biting, and dishonoring of others, that's going to keep you small and keep you behaving the same way.

Abiola: One of your books is named *The Unmistakable Touch of Grace*. How do you define grace?

Cheryl: I define grace as a benevolent force of energy that is always available to all of us. We don't have to do anything to earn it. We don't have to work hard to earn it. We don't have to be good enough to receive it. Grace is this divine energy that we live within, and the more we recognize that we're co-creating with this energy, the more our lives can begin to reflect what's important to our souls.

Abiola: Lovely! If our politicians found a way to look at the world through the lens of grace, that would be a great help in the world right now.

Cheryl: Well, if most people period could really recognize the power that their thoughts and their state of mind has – on not only on their lives, but the lives of others – we'd be living on a very different planet.

Abiola: Let's talk about your project with Louise Hay, the grande dame of affirmations.

Cheryl: Louise and I spent about nine or ten months traveling together and we had a series of conversations that turned into this incredible book, *You Can Create an Exceptional Life*.

Abiola: We need more intergenerational collaborations like that because we have so much to bring to each other!

Cheryl: I so agree with you. We, the younger generation, and my generation, really neglect to realize the kind of wisdom and powerful experience that can come from spending time with elders.

Abiola: Think about how popular Betty White is in pop culture. I think it's because we are craving that national grandmother, the crone archetype. When I look around New York City, no one has wrinkles or gray hair anymore.

Cheryl, you've been in the presence of Louise Hay, you talk about self-care, can you share three helpful affirmations?

Cheryl: Sure, so what I use all the time, is: "My life is a constant stream of miracles." I also love: "Abundance flows into my life in surprising and miraculous ways every day." And then my favorites from Louise that I just naturally use all the time. One is: "Life loves me." I'm constantly just reinforcing that, and the other one is: "Only good lies before me."

Abiola: Oh, I love both of those. I usually say, "I love life and life loves me."

Cheryl: Me too.

Abiola: Really?

Cheryl: Yep, I use it all the time.

Abiola: Cheryl, let's talk about your wonderful relationship.

Cheryl: Michael and I have been together for a little over seventeen years. We've been married for fourteen. I met Michael through a personal ad in a magazine. I called on a dare from a friend. I basically just made a phone call to the Universe, that I'm ready to meet somebody, and I'm going to just take this action as a declaration of that. And then Michael did the same thing! Michael placed the ad because he had always been kind of shy, and he had always waited for people to approach him. He decided to be proactive and placed the ad. I responded.

He had over 150 people respond and I was the only person he called. When we met, it was like instant, and I did not believe in love at first sight. I thought it was a lovely idea; I didn't think It was going to happen to me. As soon as I saw him, I remember saying, "Please God let that be him." We had a wonderful dinner, and I knew. I drove home that night and I said, "This is the man I'm going to marry." It's been a great, soul-nourishing relationship.

We've had incredibly wonderful, great times, [and] really difficult stressful times. I wanted a partner who was committed to coming to the table and working through anything that came up because they saw marriage as a spiritual partnership. Michael walked that talk. Our relationship with each other comes first after our relationship with ourselves, and our commitment is to use that partnership as a way to grow and evolve.

Our spiritual language might be different; and so many people think that a good, healthy, enjoyable relationship is when both people are so aligned and it's not. It's when both people are mature enough to be accepting and compassionate with each other's differences.

Bombshell Takeaways:

- You can increase your capacity to receive with positive affirmations.

- You don't have to be "good enough" to receive grace.

- Be open to receiving love by being accepting and compassionate.

Bombshell Dialogue with Demetria L. Lucas: How to Receive Love and Blessings

Demetria Lucas blogs as the "Belle in BK" but her main lesson is how to be the belle of your own life. Called "the black Carrie Bradshaw" by *The Washington Post*, the educated beauty and southern belle is an award-winning journalist and life coach. Demetria's best-selling memoir, *A Belle in Brooklyn*, left fans hungry for more. She is a cast member on Bravo's hit series *Blood, Sweat and Heels*. Demetria has spent the past 10 years helping women learn how to receive more love.

Abiola: What motivated you to write your latest book, *Don't Waste Your Pretty*?

Demetria: As a life coach and dating and relationship expert, I talk to women all the time. I pinpointed some very key mistakes that we make when it comes to dating and relationships. And it's just because we were never taught. So *Don't Waste Your Pretty* is really about not wasting your effort, not wasting your energy, not wasting your looks – because that's important too – on the wrong [people].

Sometimes we meet somebody and we get so caught up in emotions that we want things to work. We want him to be a great guy and just the facts in front of us are not really panning out. He's not willing to commit. He's not treating us the way that we want. He's not picking up the phone to call. So, I'm trying to get women to see these points. Who's a good catch, who deserves their energy, and who they should just pass on by.

Abiola: I'm going to get in all your business. Your man is known in your blog as "Chocolate Boy Wonder" (CBW). Spill the beans, please.

Demetria: I'll spill some beans. We actually met on the subway a few years ago. I had gone out the night before and I accidentally spilled my drink on this guy. The next day I was headed to work and that guy and his best friend [were] standing on the train platform. I was in the train and the guy says to [his friend] (CBW), "That's the girl who spilled her drink on me [at Butter]." And so CBW gets on the train and says, "Hey you were at Butter last night?" And I'm thinking, "My God how much did I drink that I did not see this beautiful man? I walked out [of] the club and passed him by?" We sat on the train and he rode all the way to 42nd Street with me.

Abiola: I want to point out that there's a lesson there. So often we're closed off. We're on that subway or wherever and we've got that mask on. We're not open to receiving love and Mr. or Mrs. Right can be right there. Demetria, we often feel that we have to make a choice between personal success and career success. How do you balance your romantic life and work?

Demetria: I'm a work-in-progress when it comes to that. You know those clowns in the circus that have the sticks and they're rotating the plates? You really have to think, "What is the priority for the moment?" Those sticks, those are your relationships, your personal time, your work. But everything doesn't need your undivided, full, devoted attention at all times. You really have to assess what matters most right now.

I also need to say to ask for help. That's something that I had a really big issue with. I want to control everything. I want to do everything on my own. Sometimes it's just better if you can free your mind to focus on the big picture.

Abiola: Some people may feel that a bombshell like you never has fears or doubts. What do you do when you do feel sad, afraid, or nervous?

Demetria: Well, let me just disavow [you] of the notion that anything is close to perfect. [I have] fears and doubts like anyone else. I think so often we see other women who are very pulled together and we think everything must be perfect. But everyone deals with issues. I've got them, you've got them. Every single woman does.

But when I have fears and doubts I start off with a prayer like "God help me," because I recognize that I cannot do this alone. "I'm trying and I'm flailing, so bail me out." And I ask for help. I'm a life coach [and] I have my own life coach who I give a call to on a regular basis because sometimes you're very close to a situation and you can't see the forest for the trees. Sometimes other people just have a different insight.

Abiola: How did you learn to love yourself?

Demetria: You know what? It's a process. It's something that I've only come to maybe in the last few years. There are days where I'm just, "Oh, I own it. I've got it." And there are other days where I just don't want to get up in the morning. But what I try to tell myself is, just accept the things that you cannot change. Accept yourself and do your best. Work on the things that you really don't like. And the things that you really can't do much about? "Let it bang."

When I first started my blog I was really in a negative place. If you go back and read the early stuff … it's very hard for me to read. I had very cynical views about relationships, very cynical views about men. I'd had my heart broken. There were really great days and days that completely sucked. I realized that no matter what I put out there – the deepest insecurities, my deepest flaws, all the ways that I fell short – there was always someone else that said, "Me too." I was totally one of those people that was looking at other people and thinking that their lives were so perfect and then people would respond. No matter how hard I was on myself, how judgmental I was about things that I've done, someone always said, "Me too." I was like, "Okay. I am not horribly flawed. It's a struggle for all of us. We're kind of all in this thing together."

Abiola: That's a beautiful lesson. Many single women live their dating lives in fear of "the dearth of single men" or "the marriage crisis" that you and I have spoken about in numerous professional forums and panels. What are your current thoughts on the issue?

Demetria: For *ESSENCE*, I did this story once about women who thought they'd never get married. These are women who are single at 40, or women who had been widowed in their 50s, a woman who had two children out of wedlock. These are all people that were like, "It's not going to happen. You're going to die old and alone" – all the horrible things that we say to women. But this woman said to me, "I was one woman looking for one man and there are six billion people on this planet. Three billion of them are men. I do believe I can find someone." And she did. Think: Instead of "there's a lack of men" or "there aren't any good men," you need to find one great man for you if you're a heterosexual woman. And that's totally possible. I really do think that everyone can find love.

Abiola: I think so, too! What makes you a bombshell, Demetria?

Demetria: I work very hard to cultivate a confidence in myself, to walk the talk, and to accept my flaws. I think it's recognizing that I'm not perfect, that I'm a work-in-progress but I'm trying. I'm not feeling sorry for myself. I'm actively trying to do something to improve myself and hopefully help others improve themselves as well. I think that makes me a bombshell.

Bombshell Takeaways:

- Let down your guard to open yourself up to loving and being loved.

- There is great power in actively tuning into your best good.

- Don't be afraid to put yourself out there – the good, the bad, and everything in between.

Secret of Receptivity Resources

1. *In the Spirit* by Susan L. Taylor
2. *Outrageous Openness* by Tosha Silver
3. *The Desire Map* by Danielle LaPorte
4. *Ask and it Is Given* by Esther and Jerry Hicks
5. *The Sacred Bombshell Meditations* by Abiola Abrams (audio)

Receptivity Affirmations

1. Great things pour into my life from every direction.
2. It is delicious to desire.
3. I am grateful that my needs are being met.
4. It feels good to count my many blessings.
5. I deserve the very best and I am worthy.

Four

The Secret of Emotions: The Power of Your Feelings

The Sacred Feminine Law of Emotions

The Sacred Bombshell gives herself full permission to feel her feelings. She believes that she has a right to feel and to emote. She knows that the way she feels is a barometer. Her feelings indicate how aligned she is with her Inner Wise Woman. She respects herself enough to honor her feelings by acknowledging them. This is sacred self-love.

Historical Bombshell Mentor: Marilyn Monroe 1926-1962

The real Marilyn Monroe was nothing like the dumb blonde she portrayed. The sex symbol was the second woman ever to lead a production company. "I am not a victim of emotional conflicts. I am human," she revealed in **Marilyn: Her Life in Her Own Words**. Norma Jean Baker knew how to exude sensuality and use it at will. Over 50 years after her death fans still speculate about every aspect of her life. The shrewd comedic actress's life philosophy was: "If I'd observed all the rules, I'd never have got anywhere." Indeed.

The Emotions Declaration

I am a passionate woman with a wide range of emotions. The rage of zest that I bring to everyday affairs feeds the very energy of the earth and in return I am refilled. Passion is the fuel that makes everything worth experiencing happen. In my previous blind dullness I shied away from this passion, these feelings and emotions. Today I am awakened from this lull with the bells of my heart screaming that I live my most passionate life now.

I once believed that those who were in touch with their emotions and feelings were privy to a knowledge that escaped me. Today I am in on the secret. I will acknowledge and accept the way I feel. I will express my anger, joy, sadness, and love fully, healthily, and honestly. Passion is contagious. With this knowledge I will choose carefully the energy I bring. With honest expression I have no need to lash out or victimize others with my feelings.

A fire burns inside of me and I use it to meet the Creator's glorious dreams for my life. This is a fact that previously intimidated me. I am no longer intimidated. I have a will to explore, a passion to express, and a zest to approach my ideals. I rise to the challenges that I encounter. I delight in the sweetness of this vigor because I am a passionate woman. For this I am so grateful.

And so it is.

My Big Fat Bombshell Diary: Feeling My Feelings

The practice of feeling your feelings is not easy. The first year I decided to feel my feelings rather than trying to avoid or numb them was a doozy. I happened to bury six close family members and one friend in those 12 months. I also had my second breast cancer scare while my entire immediate family was out of the country. If ever there was a time to cry into a box of cookies, that was it. I was extremely stressed and anxious, but I found that eliminating sugar and working out helped me to cope in a healthier manner.

A Course in Miracles teaches that there are only two true emotional energies: love-based emotions and fear-based emotions. When I was a teen who was given steroids for my skin conditions, I didn't realize that eczema was a physical expression of my sensitivity and anxiety. I saw no correlation between a stressful day of being so bullied that I became a functional agoraphobic – feeling like the consummate outsider in school — and numbing out on Cheez Doodles at home. My social anxiety made certain interactions crippling.

My theatrical show *Goddess City* won accolades when I was only 26. The play included challenging topics from rape to abortion and we hosted healing discussion forums. Did I enjoy it when *Cosmopolitan Magazine* selected me as a "Fun, Fearless Female?" No, I chided myself for being a slacker. I compared myself to my icon who had written a Broadway play at 25. Insecurity often disguises herself as perfectionism. Perfection is the enemy of joy and forward motion. The word "emotion" literally has *motion*, or movement, in it. I was stuck in anxiety.

Whereas depression is a condition where people continually lament the past, anxiety is a condition where we are worried about the future. We are all under tremendous stress. This is compounded by the fact that we are reachable 24/7. For the first time as an adult, in 2012, I started to take weekends – Saturday and Sunday – mostly off. It was life-altering and felt decadent. When our bodies don't get to recuperate by tuning out naturally, we force them to tune out with whatever life-avoiding addictions we choose.

This brings me to my other addiction of choice: workaholism. Busyness is respected in our culture. In fact, over-working is the most accepted addiction, particularly in the Big Apple where I live. My corporate buddies are seen as slackers if they take a lunch hour. Although I worked for myself, I operated in much the same way.

The year after my first marriage completed itself was incredibly productive for me. I completed my master's degree, wrote a novel, taught in Nigeria, hosted a TV show on a major cable network, wrote and directed an award-winning art film, contributed to anthologies, and curated a two-museum film festival. That's just for starters! This is not because I am a whiz kid, but because working non-stop is a way not to feel. It's a means of ignoring yourself and whatever you are experiencing. Addictions are a means of avoiding intimacy. I was dishonoring my feelings of grief, anger, and betrayal. My body even manifested malaria to force me to relax and honor myself with care. The go-go-go was full-on masculine energy. The move to self-care is femergy.

The funny thing is that after the Cheez Doodles as a kid and the French fries and workaholism as an adult, all of my problems were still there. I just felt self-loathing on top of them for overdosing on food and stress. I subconsciously built a wall of protective fat around my body to keep me safe. My recovery from these addictive behaviors involved creating new habits by finding healthier ways to deal with stressful and repressed feelings. Working out allows me to release frustration on a physical level. I became more open and communicative. I am finally able to say when I am feeling mad, bad, or sad. I also learned to be present with myself when I am feeling glad. My urgent and relentless self-care involved nurturing my body by transitioning to a plant-based diet. I am learning the power of feeling safe and free enough to be spontaneous.

I am a naturally high energy person – except when I'm not. I enjoy being giddy, "extra," and over-the-top – except when I don't. Learning my moods and paying attention to myself allowed me to honor my peaceful energy and introspective moods as well as my rah-rah-sis-boom-bah moods. I realized that as an extroverted introvert, with certain people I was holding back – not feeling free enough to be my fun and crazy self because of their low vibrating, cynical energy. Becoming myself has meant knowing that expressing the full range of emotions is healthy. Confrontation and honest conversations when necessary are also healthy.

We must learn to feel our feelings without judging ourselves as "bad" or "wrong" for what we feel. You ever see people laughing at a funeral or crying at a wedding? We are finely tuned instruments that feel a full range of emotions when we allow ourselves to. There are some cultures that are more comfortable with anger than glee. Happiness is seen as suspicious. Although I grew up with the myth of the "strong black woman," I am human and many days I feel the antithesis of strong. Feeling my feelings and honoring them made me whole. I feel less of a need to blame others for what I am feeling. I know now that I have a right to be silly and happy and pissed off and depressed and emotional!

The Sacred Feminine Power of Feelings

"How you gon' win if you ain't right within?"
—*Lauryn Hill*

"Never let them see you sweat," right? In our masculine/dominant culture, showing emotion is seen as weakness. Feelings have no value. As a result, we've lived solely in our heads rather than our hearts for far too long. Part of coming into our own means breaking our family and societal emotional habits. "You're so emotional." "Are you PMSing?" "You have an attitude." These dismissive words are used against women as a weapon when others (including us) feel uncomfortable with our feelings. These accusatory words cause shame. Shame causes inflammation. Inflammation can cause disease.

Sometimes we pigeonhole the ways we are culturally "allowed" to behave. Stereotypes like "angry black women," "hot-headed Latinas," "timid Asians," "crazy Muslims," "unstable Italian women," or "nagging Jewish women" can stymie your right to full expression. If your only tool is a hammer, you need more tools.

Have you ever been in a situation where your emotions got the best of you? If you're alive and breathing, I'm guessing that the answer would be yes. Common fears that cause anger include fear of not being enough, fear of being unloved, fear of not being respected, and fear of being alone. There are no good or bad emotions, only emotions that make us feel better and emotions that make us feel worse. There is no one way to react.

Yesterday, I told one of my coaching clients that it was important to honor her emotions. She disagreed because the Kabbalah teaches that everything happens for a reason, so in her view honoring a feeling of self-pity, for example, is blasphemous. While I greatly respect that teaching, I don't think that one invalidates the other. Honoring what you feel is not the same as wallowing or emotional cutting. Dishonoring what we feel is an epidemic that has us self-medicating as a culture and trying to numb ourselves by any means possible. Trying not to feel our feelings results in addictions to alcohol, shopping, legal and illegal drugs, gambling, TV, games, porn, love, and food.

I am intimately familiar with using food as a drug. As an emotional eater, I used food to numb when I was feeling really bad and when I was feeling really good. At any point in time, I didn't know what I was truly feeling except that I could numb out with French fries. The practice of being where I am, acknowledging what I am feeling, and staying present has been tremendously healing. This is what I mean when I say we must honor our feelings.

There's a reason why our cultural image of women dealing with breakups involves self-soothing with a tub of ice cream. We might also go out with our friends and drink ourselves into a semi-coma. After all, who wants to feel like crap? The problem with numbing out the crappy emotions is that we also numb out feelings of bliss. Those tears and laughs that we're missing are the experience of living. Those highs and lows that we are glossing over are our very lives. We don't show up for our own lives and then wonder why we feel disconnected and miserable.

Emotions – expressed openly, healthily, and clearly – are a sign of strength, openness, and vulnerability. In order to be mentally healthy, we have to have access to all of our emotions. A yin energy woman allows herself to feel all emotions from giddy happiness to anger. Your emotional energy is your power supply and all feelings deserve to be acknowledged. Being intimately in touch with how you feel makes you intuitive and vibrant.

Being in true alignment with your power means that you acknowledge that feeling good matters. In fact, you feeling good is the most important thing on the planet. If that sounds downright hedonistic, so be it. Hedonism is "a school of thought that argues that pleasure is the only intrinsic good." Why assume that pleasure is selfish? It is pleasurable to think of women being paid what they are worth. It is pleasurable to make sure that our children are well-fed and educated in healthy, violence-free environments. It is thrilling to activate my feminine power of tribe-building and support the next generation. It also feels good to get dressed up and flirt with cute men.

You ever notice that when you're feeling great life is just easier? You're radiant and in alignment when you exude good energy. Similarly, when you're having a bad day it's like Murphy's Law is stalking you. To move into a state of creating joy-filled days on purpose, listen to the wisdom of your emotions. Vibrating on the positive end of the emotional scale makes a woman vivacious. Vibrating on the low end of the scale is less healthy, but it does not make you bad or wrong. Be where you are, and trust yourself.

Every action we take is either seeking pleasure or avoiding pain, so why not go straight to seeking pleasure? Moving toward joy is a much more positive and powerful means of jointly creating your life with the Universe than avoiding pain.

Bombshell Confidential: Listen to Your Body

Emotions are information. As I write this section I am (hopefully) at the tail end of a hellish hives outbreak. Hives, for the luckily unfamiliar, are raised, red, itchy, and painful welts that kidnap your skin for as long as they want. Mine are often compounded by eczema. They can be triggered by food allergies, random allergens, and stress.

Hives produce a visually angry outbreak on the body for a reason. Whatever we don't express in our lives finds a way to express itself through the body. So with this current outbreak, yes I realize that roasting beets for the first time and not properly cleaning them might be the medical reason. That's a start – but we should always ask our bodies, "What are you trying to tell me?"

If I am honest with myself, I must admit that there is currently unexpressed frustration in my life. There is more than one conversation that needs to be had. I need to tell someone I care about, "Look, I am pissed off and hurt." My body is saying, "Wake up, Abiola, pay attention to yourself." It is also the full moon and the first day of my period, a time for releasing, expressing, and emoting. Louise Hay, in *You Can Heal Your Life*, teaches that the underlying cause of skin eruptions is often a feeling of denying one's own power.

Bombshell Playbook Exercise

Answer these questions in your Bombshell Playbook. Take five deep, cleansing breaths to get centered and begin.

1. Do I believe that my feelings and ideas matter?

2. When is the last time I felt naturally high?

3. When is the last time I felt low?

4. How do I avoid feeling my feelings?

5. What would I do differently if I honored my feelings?

Are You Feeling Aligned?

"How are you?" It's a basic question that we rarely give an honest answer to. Maybe we would get a clearer response if we asked, "What are you feeling right now?"

Our emotions provide strong inner guidance. When you are aligned with your true Self – the Self that is an expression of the Most High – you feel juicy and alive. If you want to know if you are aligned with your highest and best good, ask yourself, "What am I feeling right now?" Negative emotions make us feel out of sorts because we are out of alignment.

This doesn't mean that you ignore your bad-feeling emotions or that feeling good is the only valuable way to feel; everything we're feeling has something to teach us. It just means that you can use this inner guidance to feel yourself back into alignment. When one of my soul sisters introduced me to the spiritual teacher Esther Hicks and this process of feeling your way back into alignment it was life-changing.

So what am I feeling right now? As I write this, I am feeling sad that my hives outbreak made me miss a chance to watch the New York Mets play against the Atlanta Braves with my friends. I don't know anything about baseball but I was looking forward to fun with my girls. It's important for my well-being that I acknowledge that I feel sad (and itchy!).

What do you feel right now? Curious? Annoyed? Excited? Feeling good is our birthright, but you can't get where you're going if you don't know where you are.

From this place of feeling itchy sadness and self-pity, it is unrealistic that I could suddenly jump to feeling happy. I don't have emotional access to that place right now. I can, however, find relief from feeling mopey and alone by reaching for a slightly better feeling. I can travel from sadness to joy the same way I would travel from Brooklyn to Queens: one step at a time. This is not new age woo-woo stuff. This is listening to our bodies and hearts to know where we are.

Bombshell Tool: Plug Into Your Power Source

When there is a gap between how you feel and how you want to feel, you can bridge that gap by generating positive feelings with your thoughts and actions. When my phone is dying, I don't draw a green checkmark on it and hope for the best. I plug the phone into its power source to get re-juiced. You can do the same thing for yourself. Here's how:

- Make a list of everything you are grateful for right now.
- Take a soothing bath in Epsom salt.
- Be sweet and loving to yourself.
- Cuddle with a loved one or pet.
- Watch a funny movie and laugh, laugh, laugh out loud.
- Allow yourself to be loved and cared for by someone else.
- Kiss your shoulders and say, "Hey beloved. It will be okay."
- Find a way to help someone else.

The key to lifting your mood is to reframe the situation. I do this by finding thoughts that feel slightly better than the defeatist "woe is me" thoughts I am having. Your situation doesn't change, but your thoughts about it do as you move your focus from what you are missing to what you have and are gaining. In my current situation with the hives, my reframed positive thoughts include:

- At least I got to catch up on rest and begin to heal myself.
- This isn't the last Mets game and it will be fun to catch the next one.
- This skin condition is temperamental but temporary and this too shall pass.

- ❧ I've gotten through it before and I'll get through it now.

- ❧ What great lessons these hives taught me and how perfect that I was able to share those lessons.

- ❧ If this situation didn't force me to take it easy, I wouldn't have been available when a client called in the midst of a panic attack. I am happy that I could be there for her.

And just like that, I am feeling a little better than I was at the beginning of this chapter. There is even a smile on my face. Do I feel the best I've ever felt? No, but I do feel better and more in alignment with my bliss. I am more aligned with my joy because my main goal is to feel better. As Esther Hicks says, alignment is not about trying to feel better than you ever have in your life, just better than you feel right now. I still feel physical discomfort, but by honoring my feelings my mental state is improved. I have moved from a feeling of irritation to one of optimism.

This is a key part of emotion management. You are responsible for what you feel. Take responsibility for making yourself feel better. Feel your way back into bombshell bliss when you feel off. This is how we move from feeling powerless to feeling powerful. Feeling your feelings is an act of radical self-love. Honor yourself by feeling what you feel.

The Healing Power of Compassion

The femergetic power of empathy is putting yourself in someone else's shoes, and compassion is putting the energy of empathy into loving action. Compassion that flows only in one direction leads to being a martyr and wounded healer. We can't be compassionate toward anyone in a healthy, healing, generous way until we are first compassionate with ourselves.

The love junkie looks down on the overeater who looks down on the alcoholic who looks down on the drug addict. Hello? We're all in this together. Knowing how difficult it is for you to resist M&Ms or leave "him," how can you judge someone else for popping pills? Welcome your own vulnerability and the vulnerability of others.

When I was younger, my whole life was built to protect me from being vulnerable. My homework was always as perfect as possible, my clothes and hair were bulletproof, and I kept my friends at arm's length. No one really knew me because I didn't let them know me. I was terrified to be vulnerable – to risk sharing what I was feeling, the heartbreaks and abandonments that I had experienced. I feared that if anyone saw the imperfect mess inside me who was not always kind or nice – who felt angry, sad, and jealous from time to time – they would run screaming in horror.

We avoid vulnerability because the very word means "capable of or susceptible to being wounded or hurt, as by a weapon." Well, that sounds about as much fun as being struck by lightning! No wonder we don't want to be vulnerable. However, as famed University of Houston vulnerability researcher Brené Brown points out, avoiding being vulnerable is a false sense of safety. If we don't let anyone in, we can't let ourselves out.

The reason you spend a great deal of energy trying to avoid feeling what you truly feel is that you're afraid you will break. You won't. Give yourself the gift of allowing yourself to feel your emotions fully. Express yourself and communicate in open and honest ways. Practice listening without defending and speaking without offending. Apologize and make amends when necessary. This doesn't make you weak. It makes you beautifully human.

Bombshell Tool: Honor Your Feelings Inquiry

Honoring where I am started with very simple questions that I asked myself whenever I was feeling anxious or uncomfortable. Ask yourself these questions to help understand what you're feeling and honor where you are.

- What am I feeling right now?
- Do I have any judgment about what I am feeling?
- Am I coming from a place of love or fear?
- What do I want?
- What am I afraid of?

- What is the best way to express myself?
- What is the most loving thing I could do for myself right now?
- Who do I need to forgive?
- What do I need to release?

If it's challenging for you to know what you're feeling, consider keeping a daily feelings journal.

The Big Bad Scary Feelings: Fear, Sadness, Anger, and Anxiety

Every culture has its myths and scary creatures. In Guyana, a jumbee is a spirit or ghost that moves among the living. My dad likes to tell a funny story about a drunken playboy stumbling along on a Saturday night, singing love songs and playing a guitar. A jumbee happens upon the playboy but he's too intoxicated to notice that something is off about his new friend. The two strike up a conversation and the man lends the jumbee his guitar.

The jumbee starts playing and the playboy is impressed. "Wow. Great music," the man says. The ghost replies, "Man, you think I can play now? You should have seen me when I was alive." Naturally, our friend takes off running. The jumbee runs after him yelling, "Take back your guitar!" but the guy wants no part of any of it.

When the man makes it home, his family asks what happened. He explains that a fearsome jumbee scared, stalked, and chased him. "You lie," the jumbee shouts from outside. "I was just trying to give you back your guitar."

Have you ever felt stalked by your fears? Fear is just like that jumbee. It may be chasing us, but it doesn't really exist. We are afraid of it, but fear is just giving us a warning that we can choose to engage in or disregard.

As long as we're breathing, there is stress. Our brains go into fight, freeze, or flight mode, ready to rumble with the tigers in the jungle. Because most of us are not battling tigers, the fear and anxiety that can send our bodies into overdrive does not always have a helpful purpose.

The great thing is that we're getting more comfortable with conversations around coping with stress and anxiety. This is particularly important as we are focused on giving the picture of perfection. We put on our glamouflage to distract from the fact that we're terrified inside and we're are drinking, drugging, sexing, gambling, under-nourishing, and over-working ourselves to distract and numb from what we're really feeling.

Bombshell Challenge: The next time you are in emotional distress, feel your feelings. When you are tempted to "do," surrender to the moment and do nothing. If you feel naked, raw, and vulnerable, put a hand over your heart and surrender to that vulnerability. Ask your body, "What am I feeling? And why?"

Anger Mismanagement: Nobody Wants to Tame Your Shrew

Anger for us women is multi-layered. Many of us grow up feeling that we don't have a right to our anger, but anger is a normal, healthy part of our emotional range. I was taught that it was not ladylike to express uncomfortable emotions. I didn't want to be dismissed as "acting like a bitch," or for being "emotional," so I learned to stuff my "unladylike" anger down. Maybe you suppress your anger with distraction, denial, or addictions. The problem is, trying to close down anger is like turning off a circuit breaker that controls all emotions. You end up being numb not only to anger or sadness, but also to joy, vulnerability, and compassion. Constipated emotions also make you really pissed off.

Anger is a physiological response to a perceived threat. The difference between anger and rage is that to an enraged person, the threat doesn't have to be real, only perceived. This kind of angry mind is not rational. Rage is like a seizure. Rageaholics can't tell the difference between a real fight-or-flight threat such as, "my life is in danger" and a pretend threat. Pretend threats include: "Somebody called me a name," "Somebody smiled at my man," or "Oh no, he left his socks on the floor." These things may be reason for a conversation but not fight/flight rage, as they don't threaten your true well-being. Often when there is a rageaholic in the family, only one person gets to express their anger. Everyone else is given the task of managing their lives around the drama queen or king. Obviously, this is extremely toxic.

Directed anger, on the other hand, can be healthy. For example, the people participating with Dr. Martin Luther King, Jr. in the March on Washington in 1963 were feeling righteous anger. This righteous anger prompted the freedom fighters to use positive activism.

There is a difference between "being an angry woman" and "a woman who is angry." Anger stems from frustration, so it's natural to be pissed off from time to time. A woman who is angry feels this emotion at times, but it does not control her. An angry woman is owned by her anger. It's not fun to spend time with her because random things might set her off. Her out-of-control anger creates a hostile environment.

Every time you fly off the handle because life doesn't go your way, you are giving away your power. People who have true internal power feel no need to be reactionary. You always have a choice. *No one is making you angry. You are choosing to make yourself angry.*

When you find yourself in an emotional tornado, get still. Ask yourself, "What am I afraid of right now?" It is solely your job to manage your emotions. Be 100% responsible for the energy that you put out in the form of your emotions.

Oftentimes when that tornado starts swirling, if we get still we realize that it all comes back to primal fears: abandonment, not being good enough, being unlovable, feeling unworthy of respect and acknowledgment. Is it hard to get still when your emotions are running high? Hell yeah! But you and I both know that the other way wasn't easy either.

We're all eight years old inside. Just don't let that eight-year-old who formed what you believe about love, safety, and emotions control your adult life. We all have the same needs. We want to feel accepted and loved.

Bombshell Tool: Anger Management Techniques

🔥 **Know your triggers.** What do you do when you feel hurt? How do you react when you're afraid? When you were a child and trauma happened you had no choice. As an adult you always have a choice. You are not a victim.

🔥 **Take an adult time out.** Stop, drop, and roll out of the situation. Ask yourself, "Is this really important?" You can have healthy boundaries without shutting down. Think of it as opting out, like when you cancel a subscription. Refuse to engage without making the other party bad or wrong. Try repeating to yourself, "This is not my issue."

🔥 **Create an emotional 911 plan.** Just like we do fire drills and have an emergency plan, make a list of five "In Case of Emotional Emergency" action steps. Items can include: phone a friend, go running, sit with the pain, allow myself to cry, and so forth. Put this ICEE list somewhere easily accessible; especially if you are predisposed to addictive, habitual, or reactive behaviors.

🔥 **Emotion follows motion.** Get your anger out without lashing out at others. Write it out. Stomp pillows. Go running. Dance. Scream. Cry. Work out.

🔥 **Do a mental body scan.** Ask your body where the difficult emotions are physically inside of you. Are they in your throat, blocking your expression? Do you feel them in your belly or your bowels? Yoga might help you to drop back into your body from your mind, which may be running amuck. Speak to your body, listen, and take steps to heal.

🔥 **Take a deep breath.** Deep breathing works well to manage anger when done correctly. Take a Fat Belly Breath. When you inhale, your stomach should expand. Inhale and count to four. Hold it for a count of four. Exhale on a count of four and do it again until you feel calmer.

- ⚭ **Consider perspective and perception.** Can you activate the feminine power of empathy in the situation? Ask yourself, "Am I willing to see the situation and related parties differently? What am I making this mean?"

- ⚭ **Take responsibility.** How can you take 100% responsibility in any interaction rather than thinking 50/50? You created the world as you see it and the situation you are in. Anything less is a victim mentality. Ask yourself, "Do I want to be right or do I want peace?"

- ⚭ **Set a positive intention.** A great question for in the moment is: "What do I want to happen right now?" Another helpful question is: "What is my anger trying to teach me?"

- ⚭ **Draw the emotion.** Does that anger have spikes or horns? Is it mucky green or fiery red? Then talk to it. Face your demons by giving shape and voice to them. What we resist persists. What we acknowledge fully can more easily dissolve.

The Many Faces of Depression

The blues, funk, ennui, toska, the vapors, gloom, melancholy, despair, bummed out – our sadness is a rainbow, although our modern culture only gives it one word: depression. Depression looks different in different women and has many shades within the same woman. One woman's sadness looks like shopaholic glee. Another woman's depression looks like a heaping plate of lasagna. Yet another sister's depression looks like "I don't need anybody" diva solitude. Depression to you might mean another night, another man. Then there's the blackout drunk face of depression. Yes, women's sadness has many shades and it is okay not to be okay. It's not only okay not to be okay – it is human. Ask the sadness, "What are you here to teach me? What is the lesson I must learn?"

If you have the blues, take good care of yourself. Treat yourself with gentle love and kindness. Every day, challenge yourself to participate in the world for one half-hour more than you did yesterday. Reject the stigmas and solitude of depression by speaking to the people you love. Lean into the vulnerability. You may bend but "you were not built to break" as a beautiful singer once sang. While you are still here you have a purpose; and you are still here.

You will not snap out of it, shake it off, or any such nonsense. You are also not helpless or hopeless. For now, just promise yourself to shower, go for walks, make the bed, create a routine, and talk to someone. Allow yourself to be listened to, hugged, helped, and supported. Be honest about what you can handle and what you cannot. Write your truth until you can speak it.

Meditate. Feel the sun on your skin. Get enough sleep and go help someone less fortunate. Visit your elderly neighbor or sweep her porch. Learn something new. Ditch the serotonin-stealing caffeine. Give your Inner Bully a run for it by challenging those self-hating thoughts. Don't believe it just because you think it. Find a therapist, counselor, or coach and work through it. You're worth it. And you are not alone.

My documentary **Knives in My Throat** followed a year in the life of the courageous Taqiyya Haden as she dealt with clinical depression and suicidal tendencies. If you have clinical or long-term depression, please get professional help. Women have told me that they feel guilt or embarrassment that they cannot will or pray their depression away. It is critical that you get the help you need ASAP, just as you would if you had a raging third-degree burn. Screw stigmas.

Bombshell Tool: Healthy Self-Soothing with EFT

Emotional Freedom Technique is a scientifically proven way to rewire the brain and interrupt anxiety, panic attacks, fear, social anxiety, phobias, compulsive behaviors, stress, and trauma that works for many people. This self-care tool combines modern psychology and ancient acupressure. You tap on specific meridians, or access points, on your body while repeating phrases related to your current issue or emotional state. It sounds simple, but this process has been life-altering for me.

Whether you are dealing with relationship drama, money stress, career anxiety, or mild depression, this acupressure technique may be helpful and healing. EFT can help you maintain a healthy state of mind. The great thing is that you can do EFT tapping yourself. You repeat a script as you tap on the specific meridian points with the middle and index finger of either hand. The meridian points are the top of the head, the inner eyebrow, the side of the eye, under the eye, under the nose, the center chin, the collar bone, and the underarm.

Life is beautiful when you feel your way back into alignment with the true Sacred Bombshell you are. Check SacredBombshell. com for EFT scripts and videos. To learn more about acupressure and this energy-healing technique, Nick Ortner's book, *The Tapping Solution: A Revolutionary System for Stress-Free Living* is unparalleled.

Bombshell Dialogue with Christelyn Karazin: How to Deal with Criticism and Shine Brighter

Christelyn Karazin is a writer, public relations specialist, and one of the foremost experts on interracial relationships. Her site, BeyondBlackWhite.com, enjoys blockbuster popularity. She is also the co-author of the popular advice guide *Swirling: How to Date, Mate, and Relate Mixing Race, Culture, and Creed.* This well-known online personality is also the host of a multicultural dating show called *Swirlr,* linked to a dating site of the same name. Christelyn is part of a movement called Black Women's Empowerment – bloggers and writers who are presenting their own brand of accessible feminism.

She came to national attention with her No Wedding, No Womb movement, aimed at getting men and women to take responsibility for creating two-parent homes before having children. Critics feared that the project might demonize single mothers and argued that the idea was heterosexist but she remained undeterred in her positive mission. Because Christelyn addresses race and gender, she is a target for vitriol and controversy, yet this woman manages to be a decent, and loving human being while having the ovaries to address her detractors directly.

Abiola: You're not afraid to take on controversial topics. Your No Wedding, No Womb campaign was a huge initiative. From your site: "No Wedding, No Womb is a primary call directed to the black community to take action against the rampant births of children who are born without physical, financial and emotional protection. NWNW calls for both men and women to put the needs of children first, and advocates that couples abstain from having children until they are emotionally, physically, and financially able to care for them."

Christelyn: No Wedding, No Womb was just a byproduct of what I had been seeing at the time. The black community in America [when] I last checked had between 70–80% out-of-wedlock birth rates. This is devastating to us. I thought there was strength in numbers, so I got the bloggers together. Pulling from my public relations and magazine writing backgrounds, I said, we'll pick one day where we'll all blog about [it]. And it went viral: 100,000 tweets in one night. It was trending on Google. We were covered in the **Associated Press**, **ESSENCE**, newspapers and blogs all over. We got a lot of good press but we had a lot of people who hated the message, who thought that I was demonizing single mothers and that I didn't know what I was talking about.

Abiola: You started as a single mother yourself.

Christelyn: Exactly and I was like, who better to tell the story than somebody who has lived this? There are always going to be people who have something to say. It was a good experience for me because it toughened my skin. I'm a very sensitive person and seeing all this stuff, the criticism ... I'm not completely immune to it but it's toughened me.

Abiola: How do you, as a blogger and public person, deal with criticism without letting it get into your soul? How do you realize that it's not personal?

Christelyn: First thing you do, close the laptop. It's magic because when you do that it goes away. [Second,] get some perspective, stop reading. After a while you realize the type of people who don't like you ... are just miserable anyway. Nothing makes them happy. Everything they say is negative. It's really easy to trash people now. The third thing is focus on the people who love you. Maybe I have 100 really earnest haters. Any time the media says anything [about] me they are committed to hating me. Oh hey, but my Facebook page has 30,000 fans. The blog gets 500,000 page views a month almost. Two years later the book is still selling. I have to focus on those things. I have an awesome life. My life is not perfect but it's awesome. I have a beautiful family who loves me. I have a supportive husband. I can't complain.

Abiola: That's exactly it. Focus on the love, not the fear or hate. Many of your critics would probably have a problem no matter what you said. For some, negativity is their vantage point.

Christelyn: They don't want to be won over. They don't want to like you. [Some] who are critical of me will say, "Christelyn is ugly and [that's] the only reason she does this. She knows that no black man wanted her."

Abiola: That's ridiculous because you're beautiful!

Christelyn: But for them, that's their argument. So I just have to look at myself in the mirror and check: I'm pretty symmetrical. No weird things, good skin. I'm not ugly and I just have to laugh at that.

Abiola: Well, where do you get the courage to get up in the morning and say, "I'm going to go out there again?"

Christelyn: My mom was one of those people that would just say what was on her mind and didn't care. When I watched my mom do these things I was like, "Oh my God, doesn't she see the reaction that she's getting?" [Then] I was like, "How can I do what she does? How can I say what nobody wants to say?"

I've always been like that. I stand up for justice. If there was somebody who was bullied on the playground I would always stand up for them. I never back down. If I see something that just isn't right I'm going to say something. I think it is part of being a good person. There are so many people who just don't want to get involved. Sometimes you have to get involved.

And then guess what? You give other people the courage to stand up. Then all of a sudden the bullies are outnumbered because you stood up and you emboldened others to also get that courage. I got a note from a black girl who is in medical school and who was on the fence about dating a fellow student because he was white. She said, "You gave me the courage to date him and guess what? We're getting married!"

I get notes like that constantly. "Thank you for sticking your neck out because now I'm not afraid anymore." I'm sure you get that, too. People are saying, "You made me think this, or do this differently." It's so fulfilling.

Abiola: Yes, it is fulfilling! Whenever you come from a place of service, that makes you stronger because it's like, I'm not just speaking up for me. You're in service to a community to hopefully make someone's life better. You've blogged that there's your outer yoga, your garden, and your inner yoga. How you deal with difficult emotions?

Christelyn: I have different people who I talk to. My husband is very problem-solving oriented. I have my girlfriends that I cry to. The people who I've formed friendships with, they know what I'm talking about. They're like, "let's hash it out" so I'm not doing something stupid like writing a blog post about how much I hate this person.

Abiola: Online dramas or work-related issues have nothing to do with your everyday life. They don't stop you from being a wife and being a daughter. Someone's ridiculous comment has nothing to do with who you are as a person. It's not personal because if it wasn't you they would be saying the same things to someone else.

Christelyn: Exactly. Just block them.

Abiola: Let's address one of the hot topics you've covered. Your title is *Let a Man Feel Like a Man*.

Christelyn: We live in a society where we are striving towards equality and I think that's great. However there are certain things that are innate: [Yin energy] women like to feel feminine and [yang energy] men like to feel masculine. It's yin and yang.

Abiola: This part of what this book is about!

Christelyn: A [yang energy] man wants to feel like he's needed. He wants to feel like he's capable of taking care of you; and it's not necessarily financially but emotionally and physically. He wants to go out and chop your wood. And the more feminine you are the more it stirs that attraction.

You're a very feminine woman, Abiola. You are desired. You spark that desire because men want to take care of you. And part of being feminine is to be able to trust and surrender that "I can do everything" over to someone else. That's scary because you've got to make sure that the person you are surrendering some of that power to is worthy of you.

Abiola: Choose your partner carefully. What makes you a bombshell, Christelyn?

Christelyn: I stopped trying to fit the mold of what beautiful was supposed to be defined as and just focused on being the best me I could be. And that was with everything – intellectually, emotionally, physically. Instead of trying to look like Beyoncé, I'm going to be the best version of Christelyn I can be. I'm going to be a damned good Christelyn. Focus on being the best version of yourself.

Bombshell Takeaways:

- When you stop trying to fit the mold, you can focus on being the best *you* possible.

- Criticism is not personal, and there are always going to be haters.

- When you stand up for what you believe in, you embolden others to do the same.

Bombshell Dialogue with Alexyss K. Tylor: How to Express Yourself and Own Your Voice

Alexyss K. Tylor is known for being a "Vagina Power"–shouting YouTube star and business woman who created a viral brand. Her brazen personality and "not safe for work" content have many women affirming, "Yes, thank you" while others are left perplexed. Alexyss, however, has remained steadfast in her goal to educate in her own authentic way. The Atlanta native has created her own line of nutritional supplements and organic butters and oils for skin and hair. Alexyss is also a medical intuitive who gives private tarot card readings. Alexyss is most importantly a mother. This gutsy woman had the blessing of reuniting with her son when he was released from prison. As a result, Alexyss has made educating parents about dealing with troubled children and jail culture a part of her personal mission.

Abiola: *Clutch Magazine* sexpert Arielle Loren named us both in her "10 Ten Black Women Teaching Us About Sex" piece. The reducing of shame and stigmas is so critical and I want to hold a space of honor for you, Alexyss. You are so transparent and outspokenly honest about what you have experienced. How did you become so courageous about speaking your truth?

Alexyss: Being abandoned by my mother. She told me when I was around nine that I was the product of a rape and it made me feel very unwanted. My mother taught me my vagina was shameful. I was taught it was worthless. My whole existence was shameful. I was an embarrassment to her. She was very abusive. And I would be like a little puppy. Just excited inside like, "My mom's here and she's so beautiful." I wanted her to hug me. I would just stand there and wait for her to see something in me. I was just heartbroken. But even as a grown woman, my mother would still play those games and, like, punish me and want to ridicule – literally destroy me, and take the courage from me to speak my truth … because my mother never told her truth.

Abiola: You've been through so much. Where did your knowledge of Vagina Power come from originally?

Alexyss: From being hurt so much.

Abiola: But a lot of people stay in the hurt. You've told me you dealt with depression, but you were able to know where the light is. A lot of people don't even know where the light switch is to say, "There is power within me."

Alexyss: I didn't know where the light was either all the time. I just had to have faith. I didn't have anybody. All I had was my higher self and my ancestors. That made me grow more spiritual. So I have my altar set up – you know, I talk to my ancestors. I reference them. I owe them because no matter what they went through – the African ones, the Native American ones – they stayed alive long enough to get me here. I owe it to them and I can't give up. I know I have a mission and a purpose.

And then I was responsible for [my son.] So, I had no choice. I just had to go within myself. I realized [there's] more protection for me in truth than in lying.

Abiola: So if somebody wants to tap into her Vagina Power, how would you recommend she go about that?

Alexyss: First, Vagina Power is not about physical sex and using your vagina to manipulate or get a man or anything like that. Many people don't consciously realize that they don't know who they are and they don't know what they are. Ask somebody, "Who are you?" They are going to define [themselves by] their money, their education, who they know, where they work. I'm not talking about that. That's a projection of that false self and how you have to move and function in this matrix with the rules of this matrix that are an illusion.

Abiola: Can you also speak about the connection between Vagina

Power and celibacy?

Alexyss: I felt that men were tricking me and lying to me. That's the time I became celibate. That was almost eight years ago. I realized, I'm always picking these men that want to act like they love me and then they want to imprison me. I'm always the common denominator. I realized, wow, Vagina Power! That's when it came up and I was like, "I'm going to do this Vagina Power show." I was angry from being abused all my life.

I felt then that this was all spiritual, psychic, emotional – and it was happening because I always felt powerless. So nobody was going to touch me because I had attracted the wrong people. Realize that in your vagina is the world of all worlds. And it holds the knowledge of all things because it's connected cosmically to the Universe before it comes physical.

That's where that knowledge comes from. In that pain and that celibacy. Everything I talk about now, all the projects [that I am] creating with my son, expanding the brand, adding to that umbrella of Vagina Power, actually came from me being celibate. Other than having sex with the Universe and having sex with myself. (laughs)

Abiola: You teach women how to do healing with their menstrual blood. When and how should women do this practice?

Alexyss: If you have mental, emotional issues or psychic attacks ... or things you're carrying that you want to release. A lot of stress, a lot of pain. It's good to use a menstrual cup. You can go into your yard and you can use herbs with it, too. Mix the herbs and really listen to your own spirit to create your own elixir. Then dig a hole in the ground. You pour [in] all your prayers. Pour as you're saying what you want to pull out of your body and release because that blood is attached to your soul. You want Mother Earth to absorb everything that you're releasing in the blood. Pour it in that hole in the ground and cover it. You can make that a sacred place where nobody goes or you can plant in that area and make a garden around it. That's your sexy witch space. (laughs) We're still sexy and we are witches and we're in Vagina Power.

Abiola: Yes! (laughs) This is our knowledge that we have lost and it's important to reclaim it so that we can pass that knowledge forward. You first came to the forefront with your relationship advice. What are your top love tips?

Alexyss: You've got to love and respect yourself first. You've got to heal your little girl wounds. You've got to heal your issues around daddy and men, and you must realize that you are moving from the laws at all times. Whether it's a good man or a bad man, you are a goddess so you have created that power play. You have power to use that Vagina Power to manifest what you truly want. You really do make that happen.

Abiola: So much of what you reveal is about post-traumatic disorders. There is the energy of trauma in our communities and people are just passing that on for generations without talking openly the way that you are. Part of healing is saying, "This happened to me. I will not play the game of denial. I will not play the game of shame. And I'm going to shine a light and move toward my healing." You are the person that is standing up and saying, "This happened to me and I will not be silent." So, what makes you a bombshell, Alexyss?

Alexyss: I've gone against the grain and fallen in love with myself when everybody said there was nothing to love. And I've respected myself although all my life I've been told that I don't deserve respect. I respect my voice and I use and direct that voice the way that I want to when my mother [told me], "You are always seen because you're too dumb to be heard."

Bombshell Takeaways:

- No matter what happened to you in the past, you have the power in the present.

- Don't ever be afraid to use your voice.

- If you were not parented the way you needed to be, re-parent yourself.

Secret of Emotions Resources

1. "Gifts of Imperfection" by Brené Brown (e-course)
2. *Up Thoughts for Down Times* by Les Brown
3. *Shakti Mantras* by Thomas Ashley-Farrand
4. HappyBlackWoman.com, run by Rosetta Thurman
5. EmotionalNudity.com, run by Jai Stone

Emotion Affirmations

1. I feel my feelings.
2. I have a right to express my emotions.
3. I love, honor, and accept myself.
4. I am worth loving.
5. It feels so good being emotionally naked.

Five

The Secret of Self-Devotion: Unconditionally Loving You

The Sacred Feminine Law of Self-Devotion

The Sacred Bombshell loves, honors, and cherishes herself unconditionally. With activated self-devotion, she understands that her
life is a mirror, reflecting how she feels about her Self. Thus, she is
devoted to loving and accepting herself first. This allows her to live
a life of passion, joy, and service. When she feels a dearth of love
on the outside, she loves herself more on the inside. This is sacred
self-love.

Historical Bombshell Mentor: Zora Neale Hurston 1891-1960

Fearless folklorist Zora Neale Hurston was a maverick in her
time as a writer, anthropologist, and world traveler. The Barnard
graduate committed several years to embedding herself in Voodoo
culture, becoming a priestess during her studies. Her personal
stories are even more fascinating than her colorful creations. Zora
was always ready to "jump at de sun." As she said, "Sometimes,
I feel discriminated against, but it does not make me angry. It
merely astonishes me. How can any deny themselves the pleasure
of my company?" Ever courageous and outspoken, Zora remains a
Harlem Renaissance icon.

The Self-Devotion Declaration

I am enjoying the love affair of a lifetime. My beloved smiles at
me from the mirror. She is strong, graceful, and complete, with a
generous heart. I am the lover and the loved. My devotion to my
Source is mirrored in my devotion to my Self.

I am love. My oneness with my Creator reminds me to spread
kindness and hope under the dreams of all whom I encounter. I run,
laughing, from complainers as if they have set fire to my feet. As is
the golden rule, I will love my fellow beings as I want to be loved.

I adore myself with more love than I ever thought possible. This devotion is fuller than romantic or familial love, yet it enhances both. I release judgment, freeing myself and those around me. Like a light bulb screwed into its power source, I love unconditionally, shining my light on those who would curse me. They are deluded as I was, believing the laws of separatism and competition.

Previously I believed the lie that I was separate from that which created me. I was lulled by the falsehood that I was separate from my brothers and sisters. Now I know that I am loved unconditionally. I return this unconditional love to every person I meet. I attract what I am and I am love. For this I am so grateful.

And so it is.

Do You Love You?

We women are so brutal to each other because we're brutal to ourselves. The Hindu-derived salutation "Namaste" means "the divine in me sees the divine in you." The way we treat each other as sisters, as girlfriends, is more like, "the loser in me sees the loser in you." In other words, "I'm nothing so if you look like me obviously you're nothing, too."

Do you feel unconditional self-devotion? Let's not confuse self-devotion or self-love with vanity, narcissism, and selfishness. The seeming overconfidence of the vain and narcissistic often just hides low self-esteem. Unconditional self-devotion is loving, honoring, and accepting your whole Self.

Some of us might mistakenly think that self-devotion looks like a loud, flashy, "deal with me, honey" reality TV character. Self-love is not the same as conceit. People who are conceited see themselves as being the number one doll while looking down on everyone else. People who love themselves don't bully, belittle, or look down on others. They don't need the approval of an audience. They are not in competition. Self-loving individuals don't need to leech energy from others; they are directly tuned into the Source.

Erin Myers, a psychologist at Western Carolina University, conducted a study which revealed that self-aggrandizing individuals merely present a well-constructed façade to mask deep feelings of inferiority. She told the website *LiveScience* that "narcissistic individuals may not really believe they are as great as they claim to be."

So how do we know whether we love ourselves or not? For most of us, our supposed self-love is shallow and conditional. We feel loving toward ourselves when we have a good hair day. We feel a semblance of self-worth when the person we like treats us like we're worthy. We like ourselves more when our jeans fit well.

It is impossible to love anyone else and hate yourself. How can we begin to even consider unconditional love and devotion in relationships when our primary relationship – the one with ourselves – is so frigging conditional? We say: "Self, I will love you if your body is perfect, your career and bank account are working, and the people I love agree that you are worth loving." This is not self-love or even self-like.

Bombshell Challenge: What if you were madly, truly in unbelievable love with yourself with deep, spiritual, and bountiful devotion? What might that look like? Live it for one day. If you can't do a whole day, start with an hour.

The Sacred Feminine Power of Self-Devotion

A few years ago I was confused about what it meant to be a self-devoted, self-loving, self-caring, self-adoring woman. I was overweight and unhealthy. I felt that the word "fat" was abusive, so I removed the word from my vocabulary but lived it anyway. Guess what? I knew that I was overweight and I didn't care. I just bought bigger clothes. The clothes were cute and so was my hair and makeup – so what?

Meanwhile, my health tanked. My salty, fried, and packaged food was delivered and my laundry was picked up, so I barely left the house. My blood sugar went into overdrive. Any heavy meal would knock me out. I had sleep apnea, crazy food allergies and sensitivities, and acid reflux. Still, I was not only a productive member of society but was succeeding in many ways.

My refusal to consider my health was a rebellion against my prior obsessions with dieting and body image issues – but was also an obsession in itself. I didn't want to deprive myself of cookies, West Indian rice, French fries, and queso. Eating those foods felt to me like joy. I told myself that it didn't matter because I looked good, felt good, and loved myself. Being fat was my personal "f—you" to every component of society that tells us women to hate ourselves. Unfortunately, the only one I was hurting was me.

While I might have painted a picture of loving myself that even I believed, I was treating my body and my Self terribly. I was spelling love c-o-o-k-i-e. They say that the opposite of love is not hate but indifference. I was treating myself with indifference. You can't love yourself and not properly care for your body.

Working with an intuitive coach combined with my own research and practices of self-care helped me to change my body and my worldview. I also came to terms with my addictions to food, sugar, work, and people pleasing that were keeping me small. I faced my history of disordered eating and the triggers that were creating that behavior. As they say in the recovery movement, addiction is not the problem – it's the solution that the addict creates for the problem. When you love yourself you release all barriers to being the shining light you were born to be.

I was inadvertently taught to love myself with food, shopping, and achievement. This left me unhealthy, broke, and burnt out. Luckily I also had other lessons. My parents taught me that I was beautiful, smart, creative, and could do anything, and they made me feel prosperous. They said, "God is within you" and "I love and support you unconditionally."

Life comes down to a series of choices, and we can always make different choices. As for the belief that we are unworthy, a belief is a thought that we keep thinking. Many of us are excellent at hiding our self-esteem issues – even from ourselves. We say "I love myself" while practicing self-hating behaviors. We dress up to resemble self-esteem while indulging in toxic relationships and ingesting poison.

Bombshell Exploration: Give Yourself a Gift

Cost has nothing to do with buying a loving gift for yourself. The gift can be a star sticker that reflects who you're becoming or an experience like hiking in your local park rather than a material object. Many women remember buying themselves the first designer bag or car – things that signify outward success. That's fun, too, but I remember buying my first original piece of art. This was a soul-enriching rite of passage for me. Follow the yearnings of your heart.

My parents somewhat "spoiled" me whenever they were able to. Still, there were toys that I lusted after that I was not able to have. Instead of living in a Barbie Dreamhouse, for example, my dolls rocked out in a townhouse I made by pulling all the books off the bookshelf. I had a cool kiddie kitchen set but the stove didn't turn on like the Easy Bake oven. The alternative was that I got to hang out in the real kitchen with my mom, mixing cake batter and cutting vegetables from the garden. Still, I never got over not having an Easy Bake oven. How exciting would it be to buy myself one now? As a grown woman, do I need to cook with a light bulb? Of course not. The grownup voice in my head says that this is something I can buy for my future daughter. The bombshell voice in my head says screw that! If you want a frigging toy oven, buy it for yourself. Join a Meetup.com group or forum of other toy-oven-obsessed adults online if you want to. What's the worst that could happen? Light bulb cooked kale chips, here I come!

Awkward Author's Note: My mom and sis have since confirmed that I did have an Easy Bake oven. I didn't even have to share it because my sister had her own Holly Hobbie oven. Whoops! But the lesson still stands! Give yourself a meaningful gift.

Bombshell Playbook Exercise

Answer these questions in your Bombshell Playbook. Take five deep, cleansing breaths to get centered and begin.

1. How were you taught to love yourself?

2. What messages did you receive about your self-worth from your family dynamic?

3. If you could re-parent yourself, what would you like to teach you most?

4. How can you show yourself that you are enough?

5. What would you do differently if you believed that you are worth loving?

Imagine a Bombshell Who Adores Herself

How do you know if someone loves herself? No hairstyle, religion, or ethnicity has ownership of self-love or a greater propensity toward self-hatred. The best way to tell if a woman loves herself is by how she treats herself and others. She makes self-loving choices.

A woman devoted to herself makes as much time for herself as she makes for the people in her life. She listens to her intuition and her emotions. She believes in herself enough to invest time in her passions. She treats her body like a temple. Self-loving women enjoy their own company. It is a radical act of self-love to say yes when you mean yes and say no when you mean no. Boundaries are essential. When we know that we are worthy, we stop playing invisible and inconsequential. We become the women we were born to be.

A woman who loves herself believes that she is worth loving. She knows that her presence is a gift. She invites only those who agree to share her life. She teaches her family, friends, and partners to treat her well. She treats them kindly because it is a pleasure to do so. She listens and gives generously to people and causes that enrich her soul. Her chosen love treats her like a queen because any relationship we are in with others only reflects the relationship we have with ourselves.

A woman who loves herself has self-trust and self-integrity. She knows that her promises to herself are valid. She keeps her word to herself. If she says that she is going to work out she will. If she says she's not going to call him she won't. She nourishes her body with Mother Nature's foods. She feeds her mind in healthy ways. She honors her body's natural rhythms by resting when she's tired and withdrawing when she needs to.

This woman who loves herself makes time to play. Pleasure is her domain. Joy is her pursuit. She knows that the best thing she can do for her loved ones is to feel good. Therefore nothing is more important than feeling good in her skin. Self-love means acknowledging and respecting your own desires.

A self-devoted woman is also compassionate to herself. She forgives herself for her missteps and learns the lessons necessary to avoid repeating them. She knows that life is working toward her highest good. Women who love themselves don't indulge in shame, blame, gossip, or other low-vibrational thinking. The light emanating from a woman in love with herself lights up a room, a family, a community. A self-loving woman takes responsibility for her life. She understands that she has choices. Women who adore themselves love learning and adding to the wisdom of the planet.

A woman who is devoted to herself is radiant and vibrant. She is radiant because she radiates love. This woman is vibrant because she is vibrating positive energy. She is not perfect, nor does she want to be. She is not a saint nor should she be.

Bombshell Tool: The Mirror Exercise

The most sacred thing you can do is to look into your own eyes and say "I love you." Maybe you won't mean it at first, and maybe you will, but here's the assignment: Every morning look into your own eyes and say, "I love you" plus your name. Do the same at night before you go to bed.

A woman who knows her own worth and beauty is magnetic and attractive to all she desires. There is no force stronger than a woman who genuinely loves herself without comparisons to or in competition with others. If you love your own beauty there is no need to hate, reject, or ridicule anyone else's. Don't ever pass a mirror without complimenting yourself. For extra self-love points, do this naked and speak love into every part of your body. Try it right now.

How to Re-Story Yourself

Self-devotion is not lurking between your couch cushions waiting for you to find her. Your mission, should you choose to accept it, is unconditional love for you. We fall in love with ourselves the same way we fall in love with someone else – repeated actions that prove respect, care, trust, and adoration. Keeping your word to yourself is how you build up trust in yourself. Show yourself compassion. Take a vow to release the idea that you can't love yourself until you're perfect.

Self-Devotion Assessment

How much do you love yourself? When you love someone you treat them in loving ways. You give them only the very best in company, food, and affection. How do you treat yourself? Do you only accept friends and romantic partners who treat you like the jewel you are? Do you feed yourself with healthy food and positive images and entertainment? Do you affirm your own beauty?

Positive Self-Talk

Who's in charge: your Inner Bully or the highest part of your Self? We fear rejection but reject ourselves more than anyone. We fear criticism but we say things to ourselves that we wouldn't say to our worst enemies. Notice negative self-talk and use positive affirmations to counter. Be aware of your snark and self-deprecating "humor." Imagine that with every word you speak you are casting a spell over your life.

What is that spell saying? Is it saying that you are beautiful, funny, talented, creative and loveable? Is it saying that you are an idiot, poor, and not enough? For most of us, it's the second – the voice of your Inner Bully. It calls you lazy when you are burned out or stupid when you make mistakes. Instead, make every word an affirmation or prayer.

Take Risks

Risk is the only way to become more than we are. Inaction is paralyzing. The way to beat fear is to take action and risk something. If you fall or fail, so what? This is how you build up unconditional love, respect, and admiration for you.

What does it mean to take a risk? Try new things. Experiment. Flirt. Walk down the street smiling. Wear something that you would never wear. Be weird. Tell someone you love them. Confront someone who mistreated you. Apply for a new job. Try a new kind of cuisine. That person who asked you out, that coach you wanted to contact, that adventure you wanted to take – go for it!

Ask for Help

If you need help, ASK. It doesn't matter how obvious you think your situation is. I inherited a martyr gene: No, don't help me, I'll just take care of everything by myself. I don't need your assistance, attention, money, time, love…

Ask for help and then ACCEPT it. Be willing to receive assistance. Allow good things and good people to make your life better. It is not selfish to say, "Help me." It's compassion toward yourself. You are worthy of support.

Break Up with Bad

Bad could mean a bad job, friend, or lover. Everything you do is either adding to your life or subtracting from it. The company you keep is a direct reflection of how you feel about yourself.

Play, Play, Play

What role does genuine pleasure play in your life? Besides trinkets, what do you want? It's a fallacy that playtime should stop as an adult or that grownup fun time has to be expensive. Get outside and move it. Play cards or kickball. Create art. Dance.

Spend Quality Time Alone

A word about isolation: Quality time with yourself is not sitting on the sofa zoned out to the TV with your BFF, potato chips. Quality time is also not spending money you don't have. Quality time means enjoying your own company on purpose. Read a book at a restaurant. Explore a new neighborhood. Window shop for the life you're planning. Go to a music festival and make friends. No one you know understands why you would want to visit Alaska? Take a solo-cation. Will you feel uncomfortable? Maybe. So what?

Send Yourself a Card

Buy yourself a beautiful card or make one. Sing your own praises in a note and snail mail it to yourself. On days when you need to remember how superb you are, open your card and read it out loud.

Bombshell Playbook Exercise

Answer these questions in your Bombshell Playbook. Take five deep, cleansing breaths to get centered and begin.

1. What are the most wonderful things about me?

2. What would my life look like if I truly loved myself?

3. Where am I putting the needs of others above my own?

4. When I repeat the affirmation "I am worthy," what feelings does it awaken?

5. What regrets do I have and what lessons do those experiences teach me?

Bombshell Confidential: Your Yoni Power

The exquisite Sanskrit word "yoni" describes that precious area that includes your vulva, labia, mons Venus, vagina, and clitoris. The clitoris is the only body part with 8,000 incredible nerve endings devoted solely to your pleasure! Thus I call being devoted to yourself being a "yonified" woman. A couple of years ago I was a speaker on two educational panels at the Good Vibrations Summit in San Francisco. The keynote was given by the esteemed Debby Herbenick of The Kinsey Institute. There was an intersection in our work. She has been outspoken about "genital self-esteem" and in my ESSENCE.com "Intimacy Intervention" column I give advice on sexual self-esteem. Her research reveals that women who don't have positive thoughts about female genitalia have a self-critical view that affects how they see other women plus more issues with orgasm. It also turns out that men are more positive than women about the beauty of all associated lady parts.

Yonified, femergized, and vulvalicious is how we should all feel on a daily basis! The heaven between your legs is not just there to push out your children or for someone else to appreciate. This is the most pleasurable part of your anatomy. Yes! Yes! Yes! Here sits your energy center, the birthplace of your mission, the creativity gateway for all that is. She shines in nature and in art. A 42-year-old Russian woman made the **Guinness Book of World Records** for lifting 30 pounds with her vagina! You can move mountains with the energy in yours. Herein sits your yoniverse.

Why is loving your own sacred space so forbidden? I was reading someone else's self-help book about being a badass and she said, "And you won't even have to write love letters to your uterus." Why the devil not? (as my mom would say). If it's not for you, that's fine, but don't knock it for your sisters. Every part of our bodies needs and deserves love.

If These Yonis Could Talk

In 2007, I curated a multimedia art exhibit called "Hoes, Putas, and Dragon Ladies: Our Sexuality Re-Mixed" at the Chashama Gallery in Manhattan. I hand-selected women artists from diverse cultures and artistic mediums to share work about sexual stereotypes.

On our opening night, artist Liliana Velasquez presented a masterful and yonified performance. The dazzling Colombian painter, dancer, and performance artist created a work of art-life that was about yoni soul healing. She shared the stage with a woman who was dealing with the grief of losing a baby. Liliana, who calls herself the Goddess of Transformation, danced the tango while wrapping the woman in a womb made of saran wrap. The crowd spoke about the trauma of an empty womb as Liliana painted the wrapping. It was magnificently choreographed and upon completion, all present felt a renewal and healing. Liliana was at once the seductress and the motherly healer.

If these yonis could talk. There is so much broken-hearted yoni energy in want of healing. Our vaginas experience violence, hatred, scorn, and anger. Almost every woman I've asked has a personal story of an unwanted sexual experience, either taken by force or given because she didn't think she had the right to say no. Almost every woman I know also has a story to share of lost babies, babies we chose not to have, childbirth yearned for, or all of the above. Sometimes there are ugly histories that we carry in our DNA. We are daughters of rape and sorrow and slavery, but we can be the ones to evolve our family stories. We are also daughters of joy and radiance and beauty and spunk.

Yoni is my favorite word for our organs of reproduction and sexual pleasure. I also find poetry in the word "vulva." "Vagina" is inaccurate to describe the totality of your nether regions because it only describes the "sheath" area. The sometimes hilariously subversive and often crass "pussy" is lyrical enough but I don't care for it — though the naughtiness of it can be fun. "Cunt" is too loaded with other people's anger for me.

People have very personal reactions to what others choose to call their body parts. Use whatever word makes you feel most empowered, Sacred Bombshell. There's vulva, vagina, pussy, punani, and pudenda. Other euphemisms include "down there," "the v," and "it." Then there's the slanguage: flower, wee wee, coochie, pocketbook, kitty, candy, privates, plum, vajayjay, lady bits, lady parts, velvet glove, happy valley, mother of all souls, cake, gonda, concha, papaya, chocha, twat, honeypot, poontang, la pepita, cunt, scunt, pata or patacake, vag, sugar walls, the queen, love box, and so on. Nothing sets off the giggly little kid in us like hearing our bawdy national grandma Betty White call hers "muffin" on *Saturday Night Live*.

In 2006 I created and curated the Vagina Warriors Film Festival in association with the V-Day and Until the Violence Stops festival created by Eve Ensler. Our mission was to create a conversation about the violence perpetrated against women and girls. We ultimately had to change the name to the Until the Violence Stops

Film Festival because one of our screening museums would not print the word "vagina" on invitations. I guess they missed the point of the word vagina being in the title in the first place!

Loving our bodies and ourselves unconditionally is a revolutionary, evolutionary, and sacred act. "Yonified" is my name for a woman who has high sexual self-esteem. When I coach women on tapping into divine feminine power, I refer to accessing your goddess or bombshell power. Alexyss K. Tylor calls it "Vagina Power." Mama Gena Thomashauer calls it the "Power of the Pussy." Jessica Holter of the Punany Poets talks about "Flower Power," and poet Christa Bell calls it "She-ism."

We're all saying the same thing. Yes, darling! Your power center is real. Your sacred womb holds the ultimate creative life force — and you don't have to physically have the reproductive parts to have the emotional memory of this energy in your body. Here is your divine, ready-to-be-awakened feminine energy. You can be celibate, in a relationship, or single and dating (or not) and access your yoni power. Your inner strength has nothing to do with whether you are "bony" or "thick," an immigrant or home grown, vanilla or cocoa, younger or older, with a history of two partners or twenty.

A male reader called me a "sex blogging prude" because I am an advocate for celibacy and emotionally safe sex, and have only been intimate when in a long-term, committed relationship – but I am all about yoni power and a woman's right to do whatever she damn well chooses with her body. How could a woman who has had less than a handful of partners be an activist for sexual freedom? What do the choices that work for me have to do with empowering another woman to make her own sex-positive choices? They key word is choices. Enough with the slut-shaming and prude-shaming. Most of us are neither "Madonnas" nor "whores."

Writing a love and lifestyle advice column for gURL.com was eye-opening. Teen girls have the same exact questions that adult women are asking me 10, 20, 30 years later. How do I learn to love what's between my legs? Why doesn't he find me desirable? What's wrong with my body? How can I make him stay? Our mothers would have taught us this if they knew, but that's okay. No judgments. It is time for a new paradigm.

If these yonis could talk. We live in a society that believes showing sensual interaction on screen is more dangerous than watching people kill each other. We wag our fingers condescendingly about female genital circumcision and hijab in other countries, but in America we are lining up for labiaplasty and vaginaplasty surgeries. We don't ask about the ramifications of using chemically bleached tampons in our most intimate inner space – even though menstrual cups, an alternative that makes many women feel more connected to our bodies, are available in most drugstores.

This is the time for adult sex re-education. When my childhood friend first showed me a porno flick on her dad's VCR, I was shell-shocked. I questioned my womanhood because nothing on my body looked like what I was seeing on the screen. Pornography is not the place to learn about intimacy or our bodies.

Pussy power is "ha-ha funny" but do men lead with "dick power"? Heck yeah, they do. What do you think swag or swagger is? Have you ever seen a president without charismatic sexual energy? Too many of us feel disconnected from this central part of our bodies. We're used to seeing ourselves through the gaze of someone else. There's a belief that our bodies are not ours to enjoy. The media says that there's an accepted way for our vulvas to look, smell, and react. We're not so fresh, too bushy, too wet, too dry, or whatever. Yes, real life vaginas have discharge and periods. But we also have much wisdom in our bodies.

Yoni Healing

When I read about Mayan abdominal massage, an ancient belly kneading procedure that counts among its benefits increasing fertility, restoring menstrual flow, and decreasing cysts, I gasped. This process sounds like what I've been told that my great-grandmother used to do! My mother says they called it "anointing." In addition to delivering babies "Ma" was able to fix women's fertility issues with this kneading and manipulation of the uterine area. Mayan abdominal massage also includes uterine massage. It is the sacred passageway to life.

Global culture offers so many non-invasive ways for us to heal and care for ourselves. Unfortunately because of the taboo nature of real conversation about women's bodies, we don't learn about them.

- There is a Korean procedure called Chai-Yok, which is a yoni steam bath. The treatment is said to help with everything from fertility issues to hemorrhoids (practitioner Tracey Bryant explains in Chapter 5).

- *Shameless* author Pamela Madsen was able to free herself from emotional turmoil with erotic yoni massage.

- Castor oil packs on the abdomen can increase lymphatic flow and aid with menstrual issues.

- There are cuddle and snuggle parties where fully dressed adults craving non-sexual touch get together for the honor of holding and being held.

- Breast massage, popular in China, may prevent breast cancer and help to increase breast milk for nursing mothers.

- Yoni meditation is said to allow us to open our hearts.

- The yoni mudra gesture in yoga is said to be therapeutic for stress relief.

- Womb yoga focuses on a practice of postures for uterine strength.

- The Chinese Jade Egg trains the yoni in vaginal kung fu – strengthening the pelvic floor, rejuvenating the vagina after pregnancy, and keeping you moist and aroused.

- In Malaysia, Para-Tan tantric sound healing can release years of trapped shame, bitterness, and emotional trauma, restoring a free-flowing of energy.

- Native American women introduced the herb black cohosh to the Europeans as a healing agent for women's issues such as PMS, inducing labor, and menopause. Today's science finds that it behaves like estrogen in many ways.

- While nettle tea reportedly aids in fertility issues, sage tea helps with symptoms of menopause.

- With Indian Yoni Puja, the yoni herself is worshipped as a temple or sacred goddess. How healing might that feel?

The mighty yoni has been judged enough. Let us release self-judgment and come home to ourselves. Let us release feelings of powerlessness and realize that we are powerful beyond measure. Let us release feelings of scorn for other women's bodies and ideas. Most of all, let us be born into our joy. Yoni energy is chi energy. This is your life force and this is your life. How you treat your yoni is a good reflection of how you treat your Self. So how do you treat your vital, sacred space? Is she a neglected, ignored, and abandoned cave for functional purposes only? Is she plucked and groomed in a quest for perfection? Is she bedazzled and dyed, wearing masks for performance? Does she feel like a queen or a victim? Is she a source of annoyance, shame, or just tolerance? Or is she simply loved?

Only you know.

Only you.

Only.

O.

Bombshell Explorations: Three Ways to Get Yonified and Yonilicious

1. **Feeling yonified yet?** Wake up your inner Oshun, let Shakti reign, and be your own Venus meets Isis bombshell. Call in the energy of your self-loving Historical Bombshell Mentors such as Josephine Baker and Zora Neale Hurston. Ground yourself and soften your shoulders. Shift your energy to your sexy parts. How do you feel?

2. **It is mirror time again.** This time hold it between your legs. Explore your yoni area in your reflection. It's yours, right?

Develop a healthy love and appreciation for your body.

3. **Yoni tales.** When I was a kid I read in a romance novel I stole from my mom that women had "three holes." The concept had me verklempt. Three holes? What were they talking about? I could figure out that we peed through one and defecated through the other, but what was the third? It was a mystery to me. What funny yoni stories do you have to share? Share them with your Bomb Squad in the interest of removing stigmas and shame.

4. **Create vulva art.** Depictions of female genitalia in art are as old as time. After leading a healing workshop at the now-defunct Bronx women's safe space Casa Attabex Ache, I was invited to take part in a ceremony where an artist led us in making vulva lockets from clay. It was intense. Now it's your turn. Draw, paint, or sculpt her.

5. **Write a poem for your lady parts.** Let it be as fun, sacred, or silly as you choose. Don't let anyone else's judgment deter you from loving any part of you. It's yours! Get your bombshell sisters together and read your poems over libations and fruit.

Bombshell Playbook Exercise

Complete these exercises in your Bombshell Playbook. Take five deep, cleansing breaths to get centered and begin.

1. What names were you given for your yoni?

2. What name do you choose and why?

3. What would your yoni say if she could speak? How does she feel about you?

4. Tell the truth: How do you feel about your yoni?

5. List 25 non-sexual compliments that you remember receiving.

Bombshell Confidential: The Importance of Self-Pleasure

If you can't please yourself, no one else will.

Throughout history, there have been varying levels of shame associated with touching one's own body. Boys touching themselves is practically viewed as a rite of passage but there are still taboos for girls and women. In 1994, U.S. Surgeon General Joycelyn Elders was fired for suggesting to the United Nations on World AIDS Day that young people be taught to explore their bodies rather than exploring riskier behaviors.

Sex does not get any safer than just you. Feeling sexual urges is natural. If you can quench some of those urges yourself, that's the safest sex of all. The only risk is pleasure. The wondrous thing about self-touch is that as a solo sexplorer you can learn firsthand (pun intended) what feels good to you.

It is a fact that the more you touch yourself the more orgasmic your body becomes. If you needed another reason to enjoy your body, self-pleasure is a stress reliever. Dr. Gloria Brame, author of **The Truth About Sex**, explains: "People who had orgasms before important speaking engagements felt much calmer and more self-possessed when it came [time] to deliver their speeches." Wow!

Having intimate knowledge of our bodies is also insurance against all of the negative body image messages that come at us daily. When you know that you can give love to yourself, you move in the world differently. Self-pleasure makes you more comfortable in your body.

Declaring Your Love for You

A few years ago, the diamond industry made a splash by declaring that women should buy a "right-hand ring" for themselves. The campaigns were in the spirit of "girl power" and showing independence by making a decadent purchase. I don't know many people who jumped on to this trend, but I'm sure it may have been in response to declining numbers of engagements and the fact that women have more disposable income than ever before. Marketing ploys aside, there is value in declaring your love for yourself. I don't think that you need to spend thousands of dollars to do so, but if you want to, go for it!

A wedding ceremony generally consists of a couple taking vows of love, honor, and commitment (as they see it) to one another. The family and loved ones of the couple bear witness and the vows are overseen by the chosen officiate. This ritual signifies the joining of hearts, families, and goals. Whether it's a wedding, a new baby, a big birthday, or the joy of a new job, saying yes and yippee has value. Too often we amble through without reveling in our joyful moments. This is part of the reason I say yes to women having a commitment ceremony for themselves. I used to call this a self-marriage but because we have so many associations with the "m-word," some women are more comfortable calling it a "commitment ceremony."

"But Abiola," you may be thinking, "I am already committed to myself!" That's great, but more often, for most of us, we feel divorced from ourselves. We all *want* to be committed to ourselves. We aim to be on our own sides. We declare it when New Year's Eve rolls around, proclaim it after every self-help book, and then chide ourselves when we fall short. Yes, in our fantasies or in the rah-rah sister mask we lead with, we are fully committed to ourselves. The face you lead with at work, the character you portray on social media is in full love and support of herself. However, the woman you show me privately is the opposite. I see your tears and hear your sorrows when you feel that you were not there for you. I too am familiar with self-betrayal.

I am honored to provide a safe space for you to voice your fears and challenges. I hold a sacred space for every woman reading this book to rise up and become the fullest realization of herself. You don't need to call it marriage, but you do need to make a loving commitment to yourself. Put your hand over your heart and ask, "How have I betrayed you?" Oh, let us count the ways. You betray yourself when you say you will work out tomorrow and tomorrow never comes. You betray yourself when you sell out your body for the grown-up equivalent of a Happy Meal. You commit personal treason when you give your time and your heart where they are not valued. You are unfaithful to yourself when make someone your priority who only considers you an option. Looking in the mirror and hating what you see is treachery. You want others to love, honor, and cherish you when you have not done so for yourself. You are hungry for a buffet and settling for crumbs.

A commitment ritual announces to yourself, those in your life, and the very cells in your body that you matter. If you include other people in your personal commitment ceremony, you also have a circle of accountability. It hasn't fully worked out this way in modern times but this is one reason guests "witness" a wedding. If you are looking to move on to the next stage, whatever that means to you, this is a great way to proclaim it. This is an act of healing and self-devotion. This is not about being tired of or "over" men. It is essential for your mental health and well-being that this is pro-you, not anti-anyone else.

Note that this is not just for single women. Our culture likes to push the duplicitous story that being in a relationship is a panacea for all while touting divorce statistics. Having a partner doesn't automatically make you more self-honoring. I know of a married mom who had a self-marriage ceremony with the full love and commitment of her husband and children. Her adoring family was present while she made a moving commitment to herself.

There was an episode of **Sex and the City** where Carrie said that she was marrying herself. The episode was called "A Woman's Right to Shoes" and she was "shoe-shamed" for buying expensive shoes by a friend who was a wife and mother. Carrie's shoes, incidentally, were stolen at the woman's house. "Hi. It's Carrie Bradshaw. I wanted to let you know that I'm getting married. To myself. I'm registered at Manolo Blahnik," she announced.

The self-commitment ceremony we're talking about here is not about a party or gifts, although you should have whatever kind of soiree makes your heart sing. Some women have a big Marrying

Myself ceremony and party that could compete with any Sweet 16. You can have a full-on white gown wedding with 200 guests if that fits your fancy. It can also be a private backyard ceremony with a few friends – or just you and your Sacred Bombshell Sister out in nature. You can also choose to register for gifts as Carrie did. It's fun to combine a personal commitment ceremony with a birthday party.

So will people think you're weird? Some will and some won't. As with anything, when it comes to sharing your dreams with others, choose responsibly. Many people are followers who can't understand something unless they see their favorite celebrity do it. More likely you will be a beacon for the people who love you to strive to do better in their own lives. Besides, if someone thinks you're weird, so what? You're a leader, not a follower, right?

Bombshell Playbook Exercise

Complete these exercises in your Bombshell Playbook in preparation for the commitment ceremony exploration that follows. Take five deep, cleansing breaths to get centered and begin.

1. **How have you betrayed yourself in the past year?** Make a list of all of the promises in the past 12 months that you've broken to yourself.

2. **What are your new self-devotion promises to yourself?** Next to each betrayal, write out a new pledge to yourself. Be specific. If you promised to do a workout regimen that never happened, write down exactly what you will do for how long with a start date.

3. **Put these promises together.** This is a list of your vows to yourself. Some of them can be funny – as in, "I will watch only one *Housewives* show per week." Of course, most will be more serious, such as, "I will only have friendships with positive and uplifting people."

Bombshell Exploration: Your Commitment Ceremony

First, determine what kind of ceremony would mean the most to you. Do you want to celebrate with friends and/or family or solo? Do you want to be indoors or outdoors? Would you prefer a venue or your home? Do you want to spend money? If so how much? What do you want to wear? Would you like an officiate to be present? Do you want to cook for everyone? Is your pleasure to dance on a table or barefoot on a starry night?

As with any wedding, set a date and make your dreams come true. However you plan your ceremony, at some point light a candle and read your vows. Ask your loved ones for support. Then celebrate, celebrate, celebrate! Most importantly, after the party is over take action to become the woman you were born to be. Now you may LOVE the bride. Show yourself devotion, care, and compassion. Congratulations and cheers on being loved, honored, and cherished!

The Courage to Be Single: Start a Relationship with You

For those of you who are single, what I am about to say is quite revolutionary. I know that every woman's magazine, relationship book, and dating blog revolves around the search for Prince (or Princess) Charming and finding "the one." Well, I hereby decree that we need to take 12 months to be single on purpose, dating but not hunting for the one. This single year is a "you year." Until you can truly be with, love, and appreciate you, you won't be able to do that for anyone else.

Have you ever been truly single? For all the hoopla about supposedly "single and lonely" women, many women have *never been* truly single. Sure, you may check off "single" on your taxes, but many of us are either in a mindset of getting over a past relationship or moving into a new one, whether or not we're not currently shacking up. None of these relationship stages constitute a truly single woman.

So what's the big deal about being single? You have to know how to be with yourself before you can be with anyone else. There is fortitude in choosing to be single on purpose. When you jump from one relationship to another without healing, you are not taking the time to learn the lessons of that particular relationship assignment and evolve. You are stifling your growth.

We then go forward, attempting to date with a list of qualities that we're looking for without realizing that we are none of those things on the list. Clean up your mental, physical, and spiritual houses before inviting another person in.

The Goddess Year

The Goddess Year is a 12-month program that I developed for women to focus on themselves. Consider the Goddess Year to be the Year of You. It's kind of like the gap year that some European students take between high school and college to find themselves. But you don't find yourself – you create and reveal yourself.

If you have already partnered with your soul mate, you can still have a Goddess Year. Make it a year where you are unconditionally devoted to you. We all need a Goddess Year because women, and mothers in particular, often see the world through the eyes of everyone but themselves. Young men are encouraged to take time to learn themselves, "sow their oats," and be selfish, while young women are ushered toward constant coupledom.

You can't fall in love with someone you don't know – and that includes yourself. As the hub of the family, it's essential for a woman to love herself first. This is the biggest love lesson we teach by example to our daughters and sons. Many of our mothers couldn't teach us how to love ourselves because they didn't know how to love themselves.

Sure, the thought of being chronically single can be hard. The media browbeats us with the story that there are no comparable men for successful single women and #ThisIsWhyYoureSingle fears of "spinsterhood." Well if the love pond we're swimming in is too small then it's time to enlarge it. That's why I love online dating. You can see in an instant how many eligible singles there are out there. We can't see that if we're stuck in the mire of relationship jumping or bed-hopping.

"But what if I don't want to be alone?" The real deal is that not everyone should be in a relationship right this minute. Yes, we all deserve partnership and need love. This is not about a detrimental and unhealthy "I don't need a man" or "all men suck" attitude. Healthy, loving relationships are your birthright. However, if you approach dating from a place of being a needy person, you end up committing DWD – Dating While Desperate. Desperation is repellant to any mentally healthy potential partner. Taking the time to learn to be in your own skin will help you to see that and recognize your best partner when he or she appears.

Here are some "rules" for your Goddess Year:

Practice Extreme Self-Care

If you can't treat yourself well, why should someone else? Nourish the divine feminine within. Do you have a practice of meditation, gratitude, and/or affirmations? Do you take care of your body temple? Do you energize your body with nourishing foods? Are you meticulous about who and what you allow into your mental space? Do you ask for support when you need it from a therapist, coach, counselor, or clergy member?

Clear the Clutter

There are all kinds of clutter. There's physical clutter – stuff. We're aware of holding on to ill-fitting clothing, family memorabilia, files, books, and old tchotchkes. There's also digital clutter. Are there old files on your desktop or defunct connections in your phone? Delete and make room for the new. Then there's people clutter. If there are folks in your life who are not enriching you then they are merely taking up space. Cut ties with Booty Call Ben if what you want is true love.

If you want blessings to flow, make room for them! Clutter is a sign of a poverty mentality. If you are holding on to clutter you are being stingy with yourself. You can't receive big, bodacious love if you're grasping at the puny things.

Examine Your Relationship Resume

Learn the lessons of the past so that you don't attract the same situations. If you're in a relationship right now, use this as a tool to grow individually and as a couple. Write down the name of every person you have been in a relationship with. Next to each name, analyze the relationship and pay attention to the patterns that emerge. Relationship Resume inquiry: What worked in this coupling? What went wrong? Where do you take responsibility? What did you like and dislike about the person? What positive and negative qualities did they have of one or both of your parents? What positive and negative traits of yours do they mirror back to you? What are the lessons?

Date Promiscuously

One of my favorite prescriptions for the Goddess Year is: Date Promiscuously, Love Monogamously. When I say date promiscuously, I'm not talking about sex. Write this down: Dating is not sex. I am talking about dating. Go out. Date outside of your usual type. If you usually go for tall, nerdy, stock-broker types, try a stocky creative. After all, it's just a date, right? The pressure is off because this is your year of living single!

So often as single women we approach every date with fingers crossed that this could be "the one." I can smell the desperation from here, and trust your bombshell sister: Desperation is never sexy. If you happen to meet "the one" while you are enjoying your year of single living, tell him or her what you're doing. A good person will love and embrace your independent spirit. An even better person won't mind waiting a few months to have you all to him- or herself.

Make a Beach Bucket List

We all know about the bucket list — a list of things you want to experience, accomplish, or attempt before you die — right? Well, let's accelerate that. The beach bucket list is a bucket list hyped up on speed. Make a list of 52 things you have always wanted to do — from the simple, like (on mine) learn to swim, run a 5K, eat with chopsticks, and become skilled at false eyelashes, to the daring, like (not on mine) bungee jumping or learning Mandarin. Now embark on one of these things every week. That's right, every week. Of course, be conscious of your budget and current living situation, but the point is to push your nerve into overdrive.

Warning: This is intense. While a bucket list could take a lifetime, the beach bucket list is a living, breathing action plan. So many of us are raised to be people pleasers. This is the year of pleasing *you*.

Thou Shalt Not Go It Alone

Everything is better with support. Partner with your best friend, sorority sisters, book club, or Bomb Squad to do the Goddess Year program. An alternative is to meet new friends to share these experiences with. Maybe all of your friends are married and you're the only singleton, or maybe you've moved to a new city. Go to Meetup.com and find a new group of friends.

Explore and Embrace Your Sexual Self

Listen up, goddess. There is a whole host of stores that make buying and learning about adult toys and self-pleasure safe and fun. Again, if you can't please yourself, how can you expect someone else to?

Throw a Coming Out Party

When I told my friend Nathan Seven Scott — writer, coach, and wise man — that I wanted a coming out party, he thought that I was going to make an announcement. That's not what this kind of coming out is about. I'm not suggesting you alter your sexuality. I'm talking coming out in the sense of the Diana Ross anthem: "I'm coming out / I want the world to know / I want to let it show." You are coming out as your Sacred Bombshell self and you are inviting the world to witness it. You're a new woman. Announce it and be accountable.

Consider Celibacy

Whether you are celibate or not is your choice. How you approach your Goddess Year is up to you, but if you're always dating or having sex, take a time out. The point is to be single on purpose with the goals of self-knowledge and personal evolution. If you are out there exploring, be sure to play it safe. Here's the Sacred Bombshell definition of safe sex: sex that is physically, mentally, emotionally, and spiritually safe for you.

The interesting side effect of being single on purpose is that you become irresistible. A woman in love with herself is magnetic. The Goddess Year is not about avoiding true intimacy but welcoming it. When you learn to be authentically yourself, you give others permission to do the same.

Passion up, goddesses!

Bombshell Dialogue with Reverend Kia Granberry: How to Have Crazy Faith

Kia Granberry may look like a model or pop star, but the high-energy 28-year-old is actually an ordained minister. Kia has battled blindness, hearing loss, and extreme pain but she is standing strong. Her #holdFAST social media movement of fasting and prayer has galvanized people across six continents. (Come on, Antarctica!) Reverend Kia wants to be called "just Kia" to remain accessible. Find her ministering at Mount Moriah Baptist Church in Georgia. She is the first woman to preach at a gospel church founded by slaves. Kia is planning her second annual Mosaic Women's Conference. Catch her Twitter sermons @LiveLoveKia or even submit a prayer request with #KiaPrays.

Abiola: Kia, you say that your mission is helping singles and women to fall in love with themselves. I love that. We have the same mission! Is it true that you had a challenging time growing up?

Kia: Well, I was raised by my mother [in] a single parent home, my sister and I. I didn't recognize it was challenging growing up. We always had most of the things that we wanted and everything that we needed. But I recognize that we may have not lived in the best neighborhood early on. I can remember gunshots or being able to identify the drug dealers and the prostitutes when I was young. I always knew that I wanted something better for my life.

Abiola: You say that you have "crazy faith." How inspiring! You have been through a roller coaster ride with your health.

Kia: I was in graduate school at the University of Chicago. When I came back to Atlanta I still wanted to party. I was getting close to deciding to answer my calling but I was like, "Let me have just one last hoorah." So my best friend and I [drove] to Atlanta.

I couldn't see out of one eye and I couldn't clearly see out of the other but I [didn't] tell her. She figured it out because I couldn't buckle my sandals.

We went to the doctor and I was diagnosed with multiple sclerosis. I went through blindness four times. I had eggshell lumps all over my body. I prayed that I wouldn't have to take treatment but I got so sick that the doctors convinced me to try it. And because I asked God not to let me take the treatment, He wouldn't let it go into my body. The doctors were like, "We don't really know what's going on but we're going to try another treatment." I was like, "I don't want to try anything else."

I took myself off treatment and now through fasting and prayer I'm more healthy than I was before. There's nothing wrong with my vision or my hearing. I don't have any pain in my limbs. And what's more, my brain looks different than it's supposed to look for someone who has multiple sclerosis. Essentially, I don't typically have enough lesions in my brain to qualify to be diagnosed. I went to the doctor and the medical professional who was in the room was charting my medical history. She asked when was the last time I had an episode, was I symptomatic? Then she paused and said, "Well, I'm not going to write it down. It's not a medical issue anymore so we don't have to document it."

I was like, "Is she saying that I don't have multiple sclerosis anymore?" Because she just said it so casually. So she told me I don't have any medical issues anymore. I was so free in that moment because I felt so healed for so long but to have the doctor say I have no medical issue anymore was a really crazy moment.

Abiola: What a blessing, Kia. You're basically healing yourself.

Kia: God is healing me. I can't describe it.

Abiola: I'm just humbled and awestruck by that. So many women, Kia, suffer from self-hatred and inferiority complexes, feeling judged, trying to please others, feeling lonely or inadequate.

Kia: I was dating a guy a couple of years ago. I really thought that this was the person I was supposed to spend the rest of my life with. I found out that he was sleeping with two people that I didn't know about. He attacked me and it was a violent alterca-tion. I can remember looking at myself in the mirror with a black eye. I went to the hospital not believing that this was my life. How did I get to a place where I was so dependent on someone who could do that to me?

It took me fasting and praying. It took me a while to heal from that situation. A lot of our brokenness comes from the fact that we're trying to fix people. I encounter a lot of women who don't love themselves, don't feel powerful, don't feel significant, and don't feel valuable because they're pouring all of that energy that they should be pouring into themselves into people who don't love them. My encouragement to all single women is to make sure that you're whole first because you can't have a healthy relationship if you're broken.

Abiola: I saw women sharing your domestic violence video on Twitter. One woman tweeted, "She looks nothing like what she has been through." We have a picture in our heads that an abuse victim looks this way or an educated woman looks that way, when low self-esteem and abusive relationships impact every sector.

You did a Twitter chat with motivational speaker Sophia A. Nelson about therapy. When it comes to depression and other mental health challenges, in your opinion, is prayer enough or is therapy also needed?

Kia: I have a background in psychology and behavioral science and prayer is so important but we also need to seek medical, professional help when necessary. I'm not one of those people who thinks that [there's] only [one] way that God will send heal-ing. I believe that He uses prescription medicine, that God uses doctors, that God uses psychiatrists and psychologists to heal people.

I think it's important that people who are struggling talk to someone more than your pastor. Hear me clearly: All pastors are not trained to deal with psychological issues. If you have a serious psychological issue, you need to go to someone who's trained. You wouldn't allow your pastor to perform open heart surgery because he's not trained. We need to take mental illness as seriously as we do physical illness.

Abiola: Yes! If you broke your arm you would go to a specialist. What do you think about the connection between abundance and spiritual life?

Kia: That's the season I am in now. I had all the money I ever wanted last year but I wasn't living an abundant life because I wasn't doing what God called me to do. God wants us to prosper; He wants us to live an abundant life. That's what His word says, but I also think that sometimes we miss out on God moments by wanting so much physical wealth that we neglect the spiritual wealth.

Someone hacked into my account recently and so all of my money was gone in an instant. While I've been navigating that, I still have bills due but I've been making it every day. My bank account doesn't look abundant at the moment because someone took the things that I worked for but God has been giving me everything that I need day by day.

Abiola: I remember seeing on your Tumblr that you're into Audrey Hepburn (as am I) and that you were a fashion designer. Let's talk about inner and outer beauty.

Kia: I think that inner beauty is just undeniable. I've met many beautiful women who are broken. I don't want anybody to think that fashion-standard beauty is the answer. And that if you don't look like someone in a magazine that you'll never be happy or that you're not valuable. Because a lot of those people are killing themselves to look that way and they're not happy.

Inner beauty is so much more attractive. It's what draws your abundance to you. When you love yourself then you can then love your neighbor. First of all is to love God, but you can't complete that commandment if you don't love yourself first.

God created you with His hands; you're His workmanship. He loves you and you are amazing and so you don't have to look like Beyoncé. Abiola is gorgeous, Kia is beautiful, and you who are reading this [are] beautiful too. The same God that created those people that you idolize created you. He used the same tools.

Abiola: What about people who would say to us as we both preach self-love, "Well, Kia and Abiola, you're still styling your hair and wearing lip gloss."

Kia: It goes back to loving yourself. When you love something you take care of it. And so I think that if you feel like you want to adorn yourself, or you want a necklace, or you want to style your hair, that's the bare minimum. I can't imagine saying I love myself and I love my hair if I don't take care of it.

I am always perplexed that people pose those questions because self-love is not just something that happens inside. It happens inside but manifests outwardly. If I had millions of dollars I'd probably use a million-dollar skin cream but I don't. I take care of myself within reason but when you love yourself or love anything you take care of it.

Abiola: Yes, and look how much God shows us beauty. Have you ever walked past a field, looked at flowers, and seen how bountifully and appealingly they're made? It's all an expression of God.

We're redefining bombshell as a woman who loves herself and owns her destiny. What makes you a bombshell, Kia?

Kia: I have gotten to a place where I love me and I love what God has done for me and you can't convince me otherwise. I did a women's conference that I offered at no cost. I just really wanted people to be able to come and be poured into.

I love myself. And I think it's so important that you separate "loving yourself" and "owning it." There are some women who own their success but don't really love themselves. And there are some women who love themselves but haven't quite mastered owning their destiny.

At one point I owned the success that I was able to accomplish at a young age but I didn't love myself. Then I went to a place where I loved myself but didn't really care what I did for a living. Now I love myself and I'm owning the fact that I'm about to write a book and I'm about to take my conference to the next level!

Bombshell Takeaways:

- The way you feel about yourself inwardly manifests outwardly.

- Your self-love and inner beauty draws your abundance.

- Loving yourself and "owning it" aren't necessarily the same thing.

Bombshell Dialogue with Tracey Bryant: How to Love Yourself from the Womb-side Out

Did you feel that? The vibration in the room just reached new heights and we are all uplifted. I met the "Honey Diva" when she interviewed me for her HoneySoul Radio show. Tracey Bryant is a recognized sexual empowerment coach, tantrika, and healer. She is the owner of Honey Luv Lingerie & More, a boutique that services women in the areas of romance enhancement and relationships. A former sex worker, Tracey is now on her own healing journey. She studied sociology and human sexuality at McNeese State University.

> **Abiola:** Goddess Tracey, on your blog it says that sex and spirit are one. One of the books in this Sacred Bombshell Handbook series will definitely be on that topic. For the uninitiated, can you please explain sacred sexuality?

> **Tracey:** Well, sacred sexuality is honoring Spirit and sex as one because everything is born out of sex – even the soul. Sexuality is natural. It is human but is also represented by Spirit because all of us have gotten here through sex. Every last one of us has gotten here by the combustion of the orgasmic universe. It's very important that we learn that sex is also a very real part and a representation of who we are as individuals as well as in human consciousness.

> **Abiola:** Take it deeper for us. As a tantric practitioner, what is Tantra to you?

> **Tracey:** Tantra is a 3,500-year-old system that is actually a way of life. It does not necessarily equate [to] sex. It's finding your compassion. It's a way of tapping into your source, tapping into your spirit and identifying with that spirit with another person, another lover. It's a very spiritual component that has a sexual component to it. Tantra is really the essence of being able to

communicate on a very compassionate, spiritual, vulnerable level.

Abiola: Yoni steaming is a personal care service that has been catching on. I'm so happy to see that this is something that you offer.

Tracey: Yes, first I need to give you a little back story. Healing is a lifetime process. I have womb trauma. In my desire to heal myself from sexual violation, I started learning that I have issues in my womb. Through my research, my education, and dealing with women one-on-one I was recognizing that we all have most of our blockages in our womb area. That's where our life force and our creative energy is stored. That's the sacral chakra area. We women store all of our stress, all of our pain, all of our emotional dysfunctions in our wombs.

Healing myself, I had to start communicating with her. I needed to tell her, "I apologize to you for disrespecting you, for making choices that disrespect your presence." I had to start really forgiving myself for things I had done; from [abuse] I had self-inflicted by putting myself in situations that were not healthy for my mind, body, or spirit – or my womb. I needed to cleanse.

I went to Atlanta to the Yoni Steam Institute and I became certified as a yoni steam practitioner and a womb wellness educator because I recognized through some of my social advocate work that many of us women have some type of sexual violation or abuse history and I want to be a source of healing.

Abiola: Thank you for sharing your history for the healing and benefit of other women. I know that you also do yoni smudging.

Tracey: About five or six years back I was burning my frankincense and myrrh and I had it in my little coal pot. I was smudging the house and thanking those who came before me. I said, "Well, let me bless my yoni." I put the pot down on the bathroom floor and I squat[ted] with my knees down over it and

I started praying. Come to find out as I started researching that it's something that women did years ago! The yoni steaming, the yoni smudging, the praying to the womb – these were ancient. Also, the frankincense and myrrh is antibacterial. They're also detoxing and cleansing the area as well.

Abiola: You were tapping into your ancestral knowledge!

Tracey: Yes, and yoni smudging actually is a way of you blessing your yoni, paying homage, honoring her. Sometimes when women do smudging tears will fall because we haven't been taught to be intimate with our wombs and our yonis. The only time that we're really recognizing them is when we're on our menstruation, when we're having sex, or when we're having a baby. Those are times that we don't have any type of real personal relationship with our yonis and our wombs. However, she's speaking to us all the time and a lot of times we are ignoring her. That's why we have so many fibroids and ovarian cancers and cysts and endometriosis because she is crying out for help. She's speaking and we're not listening.

Abiola: So true. How do you do this process with your clients?

Tracey: First of all, I do a whole spiritual crystal bath before I even deal with you. I do some meditation before our energies even meet. I, as the practitioner, have to be very prepared because this is spiritual work and is healing. When we are doing this work we are healing together. We are just not healing you. When it comes to the womb we are healing the women before you as well. So the trauma and things that happened with your mother, with your sister, to your aunt, with our great-grandmothers – we are healing all of that.

First, we do some womb yoga, yoni yoga. We do stretches, deep breathing, and meditation, to get you tapped into that energy of the womb. At that point you go on a massage table and I do womb stimulation. That is where I take essential oils and I make steam and I actually do a womb massage. I massage your ovaries, your fallopian tubes, and your womb. Now, the whole time I'm doing your massage I'm meditating and praying over you silently. At that point you get a clay pack. I put that over your womb. The clay pulls out toxins.

Now remember, the yoga and the deep breathing is moving the energy in that area. Then you lay down and get your womb stimulation, which is your massage, so now we've actually activated the energy in your womb. Then I put crystals, a crystal grid, on your womb so that the crystal tones up your yoni. It actually vibrates with the energies.

From there I'm doing reflexology. So, while you're laying back and you're in a very meditative state and toxins are being pulled out of your yoni due to the clay and you're also getting a recharge from crystals, I am working on the pressure points of your feet so that we can release some of the trauma.

After about two minutes, [the client] sits on a yoni steam stool. It's considered an altar. If you have any challenges or conditions we use specific herbs to help heal those areas, but mostly it is for cleaning, strengthening, toning, detoxing. It's hydrotherapy and an herbal infusion going up into the yoni, the vaginal canal, the uterus, and the fallopian tubes. While you're steaming, you're breathing, you're drinking herbal tea, you're just relaxing, and you're really getting tuned [in] to your sacred center.

Abiola: Wow. Beautiful. You recently had a show about self-pleasure for healing sexual trauma and I know this is very personal to you.

Tracey: Western society usually tries to cure the symptoms instead of touching the root cause. Healing is three-dimensional: mind, body, and soul. You can't just heal the body and not correct the consciousness of the mind during the sickness. That's what where I come in. I'm doing more soul work – more spiritual, sexual soul work.

So with self-pleasure in healing sexual trauma, I found it to be significant for me because I had remained abstinent for four years. I said, "Well, it's not that I don't want sex because I do and I understand the energy of sex. I want to still have pleasure, but I'm just not ready to embrace someone else giving it to me right now because I have some soul work to do." I began pleasuring myself to the point that I started extending myself into a higher consciousness of sexual awareness.

I might take my aromatic bath with my essential oil and I'm just loving myself up. I'm romancing myself. I'm oiling my body down with nice essential oil and I'm telling myself, "You're beautiful. I love you so much. I want the best for you. You are so worthy." At that point, I will lay down and I usually have a rose quartz yoni egg I use. I will stimulate my yoni area; as I'm stimulating, I'm still saying affirmations, telling myself how beautiful I am, how I belong in the space of abundance, and how all things that are good are going to come to me. And I tell my womb I love her. She deserves the best.

And as I breathe in, I breathe in joy, love, and abundance. And as I breathe out, I breathe out bitterness, grief, shame. And I do that maybe 20, 30 times until I actually transcend with myself.

Abiola: You've got conjure-women healing magic right there.

Tracey: Yes, ma'am. We are the magicians. We are the Aladdin. We are the genies in the lamp. Rub it the right way, honey, and she will give you what you want. It's the most powerful force in the universe. You can draw anything to you during a great sexual experience, during sexual meditation, sexual breathing, and through the ability to have orgasm with your lover, being consciously connected with the same goal. You can draw in to you faster. And it is prayer. It puts you in the space of abundance because that's what it is. It's creative force. It's how we're created. Everybody thinks intuition comes through your mind. No. It comes from the energy of the womb. When you're not feeling comfortable and [get] a negative vibe, where do you feel first? And appetites. All appetites come from the area of our stomachs, in our wombs.

Abiola: A lot of women are comfortable giving love but not necessarily receiving love. Feminine energy is receiving love, being vulnerable. We think that's weakness but there is power and strength in being vulnerable and—

Tracey: In receiving! That's powerful. Feminine energy is the abundant energy of the universe.

Abiola: The more you tap into your femergy, the more soft, the more receptive, the more vulnerable you become. All of a sudden, you are incredibly magnetic. Your phone will start ringing off the hook.

Tracey: Yes. Once that switch has been turned on and you start tapping into that personal body, that personal power, and the goddess energy – do not be afraid of it. That's what happens a lot of times. We'll get scared and we'll shut down because that's not a space that we've been taught to be in. We're not taught to be powerful and vibrant and receive all of this love and to have a voice. We're not taught to have a vagina and a voice. We're just taught to have vagina.

Abiola: Powerful. I've been writing and talking about goddess energy since I was a really young woman. Goddess is a term that people – women – are terrified of. Can you define what you mean when you say goddess?

Tracey: Well, one of the reasons we are afraid of that word is because that word has been hidden from our vocabulary. That word has been downplayed and downsized. Search "goddess": love goddesses, Egyptian goddesses, African goddesses, Chinese goddesses, Indian goddesses. You will see that goddesses have been around since forever.

I want to recommend a book called ***When God Was a Woman*** by Merlin Stone. That book opened my eyes to our worship and how the goddess was revered, how women were revered. It actually goes right back to the womb. It's the life-force energy. The ability to be able to give birth is the closest thing to God that there is. So, that's why when you tap into that goddess energy and you understand that, then you are closest to God. You give birth to ideas. You give birth to children.

Abiola: Yes. It's important also for us to point out that this doesn't negate or take away from anybody's religion or religious practices.

Tracey: It has nothing to do with religion. It has to do with what's in the energy. It has to do with reverence [for] the female.

Abiola: Tracey, you have a very strong social initiative within your work. Your rape crisis volunteering; Oasis, a Safe Haven Crisis Center for Survivors of Domestic and Sexual Violence; your work with the Southwest Louisiana AIDS Initiative. You are also the founder of the Love on Lock Down Prison Ministry. Why is it so important for you to be a social activist?

Tracey: In my healing work I had to identify with other sisters who were also in an area of crisis and needed someone that just understood. Sometimes healing is just listening, just being an advocate, and saying, "I'm here for you. Here's a hug." So, it's very important that I not only deal with the pleasure and the orgasmic experience of sex, but I also have to go on the other side and say, "There's issues over here pertaining to sex."

Abiola: What makes you a bombshell, Tracey?

Tracey: What makes me a bombshell is my humility to admit that I've had some bad experiences and to own those experiences and understand that those experiences do not define me. The strength of spirit to be able to push through those experiences and say, "I'm still worthy." Also, just identifying with my personal freedom, not allowing childhood situations or conditions [to] keep me down. Being able to process the pain and heal and have enough compassion to still want to see my sister shine.

Bombshell Takeaways:

- ✒ Healing begins with loving up on yourself.
- ✒ There is powerful ancient wisdom within our bodies.
- ✒ Lifting others up as we become healed empowers and heals us all.

Secret of Self-Devotion Resources

1. **Soul Purpose** by Jackee Holder

2. **Love Yourself Like Your Life Depends On It** by Kamal Ravikant

3. **Broken Open** by Elizabeth Lesser

4. "Inner Mean Girl Reform School" by Amy Ahlers and Christine Arylo (e-course)

5. TheAJZone.com, run by A. J. Johnson

Self-Devotion Affirmations

1. I choose to love and accept my body.

2. It feels good to love who I see in the mirror.

3. Nourishing my body feeds my beautiful soul.

4. I love my body and my body loves me.

5. I treat my body like a temple and my Self like a queen.

Six

The Secret of Fullness: Brazenly Full of Yourself

The Sacred Feminine Law of Fullness

The Sacred Bombshell finds her fullness when she dares to stop playing small. Imagine a woman who is full of herself, loving pleasure, living courageously, and seeing life as a spontaneous adventure. She becomes a soul sister – a sister of the soul – by awakening to her own. This wholeheartedly femergetic woman is a light-bearer and beacon. This is sacred self-love.

Historical Bombshell Mentor: Pam Grier, born 1949

Pam Grier declares, "I thought I would be 'Sheena of the Jungle' as a little girl." The regal energy in her autobiography **Foxy** is the same bombshell energy she made her mark with playing bad-ass heroines. The image of gorgeous Grier with a gun and huge afro was simultaneously shocking and titillating to audiences in the 1970s – and today. Pam is no black Barbie, however. She lists among her interests: history, economics, veterinary science, art, and philosophy. This former farm girl proudly remains close to the land, caring for her horses and savoring green tea.

The Fullness Declaration

In this moment I enthusiastically step into my full greatness. I am a woman who is filled with my own power, full of my Self. I smile at those who find me too much and keep stepping, head held gloriously high. The world has been waiting for me to stop playing small. Thankfully, that day has come.

My fullness is the way. I live fully in my pleasure, dance daily with my passion, indulge in my play, and make positivity my way of live. This is living large. Previously I believed the lie that it was polite to play small. I shrank myself to appease others and to fit into boxes. I didn't stand out or make waves. I thought that this was the way to feel safe.

Today I realize that I am safe in my majesty. It is safe to be fully me. It is safe to hit my high notes for I am in tune with the highest part of my Self. I am in tune with my soul and my soul's hunger is fulfilled. The world is my playground and it is safe to be spontaneous.

A courageous woman is a fearless outlaw who dares to indulge in pleasure and want a passionate life. The Sacred Bombshell knows that she must have the brazen spirit to release the life she is living to claim the one she wants. She is a queen, boldly moving beyond her old borders and ripping down her old barriers. Fearing less and moving forward with full-hearted courage is the only way to become the woman she was born to be.

Whatever I take in is what my spirit, mind, and body, are made from. I readily take in pleasure, passion, positivity, and play. It is safe to live full-out. My life is my love letter to that which made me. I live on purpose and I am full. For this I am so grateful.

And so it is.

The Sacred Feminine Power of Fullness

"And the day came when the risk to remain
tied in a bud was more painful than the risk it
took to blossom."
—*Anais Nin*

Women have voracious appetites. That's right. We're hungry and we want to be filled up – with life! Previously, the mere thought of this was unladylike and therefore forbidden. Natural bodily needs for food, water, and sex are recognized human appetites. Those are a delicious start, but we're hungry for so much more. Yes, bombshell, we are starving for our sacred selves. We try to fill up but we're still hungry because we're trying to satisfy our inner hunger with outer things. We are ravenous for pleasure, passion, positivity, and play – the Fullness Four – not the shallow, empty-calorie experiences we've been indulging in.

When I was in my 20s I used to take unhealthy appetite suppressants. Suppressing your appetites is draining you. You're suppressing your appetite for love and joy, denying your hunger for pleasure and fun, ignoring your thirst for enthusiasm and passion. We don't need appetite suppression, we need appetite acknowledgement and appetite fulfillment. This will not come in a pill. The difference is being full of yourself vs. full of your Self. Are you full of your Self? Or are you trying to fill yourself up with food, Facebook, alcohol, gossip, and other behaviors that will never fill you?

Motivational teacher Lisa Nichols is full of herself and that's a good thing. Broadcaster Gayle King is also full of herself and she deserves to be. Lady Gaga is clearly a woman who is living in her fullness. Comedic performers Margaret Cho and Ellen DeGeneres seem pretty filled up with themselves, too.

Most of us were taught that it was a bad thing to be "full" of ourselves. The term is used to mean someone ego-based or conceited. Any woman standing fully in her personal power was met with "Who does she think she is?" If you hear someone say, "She thinks she's cute," they mean, "I think I'm ugly." They are saying: "How dare she think that she can be more, do more, have more? How dare she think that she matters? Didn't she get the memo?" Stop pretending that you are powerless. Give up the idea that your hunger is acceptable. A woman filled with her essence is radiant and vibrant.

Feeling like you're missing something, being empty and depleted, is the opposite of being full. I spent a long time in this mindset: hungry for myself instead of being full of my Self. I was always trying to fill other people up but you can't give from an empty fridge. Like many of you, I thought that the gracious thing to do in order to be accepted was to play small. After all, a full and powerful woman is dangerous. Wasn't almost every fairy tale queen evil? So I played small. I had glimpses of passion, moments of pleasure, dalliances with play and positivity, but I didn't permit myself to come from this energy of fullness permanently. That, I feared, would be too much. As spiritual guru Marianne Williamson says, we're not really afraid that we won't measure up. Deep down we are terrified that we are powerful. Holy crap! Owning that fact meant that I would have to do something about it.

Playing small manifests in different ways for different women. Playing small includes not being vulnerable with your loved ones, not going for that raise, not treating your body like a temple, not doing your writing, knitting, or teaching that you are here to do. I made a decision a couple of years ago to stop playing small. I have too many (hypothetical) curves to fit in a box. I released my victim mindset and the reasons why it was everyone else's fault that I had to play smaller than my full, juicy, bombshell self. I accepted my right to live in the sacred space of welcoming pleasurable situations, passionate work, positive experiences, and playtime. With that came harder decisions, like releasing certain relationships and comfortable situations.

We all have a deep-seated fear of being unlovable. We feel that if we can find the right masks, toys, or uniforms then people will love us. It doesn't work that way. Until you love yourself, until you are filled up with you, haters will keep appearing and finding something else about you to dislike. So charge up your fullness muscle. No more playing small. I want you to be full of your Self. I want you to be so full of you that there is no room for anyone else's opinion of you. Your Inner Bully will have to retire. Your detractors will dissolve.

How do you access your fullness? Start by allowing yourself to embrace the Fullness Four: pleasure, passion, positivity, and play. There is no way to live with the Fullness Four and play small at the same time. These are the gateway drugs to happiness, bliss, ecstasy, fun, and joy!

Why Are You Playing Small?

"Well-behaved women seldom make history."
—*Laurel Thatcher Ulrich*

Let's go deeper into how to "own your bombshell" and stop playing small. This lesson is the one that says, "Yes, *you* are the one that you've been waiting for." This conversation is about how to rise and shine. Our objective is for you to create a pathway to becoming the woman you were born to be, to do the things that you came to do -- for you to become you. Depending on the bombshell, this fullness does not have to be loud. It can also be quiet contentment.

My typical coaching client (although there is nothing typical about these Sacred Bombshells) is the woman who looks like she has everything going for her on the outside but on the inside she feels like something big is missing. She is not rising to her shine. She is not fulfilling her potential. She is not living her truth. She is not owning her bombshell. We play and work together for a minimum of 12 weeks with the Bombshell Breakthrough Process – customized for her needs. The goal is for her to have a breakthrough and begin to step into her fullness.

A common issue that got-it-going-on women tend to experience is Impostor Syndrome – the feeling that she does not have a right to her majesty (see Chapter 7 for more on Impostor Syndrome). She fears that if the people who praise and applaud her saw the mess she imagines herself to be, they would be appalled. At first, if I say there's a self-esteem issue at the base of feeling like an impostor, some of you amazing women get upset with me. But my dear Sacred Bombshell, self-esteem outages take many forms. Imagining that you're not good enough for the accolades that you receive or for the life you are living or wanting to live means that you see yourself as deficient, insufficient, broken, secretly wounded – a closet failure who only looks like the world's biggest success to everyone else. So why do you play small?

You Think Following the Rules Will Keep You Safe

You, like the rest of us, are always either seeking pleasure or avoiding pain. That's the pleasure principal. If you are playing small, you are avoiding the potential pain of being out there. You don't feel safe so you want to stay in your comfort zone.

We forget that the whole point of "the rules" is to keep everyone else safe from your big ideas, to keep us uniform, to keep us from standing out. "I can't do that with my house, with my clothes, with my relationship, with my career, with my website, with my whatever ... because *it's just not done.*" The rules say it's just not done. The rules — take a breath — the rules may keep us safe from your genius. Sure the rules might also keep you safe from potential mistakes. But if you live long enough you realize that *there is no safety*. Like the saying goes, "We plan and God laughs." You are here to evolve. That means becoming comfortable with the fact that there is no safety. You might as well go on and be yourself. You might as well fulfil your purpose. You might as well shine like your Creator made you to.

You Are Afraid

You just said, "Duh, Abiola. I'm terrified." At a meeting with my uber-coach and sister bombshell Rha Goddess (yes, coaches need coaches), she explained that I needed to triple or at least double my fees in order to best maximize my time and serve my clients the way that I prefer to. She asked what would be the problem with me tripling my prices. You know what my answer was? "Nothing. Except for sheer terror" – and I teach this stuff! We all have fears of failure, fears of rejection, fears of success, and fears of fear.

You Believe You Are Flawed at the Source

Well, I can tell you right now that your Source is not flawed at all. Your Source is what makes the seasons change. So no, you are not the one flawed, broken thing God made.

You Don't Really Believe in Yourself

You may have a lot of pomp and circumstance and that can look like perfection: the perfect hair, the greatest apartment, the most fabulous car, and pretty nails. Unfortunately, if you believe yourself to be a loser you will have to keep losing to prove yourself right.

You Have a Low Happiness Set-Point or Success Set-Point

We delved into this concept in Chapter 3 with the idea of the Heart Ceiling. You are comfortable with a certain amount of happiness or success. When you surpass that, you self-sabotage to bring yourself back to the low standards to which you are accustomed. Take a breath.

You Think Living Your Shine Will Make You Less Lovable

Who wants to be unlovable? I'm not raising my hand. Are you? Nope! We all want to be loved and if you think that standing out, standing up, and shining is going to make you less lovable, then you're just not going to do it. The good news is that it's not true! You are more lovable when you are true to yourself.

You Have Not Given Yourself Permission to Stand Out

Winners and successful folks are weirdoes and oddballs. They're different. They stand out and they embrace that. They don't try to fit into the box. Give yourself permission to stop dressing yourself, your home, or your life like a catalogue. Color outside the lines. You have to give yourself permission to create a customized journey with you as a stand-out star. Write yourself a permission slip to shine. Remember the one you signed at the beginning of this journey? Revisit it. Reaffirm the commitment to yourself.

You Experienced Failure, It Hurt, and You Don't Want to Feel That Again

Someone in your childhood said that it was not okay to fail or stand out and you believed them. Maybe it hurt to fail, and you were made fun of when you stood out. Luckily, you can take the lessons of the past and use them to shine even brighter.

Bombshell Exploration: Feel More Power-Full

Write out your top 10 most regrettable moments, situations, and experiences that you blame on someone else. Take full responsibility for each. Next time you feel powerless say, "I am open to seeing this situation differently." Ask yourself, "What's the payoff for me remaining powerless?" What benefits do you receive from seeing the world through victim-colored glasses? Do you get to blame or shame someone else? Do you get to feel superior for being one of the "little guys"? Examine this belief system. Release the need for control. Everything comes and goes. What was certain yesterday is a distant memory today. Look at how powerful newspapers were, and what an innovation fax machines were in our recent past. Relax into this knowingness that things are transient. You are no less powerful than anyone else. We are all powerful and powerless.

How to Stop Playing Small and Own Your Bombshell

"Decide that you want it more than you are afraid of it."
—*Bill Cosby*

Start with Why

You want to step into your greatness but why? Ask yourself, "What am I hungry for? Why do I want this?" Knowing why you want something can help you determine if a goal is just a fantasy that you think you should want or if it's in alignment with the yearnings of your heart.

Get Comfortable with Being Uncomfortable

Hang out with people you normally would not be around. Expose yourself to new situations. Say something in a group where you would normally be too terrified to speak. If you feel like, "That's not me. I wouldn't do that," that's not a reason by itself not to do something.

"What am I afraid of?" is a question that you can ask yourself when there is a chance to rise into your shine. Take the next step to go out on that date, give that speech, ask for the raise, step up to the plate, confront your friend. Then here's the best question: "What is the best thing that can happen for me taking this step?" That felt good, right? Take a breath.

Choose Your Company Carefully

Choose your tribe with care. If you surround yourself with people who insist that life is small, you're going to keep reflecting that back. We all have judgmental people in our lives that we are related to or have been friends with for a long time. Limit your exposure. Treat them like salt. A dash of salt adds flavor; too much ruins a dish. The same applies to your snarky, salty friends. Stay away from fearful people. Fear is contagious. Spend time with those who believe in themselves and you, people who are not afraid to say, "Hey this is what I am going to do," and then do it.

So that you're also positive company to be around, release the need to be judgmental. You have to eliminate your judgment of others because what you're afraid of is judgment. If you're judging others, of course you're going to be afraid that they're judging you. You know how you rip other people apart for not looking right, believing what you believe, presenting themselves appropriately? Screw appropriateness.

Choose a "Playing Big" Fullness Role Model

When I first started to give talks about how to stop playing small, I wondered about the words "playing big" because, well, I don't want you playing at anything. I want you doing it. I want us doing it. But it really is playing big because the world is a stage and we are all players on this journey. So, yeah, play big. Play full-out. Don't get stuck in the illusion. See beyond the story that you you're insignificant, that you must follow the rules. See that you are a spiritual being having a human experience. And so, why play small?

My "Playing Big" role model is E. Jean Carroll of *Elle Magazine*'s "Ask E. Jean" column – the longest running advice column in America. When writing this book I was embarrassed to be finishing eight months later than my original goal. E. Jean sent me the most supportive messages! She insisted that I put my bombshell self on the cover when my original cover girl was a model. The over-the-top writer is witty, generous, fun, and her own kind of woman. She's also an entrepreneur and life coach with a matchmaking site at Tawkify.com, ready to help those "whipsawed by confusion."

Remove the Victim-Colored Glasses

If you are seeing your life through victim-colored glasses, you are forgetting that you have choices. You're not making decisions because you think you don't have a right to make choices. You see yourself as a victim of your whole drama rather than seeing yourself as a star and a heroine. Take the victim-colored lenses off and take responsibility because if someone else is responsible for your life being the way it is then only someone else can fix it. We may not have a choice in everything that happens to us, but we always choose how we respond, rebound, and move forward.

Commit to Yourself

To rise into your shine, you have to be committed to you. There is nothing wrong with being different because this world needs every single one of us. We need queen bees and worker bees. Everybody is important. We all have the potential to shine. So when I say rise into your shine, I mean with whatever you do. If that means being the best mommy in the world, that is rising into your shine. If it means becoming a rocket scientist, do it. We all have different callings, so whatever yours is, step into it.

Be Grateful

If you are not grateful for what you have and where you are right this minute, you will never be happy. You just won't. It's not possible. Whenever you acquire whatever it is that you think will make you happy, you won't be able to appreciate it if you don't know how to be grateful and you will still see yourself as lacking.

Act As If

Dress, speak, and live as if you are who you want to be. Get your updated vision of yourself into your bones. Put on your new story. Wear it. Live it. Be it. You may be walking through someone else's story of you. Rewrite yourself, reinvent yourself, and step into your greatness. Step into the feeling. It's not enough to do these assignments on paper because you don't live on paper. Just be it.

Build Self-Trust

You probably don't trust yourself – most of us don't – but self-integrity matters. If time and time again someone says, "I'm going to be there for you" and then they aren't, you don't trust them. So if you say you're going to do something for yourself, do it. Here's how you build trust in yourself: pick one small act of self-care that you can commit to daily and do it. Perhaps for the next 40 days you will: do yoga videos, get eight hours of sleep, or eat only healthy food.

Risk Failing Greatly

Become comfortable with failure. I'm not telling you to stop playing small because you're going to run out there and never fail. Sometimes you will. If risk-takers were not comfortable with failure, we would not have the magnificent inventions that make our lives sing.

Eliminate Negative Self-Talk

Stop ripping yourself to shreds. That's why affirmations close each chapter. I want you to look chant these positive energy phrases repeatedly. Most of us are saying horrible things to ourselves 90% of the time, and the goal is to get different thoughts rolling around. Remember, your unconscious mind is a radio that keeps going even when you turn the volume down. You may think you're not listening, but it's still playing. So for today, decide to think one less negative thing about yourself. Micro steps.

Soften the Vibration

There's a Zen proverb that states, "Only when you can be extremely pliable and soft can you be extremely hard and strong." We're all vibrational beings. Everything is energy. Everything we want to do is energy. An idea may feel unattainable to you because it's a different energetic vibration than where you are. So soften the energy around it.

Instead of asking, "Why can't I just do that?" think, "Wouldn't it be cool if I went to that convention and spoke?" Say: "It might be fun if I felt confident enough in yoga to sit in the front." Ask yourself: "Wouldn't it be femergetic if I met the man or woman of my dreams this year?" Ponder: "Wouldn't it be divine if I released the health-blocking weight for good?" Remind yourself: "It would be such a blessing if I made this the year I healed from the heartbreak that I experienced when my father left." Soften the energetic vibration.

Face Forward

Be clear about what you want to do. Picture yourself trying to walk down the sidewalk backward. Even if you can do it, you'll run into things. You're doing the same thing when you walk into your future backward. You're trying to move forward while focused on your past. Turn around. Focus on what you want rather than the things that didn't work.

Tell Loved Ones You're Ready for Lift-off

I'm a fan of keeping your goals between you, your Creator, and people who will support you. Resist sharing your plans with non-visionary people until they come into form. However, if one of the things holding you back is a fear of outshining your tribe, then part of giving yourself permission to fly may mean having a meeting with somebody you love. Say, "Hey, I've decided that I'm going to stop playing small. I'm going to outshine everything that I have ever done. Will you still love me?" They will probably say yes and you'll have one less barrier.

Stop Arguing for Your Limitations

Stop arguing for all the reasons why it won't work and start to think about why it will. You may fall on your face but that is okay. You are unlimited. Break your big goal into 100 tiny steps.

Declare Yourself the Great "I Am"

If you want to be a writer, how do you start? Simply announce to yourself: "I am a writer." Declare yourself, whatever you are or want to be. Approach life assuming that you're already shining. You just have to see it and learn what you need to rock it. So declare yourself: "I am a professor." "I am a publicist." "I am an incredible spouse." "I am loved. I am lovable. I am worthy. I am deserving." Declare it. Own it. Be it.

People accept you at face value. Whatever you put out there and say, "This is me," we say, "Okay." So if you say, "I am a loser," we say, "Okay." If you say, "I am a keynote speaker," we say, "Oh, wow. Okay." And does that mean you won't get, "Who does she think she is"? No. You'll get that and more; I guarantee it. But that is not a reason for you to deprive us of the light you came to be.

Are You Living Your Fullness? Checklist

Fullness requires courage and full-heartedness. Sometimes you're afraid for a reason. Fear serves a purpose. It says, "Danger, lion up ahead." At other times fear gets ahead of itself, shouting lion when the speech you've been invited to make is exactly what you need to do. Fullness is having the courage to raise your hand in the PTA meeting when something isn't right. It is speaking up for someone who is not in the room. It is having the ovaries to be more than you thought you could be.

- Have you found your voice?
- Can you step out of your comfort zone?
- Do you make decisions quickly and firmly?
- Are you doing what you would dare do if you knew you could not fail?
- Do you do what you say you are going to do?
- Are you comfortable with others singing your praises?
- Are you comfortable singing the praises of others?
- Are you willing to sing your own praises?
- When opportunities arise are you likely to say yes?
- Are you a leader or a follower?
- Are you willing to go somewhere, try something, meet someone, or taste something new?
- Are you courageous enough to share your best gifts?
- Do you use your voice to bring light to taboo or uncomfortable topics?

Bombshell Playbook Exercise

Answer these questions in your Bombshell Playbook. Take five deep, cleansing breaths to get centered and begin.

1. Do I believe that I have the power to change my beliefs?
2. When in the past have I done this before?
3. What are the excuses I use to hold myself back?
4. Where am I holding back from being my full self?
5. How can I ensure that I live a more captivating life?

My Big Fat Bombshell Diary: The Consequences of Being Fear-Full

In fifth grade I was in a public school program called the EGC, for Exceptionally Gifted Children. Our teacher Mrs. Annette Feder, who is still one of the best teachers I've ever had, announced a storytelling contest. I stirred in my front-row seat. Stories were my business. I knew I had it in the bag.

We were to memorize an excerpt every day from a fable about a bickering couple. The first student who could present the whole story with flair would win the class a pizza party and win herself a trip to Africa. Africa!? I started planning the trip in my head. Aw, man! I had an unfair advantage. Helping me work on the story was a no-brainer for my writing, teaching, storytelling parents. Since I could walk my dad had been telling me Brer Nancy stories while my mom preferred to recite Shakespearean works and classical poems. I had the entire fable memorized the first day and needed no further preparation. Boom!

As I stood in front of my class ready to rock the competition, my eyes caught that girl who hated me and that boy I liked. I saw my best friend shuffle her papers. As I started to tell the story, I imagined that everyone was rooting for me to fail. Who was I to come in right away with the whole story already memorized? In my head I heard, "Who do you think you are?"

I choked. I stopped halfway through and abruptly sat down, the rest of the story coursing unsaid through my brain. Crippling fear had crushed me. My Inner Bully had won. Soon it was my classmate Marissa's turn. She stood, walked to the front of the room, took a deep breath, and began. Then she kept going, and going, and going. Marissa told the whole, entire freaking story from beginning to end – with flair - and the class broke into applause.

Fear had won but I still fit in. No one hated me for being a know-it-all. No one had to wonder why I was shining so brightly. Fear had kept me safe. Fear had kept me small. Marissa went on the trip of a lifetime while I stayed behind with the rest of the class, making Kenyan masks with clay and raffia.

Femergized Courage: Learning to Fear Less

When I revealed to a mentor that I was finally answering my sacred calling with my empowerment work, she brandished a stern warning. "Be careful. Look how they ridiculed Naomi Wolf," she said with love. "I know that this goddess stuff has always been your 'thing' but tread softly." My reply was that Naomi Wolf had much to lose. I don't. So ridicule away.

My mother came to America with spare change in her pocket. The home she left had an outhouse. I grew up in Queens, being told by people who looked like me to go back to "my country." I have never fit in anywhere. I have nothing to lose by sharing healing truths that have empowered many women. I cannot lose what is most important – my God-given power – so I let my sacred flag fly!

This is the Toni Morrison quote I shared in my high school yearbook: "And she had nothing to fall back on: not maleness, not whiteness, not ladyhood, not anything. And out of the profound desolation of her reality she may very well have invented herself." Nothing will stop me from sharing the stories that I came to tell. My work has always examined taboo topics: love, happiness, spirituality, mental health, sexuality, race, gender, and personal development. Some projects work and others don't. With each of my books, columns, blogs, TV shows, films, web series, or other productions I have had someone say, "Watch out, you don't want to do that! That's controversial."

I remember going to a puppet show with my mom when I was very small. The other kids were mystified until I started shouting, "The strings, Mommy! I can see the puppet strings." I couldn't understand why she didn't want me to tell the other kids. "Shhhh. They don't want to know," she whispered. "They just want to enjoy the show." Nothing wrong with that. It just wasn't ever enough for me.

Because my dad is a preacher, he often had church services just for my immediate family at home. It opened a window in my soul when he said that God was within me and that I could use my own words to create prayers. Then there was a moment around age 11 where it dawned on me that my body would always be changing but the real me would remain the same because God was within me. Sometimes I sat on the subway on my way to school imagining that I could see the magical energy between the passengers that connects us to each other.

Some have disagreed with me publicly only to agree privately. I understand. Being brazen enough to be who you were born to be is not always easy. The road less traveled can be a bumpy one. Nonetheless, my bombshell, it is always worth it. Know this: At times, I am terrified. You don't just believe in yourself and then halleluiah, you're healed. It's like bathing; you have to keep at it.

That's the beauty of being a work-in-progress rather than a guru. I have been on reality shows. I had a marriage that didn't go as I'd planned. I've lied about my age. I haven't finished paying back my student loans. I've been in pageants. I'm eating Skittles as I write this. I am not perfect nor do I want to be. I strive to be only my sacred, instead of scared, bombshell best. This is how I live my fullness.

Trying to live without the courage to shine is not living. It takes courage to smile. It takes courage to believe. It takes courage to get up in the morning and give it another go although you've been kicked down nine times by circumstances. It takes courage to forgive, to reach, to move forward. It takes courage to know that you are beautiful. When another woman says to me, "But I am afraid of shining too brightly," I get it. I have been there. I let the fear of "Who does she think she is?" keep me shrunken and puny until I stood to reclaim my muchness. The French root of the word "courage" is whole heart. This wholeheartedness is courage in femergy.

I believe in the fearlessness of women like my mother who left her country so that I might have a better life. If being a teacher of courage seems like a strange avocation for someone who has dealt with anxiety, it is. Anxiety is a fear-based condition. Having dealt with fear of walking out the door firsthand, I take nothing for granted. There was a time when I thought finding my courage meant bravado, swagger, and false shows of confidence. That was survival mode: functional, effective, and draining. In that mode I could make speeches and TV appearances and create while being a lunatic to everyone close to me.

The femergized courage that I have discovered comes from a different place. Now that I am able to find my joy, acknowledge my light, and activate strength from my true Source of power, I still have fear but I fear less. This kind of courage is not about powering through or barreling over anyone. It is a quiet but un-pierceable strength that I softened into myself to find. In becoming myself I have found fullness. In becoming me, I am becoming free.

Courage is necessary. We need courage to throw our names into the hat, to pursue our dreams, to love. We need to fear less in order to leave, to stay, to stand up, to call out injustice. We need fullness to stop meeting our own low expectations. Bravery allows us to claim lives of pleasure, passion, positivity, and play.

Many of us are more comfortable with the idea that we are screw-ups than with our own splendor. We are more able to receive reports of our inadequacy than our worthiness. I call on you to release this, particularly if you are raising children. Your lessons about how magnificent they can be will fall on deaf ears if they don't witness you believing in yourself. How you treat you is teaching them how to treat themselves.

As the heroine Maya Hope in my novel **Dare** asks, "What would you do if you knew you could not fail?" The answer is the same for all of us. We would live more fully. We would shine with moxie. We would accept our greatness and stop sabotaging ourselves. Forget cojones. Have the ovaries to be brave enough to become you.

I see you fully brazen, brave, fearless, gutsy, daring, courageous, full of gumption, and yonified with your whole heart.

Bombshell Challenge: When you can't be fearless, just fear a little less. We make quantum leaps with baby steps. The Japanese call this Kaizen. Take these small steps with enthusiasm. Know that life is rooting for you to expand, to take up room, to rise and shine. You are the only one voting for you to stay small. Even if there are others, yours is the only vote that counts.

The Dark Feminine

"Your life will be transformed when you make peace with your shadow. The caterpillar will become a breathtakingly beautiful butterfly. You will no longer have to pretend to be someone you're not."
—Debbie Ford

To truly live in your fullness, you must embrace your full self, including your "dark side." Your Dark Feminine is the you that you don't want to acknowledge. You may think that she's ugly, base, or unwelcome, but she demands to be seen and heard – by you. Acknowledge and love her – she's a part of you. Welcome the Dark Feminine, or as my mom calls her the "don't give a damn pumpkin." Sometimes she's the "designated bitch" – the one who stands up and says no while everyone else is silent. Other times she gets the job done. Maybe she's a star when you were taught to be seen and not heard.

The Dark Feminine is your shadow self. She is the you without the carefully constructed persona and social mask. What behaviors do you have a strong negative reaction to? Who do you respond to emotionally? Often this is your shadow suppressed in your psyche that you are projecting. It's time to kiss your "bad girl" hello. Welcome your perceived ugliness with unconditional self-love. Embrace (rather than deny) the shame, sadness, anger, and betrayal; the parts of you that you think are unlovable. These parts demand to be seen and act out when they are ignored. The unlived self chases you, haunting you like a jumbee. What you deny, hide, and ignore is a part of you. Give your shadow a voice. Carl Jung, founder of analytical psychology, called the shadow the sparring partner. Your emotional suffering is your shadow.

Call your Dark Feminine self by name. My dark feminine goddess is named Lola. Bombshell Lola came out and hosted a whole web series, *Abiola on LSD: Love, Sex, Dating and Drama*, by herself. I discussed things that still make me blush! Don't hide or stifle your shadow self for she is you. Without her you're living a constipated life – you're a bobbing yellow smiley face or dour sourpuss filled with judgment.

A woman keying her man's car because he didn't come home is out of balance. Her Dark Feminine is running things. Let your Dark Feminine be and she won't have to rebel against you. Ignoring her leads to emotional constipation and sexual repression. Instead, welcome your shadow. Reclaim the badass, dark goddess. Have empathy for the wicked witch trying to steal youth and beauty. Don't judge the evil stepmother too afraid to let down her guard for true love. Allow the bitter, jealous old crone imprisoned by her beliefs to be. Acknowledge the super villainess. Salute Miss Bossy. All of these women are us.

That bitch, ho, ditz, or ratchet chick that you ridicule and despise is triggering something in you for a reason. Instead of judging her, ask yourself where those traits are in you. When have I been a bitch, ho, ditz, or ratchet chick? What is she reflecting about me? Then acknowledge your shadow and give her room. Aren't there times when being in these energies serves you? For example, did Cleopatra, Harriet Tubman, Queen Elizabeth, and Ashanti Queen Yaa Asantewaa need to be able to access their inner bitch when necessary? What about women running households and corporations? You betcha.

Bombshell Exploration: Acknowledge Your Shadow

Shine a light on your shadow self, the dark and "ugly" parts you try to hide. Let your dark side exist. You will not be swallowed up by her because she is also you. You will still be the good girl, the nice person, or the family star. What we resist persists. By avoiding our shadow selves, we don't properly heal from the traumas that we experience. What parts of you are you hiding, denying, or stuffing down? Journal about it in your Bombshell Playbook. You can't truly love yourself unless you love all of you.

Bombshell Tool: Sacred Movement Therapy

Sacred Bombshell Movement Therapy is dance-dance-dancing in your fullness, and moving your pleasure chakra, the sacral chakra, along with the root chakra and navel chakra. Shake those hips, gyrate that booty, ripple your stomach, rotate your pelvis, and undulate your hands. Yes! In Guyana, you might move your hips to calypso, soca music, or "wining" in a "dollar wine" dance. Other cross-cultural dances to open up your comfort level with pleasure, passion, and body motion include belly dancing (raqs sharqi), burlesque, mapouka, pole dancing, twerking, and salsa. Your Sacred Bombshell Movement Therapy can be a barefoot backyard soirée with hula hoops. Yes – hula hooping counts! You can also get into your body at a woman-friendly pole fitness space like Le Femme Suite in Harlem, New York.

With this movement, all of the lower chakras – which are equally as important as the upper chakras – are engaged. You are also electrifying the heart chakra, throat chakra, third-eye chakra, and crown chakra. It is this holistic engagement that leads to harmony. "Pole activist" Sheena LaShay has a party called High-Heeled Hottie Night. (Sheena explains how she finds healing with seductive and sensual dance in Chapter 8.) Why not have your own version of a High-Heeled Hottie Night with your friends to embrace your fullness and allow more pleasure, passion, positivity, and play to flow? Create your own rules.

When one of my girlfriends was getting a divorce I threw her a Goddess Party. I invited a sexpert to give us a lesson on pleasure and passion. My goddess sister was so inspired that she threw another Goddess Party where an exotic dancer performed. Your Sacred Movement Therapy Party can be the Coming Out Party I suggested in Chapter 5. This is a grown woman playdate, and play is essential to your fullness and well-being. Make Sacred Bombshell Movement Therapy a part of your daily repertoire and you will be magnetic. Singer Shakira was right: your hips don't lie!

Bombshell Exploration: Boudoir Photo Shoot

A boudoir shoot is a sexy photo or video shoot starring you in your fullness! Women have long been taught to play the nice girl, follow the rules, and go along with the status quo. Posing in "drag" other than your own in front of a camera can make even the shyest people-pleaser feel like a brazen outlaw. A boudoir shoot can be personally transformational. You can pose scantily clad, nude, or fully dressed in "character." One of my lovely and intelligent clients wants to pose as daring Billie Holliday. There is power in claiming your vixen – and bombshell. Claiming your bombshell is owning your bombshell!

There are many reasons women choose to do a boudoir shoot. Sometimes there's a rite of passage or life event such as a significant birthday, childbirth, marriage, or divorce. Other women have undergone a body transition like releasing weight, gaining muscle, or even plastic surgery. I have seen stunning boudoir photos of breast cancer survivors. While some women set up a seductive photo shoot to give the resulting pinup shot as a gift to a significant other, I am inviting you to indulge as a gift to yourself.

I was chosen one year to be in the "Sex Bloggers Calendar" for my work as a safe sex activist. Photographer Joseph W. Carey showed up on a summer day to shoot me in my Harlem neighborhood. It was hot and everybody was outside. Terrified, I teetered out covered in a flamboyant purple silk robe, like a boxer would wear. My nerves were bubbling over on the inside but I was strutting on the outside. I threw off the robe and got into the game, posing in the middle of the street in a mini-miniskirt, cleavage-baring bustier, and fishnets. The pinup-style poses were daring, provocative, and slightly "gangsta." I began to have a new relationship with my body after the shoot.

If you're on a budget, ask a friend or your partner to photograph you. Because of the intimate nature of these photos, it is not strange to feel more comfortable in front of a hired stranger than a friend you fear may judge you. However, a part of the experience is to release the self-judgment that may be stalling your progress. If you're nervous, invite your dark feminine alter ego to step in. Snap! Your gorgeousness is captured for all eternity.

Bombshell Confidential: You Have Permission to Live

Take heed. Nobody wants to have regrets. Bronnie Ware is an Australian nurse who worked with terminally ill patients in the last 12 weeks of their lives. This was a divine assignment. She bore witness to their last wishes and most intimate sorrows. Bronnie revealed her findings in her international bestseller, *The Top Five Regrets of the Dying*. The top five regrets were:

1. I wish I'd had the courage to live a life true to myself, not the life others expected of me.
2. I wish I hadn't worked so hard.
3. I wish I'd had the courage to express my feelings.
4. I wish I had stayed in touch with my friends.
5. I wish that I had let myself be happier.

Bombshell Explorations: 25 Not-So-Random Acts of Fullness

Unbunch your panties. Unlock your fullness. Remember, you are your priority. Ready to choose sacredness over self-deprecation?

Fullness, to go deeper, is being a turned on woman, living your feminine juiciness, having an intimate relationship with ecstasy. Fullness is the opposite of self-flagellation, sacrifice, self-denial, and snark. Let's get turned up, tuned up, and turned on.

Here are some of my personal Not-So Random Acts of Fullness: I got a sacred goddess tattoo when I was not "the kind of person" who would have skin art. I left an outrageous trail of hot pink feathers everywhere I went as I wrapped my interview mics with feather boas. I wore wings around the city, taking photos in trees. I started making my own Mala prayer beads, inspired by my friend Shelley. I stayed at a hostel in Berlin for creative artists. I used colored eyeliner to create my own tribal facial markings with my friend Antoy and we wore them to fancy cocktail parties.

Here's how to be your own bombshell:

1. **What turns you on?** Bliss up your life by making a list of your every turn-on, from soft kisses on the back of your neck and skinny dipping to freshly crisp percale sheets and your baby's giggle. This list of the things that turn you on in life is your Sacred Bombshell Blueprint.

2. **Have a "Decadent Daily Dance Party."** Mine comes after my green tea, before my shower. Whip your hair back and forth. Whirl like you mean it. The average song is four minutes. You have four minutes for you, right?

3. **Take a page from Cleopatra's Bombshell Playbook.** Bathe in strawberry milk. Start with milk and honey, which was Cleopatra's recipe. Then add fresh strawberries rubbed with olive oil, which you can use to exfoliate.

4. **Be legendary in your own mind.** Whenever you leave the house, joyfully work the sidewalk like a Paris runway.

5. **Send your naysayers and supposed haters a fullness gift with the intention of love.** Expect nothing in return. Stir something fun in the recipients and get them really riled up by sending gifts like: a tiara, Hello Kitty vibrator, goddess tarot cards, or this book! They'll either unbunch their britches a bit or you'll give them something new to talk about.

6. **Blow sexy kisses at your reflection.** Plan a selfie photo shoot and let your inner supermodel all the way out.

7. **Have a Sacred Show-off Session.** Instead of bitching and complaining with your friends, be full of yourselves. Share your big bombshell miracles and teeny joys. Affirm each other's show-offs.

8. **Tired of feeling shame?** Dance divinely on the head of taboos and repression and tell all of your secrets to a sacred friend.

9. **Go for cash-free shopping.** Host a clothing, books, and accessories swap.

10. **Be unproductive.** Run away from home. Put mileage on your passport. Take an ethical observation safari in South Africa. Stomp grapes in Seville. Discover something new about your own community.

11. **Acknowledge and celebrate your lust.** Tell your sweetie what you want to do and what you'd like done in sensual erotic detail. If you're feeling shy, buy a steamy book and read it to him or her.

12. **Wear a full crown or tiara whenever you feel like it.** Wearing a crown makes it physically impossible to bow your head or lower your eyes and you naturally hold your head high. When it's not physically there, rock your inner crown.

13. **What is your super power?** Create a superhero name and character. Get a costume and do a photo shoot, or have a grown-up superhero party.

14. **Be embarrassing and emotionally intense.** Take a loud stand for an important cause.

15. **Give that old sleep shirt a rest.** Wear your favorite lingerie

just because your inner vixen is craving it. If it felt formerly forbidden to you, dress like a "scarlet harlot," "hussy," or "jezebel."

16. **Do a red wine or champagne pedicure.** The antioxidants are good for your skin and the indulgence is good for your spirit. Accentuate the soak with rose petals.

17. **Raise your bombshell I.Q. – Irresistibility Quotient.** Flirt like it's going out of style. Smile at a handsome stranger and hold it for six seconds. For an extra seductive moment, think about your yoni while talking to the person and see what happens.

18. **Put some sun in your schedule.** Grab your Sacred Bombshell Sister and go for a business brainstorm on the beach.

19. **Talk, laugh, and share.** Have a grown woman or co-ed slumber party with your friends. Many men are craving their inner yin, too.

20. **Do juicy joy experiments to see what makes you happy.** Have a "feelgasm" every time you find something that does. Be playful: blow bubbles, jump double dutch, or go on a scavenger hunt.

21. **Revise your mind.** Evolve your interpretation of strength, your perception of womanhood, your limiting ideas on happiness. Write about your new ideas in your Bombshell Playbook.

22. **Be a lifestyle passionista.** Buy yourself flowers. Give genuine compliments like water. Cook sumptuous meals. Don't save the good stuff for special times. Your life is a special time. A heart is a terrible thing to waste.

23. **Flex your fullness.** Take a naked yoga, erotic cooking, or burlesque dance class. Find your fullness at laughing yoga, nude painting, aerial yoga, trapeze, trampoline, or tango dancing.

24. **Rub more beauty into your skin along with your creams and lotions.** Make up a song about it to sing when you're getting dressed.

25. **I'm not the only passionate living coach in town.** Open

your mind. Women teaching similar lessons from succulence to pleasure include: SARK, Mama Gena, Dawn the Self-Esteem Queen, Gala Darling, Goddess Leonie Dawson, D. J. Beverly Bond, Michaela Angela Davis and more; listed in your end of chapter references.

Bombshell Dialogue with Issa Rae: How to Tell Your Own Stories

As a striking chocolate woman with short, natural hair, Issa Rae is a part of the changing face of beauty in the media. I met the mogul-in-training when she was honored with the well-deserved Reel Sisters Film Festival Pioneer Award for her standout comedy web series *The Mis-Adventures of Awkward Black Girl*. I was hosting the award show, which had honored my documentary *Knives in My Throat* a few years before with an award and discussion about women's mental health. This was the perfect opportunity to find out how this young woman so brazenly bucked the societal message that you need someone else to green light your dreams.

> **Abiola:** Issa, there is a Portuguese saying that the Afro-Brazilians use, *É Minha Cara*, and it means "that's my face." I learned it from the Thomas Allen Harris documentary. It's an expression that they use when they see something and feel like, "Yeah, that's me!" That's how I feel when I see you, Issa. *É Minha Cara*!

> **Issa:** That's beautiful. I love that. I'll start using that as soon as I can pronounce it! (laughs)

> **Abiola:** *Forbes Magazine* named you one of "30 under 30 young disruptors, innovators and entrepreneurs." You are a web TV star and now you're collaborating with HBO and Shonda Rhimes. What did you foresee for yourself when you were growing up?

> **Issa:** I wanted to tell stories. I knew that. I always wanted to find a creative and funny way to talk about my experiences. My mom said I talked too much. So I knew that the core was there but I could have never imagined that I'd have the tools to really build an audience and literally just tell my stories to millions all over the world. You can't dream of that. You can't imagine that as a

child. But I've definitely wanted to do this my whole life.

Abiola: So do you feel like you're living fully on purpose?

Issa: Absolutely. Living on purpose, with purpose, on this amazing journey.

Abiola: You are also a Stanford graduate with all of the magnificence that carries. How do you deal with the angst that can come with the pressures of everything from representation to just days when you don't feel so great?

Issa: I'm actually writing about that right now. Because there are some days where you just want to just get away from it all. I do that by writing. I keep a journal every single day. When I get overwhelmed, that is my therapy. And by hanging out with like-minded people who can relate and who I can vent to and talk about it to. I think surrounding myself with a community of people who love and support me is so, so, so important.

Abiola: This is important because your fans could be watching you, thinking, "Issa has everything going for her" and…

Issa: Don't ever be fooled. I go through it just as much as anyone else. If I can be on this journey, if I can set this path for myself, anyone can do it. I am the worse procrastinator in the world. I make excuses. I sometimes doubt myself but I just had to tell these stories. I wanted to make this happen. So if I can do it, you can do it.

Abiola: You have a book coming out with Simon & Schuster…

Issa: It's the hardest thing I've ever done in my life. It's just really trying to be in tune with yourself and figure out what story you want to tell and writing well. But I'm finding the challenge of switching from the screenwriting medium to this descriptive narrative is like … I'm trying to wrap my head around it. I feel like to really be able to do it, you really have to focus on that alone. So I'm trying to get all of my thoughts together but I love what I'm writing. It's so honest and it's a reflection of my thoughts and my observations [about] me being an African woman, an African-American woman. I'm just trying to tell it in a way that hasn't been told; that is unique and good to me.

Abiola: You do that well. As a storyteller you want to leave your blood on the page.

Issa: It's so hard. It's really hard … and especially being such a private person and being so raw and honest. Sometimes I'm like, "Hmm … I wanna delete that."

Abiola: (I wanted to delete almost every personal story in this book!) How is the HBO project going?

Issa: HBO is an amazing process so far. It's the closest thing that I can get to being on the Internet but just on television. I'm doing a show called *Non-Profit* which is set in the world that I was working in before I launched *Awkward Black Girl*. That environment is really, really funny to me and there are so many scenarios that I can come up with on the fly. It's my voice in its raw, most pure form.

Abiola: That is wonderful. I'm about women owning our greatness, owning our shine. So Issa Rae, what makes you a bombshell?

Issa: What makes me a bombshell is that I will constantly follow my passion, no matter what. There's nothing that's going to stand in the way of me and my dreams. And I will execute them at all costs. Because I never want to be on my death bed like, "Oh, I should have done that." So, I'm just living my life to the fullest.

Bombshell Takeaways:

- Follow your passion at any cost, letting nothing stand in the way of your dreams.

- Be relentless in your belief in you.

- Life is easier (and more fun!) when you can laugh at yourself.

Bombshell Dialogue with Essence Revealed: How to Cultivate Courage

Neo-burlesque temptress Essence Revealed describes herself as an "ecdysiast, performer, instructor and lover of love." Ecdysiast (I had to look it up) means "stripteaser." Clearly, there was no way that I could write a guide called *The Sacred Bombshell Handbook of Self-Love* without including a burlesque queen. Last year, Essence performed in Italy at the Milan Burlesque Awards. Burlesque is the bump-and-grind artistic combination of striptease, erotic dance, acting, comedy, and intelligent political commentary. Back in the day, burlesque bombshells like Mae West were arrested on morals charges for being so brazen!

Essence and I first met as recent college grads collaborating on my first professional writing project, a theatrical production. Today, Essence is one of the members of the popular Brown Girls Burlesque troupe. The Caribbean-American performance artist has multiple degrees from the best institutions in the land. She could be doing anything she desires. Lucky us that she chooses to entertain and teach self-love, self-celebration, and sexy empowerment as a burlesque performer.

> **Abiola:** It seems fitting that we know each other from collaborating on a project called *Goddess City*. The original name was *An Auto-Bio-Graphic Peace* because I wanted to show women that we could find inner peace by telling our own raw, naked stories. You then took your bombshell game to another level by becoming an erotic dancer. How do you "reconcile" your good-girl background with your current profession?

> **Essence:** Burlesque was actually a teeny half-step back into the "good girl" direction. (laughs) I had been a club stripper. I'm an actor so it was a cool mix of both worlds. I never in a million years thought that my life as a performer would end up in burlesque. I didn't even know that it existed. I'm so glad it revealed itself to me.

Abiola: Let's talk about the power of alter egos. Beyoncé had Sasha Fierce. My dark feminine alter ego is Lola Badass. I just now added that last name, by the way! (laughs) Essence Revealed is such a powerful name. Is "she" an alter ego?

Essence: Essence Revealed is for sure my Sasha Fierce! Our essence is who we are when we are not doing a cover for the public. It's our authentic selves. I wrote a solo show "outing" my secret life of actor by day, stripper by night, and called it *Essence Revealed*. I decided to name my burlesque persona the same thing.

Abiola: When I think of burlesque pioneers who crossed over into the mainstream, Josephine Baker and Dita Von Teese come to mind. Who are your burlesque role models and icons?

Essence: Jean Idelle, Ms. Toni Elling, and Taipai are all living burlesque legends of color that I look up to. I've been lucky enough to meet them all, too. Lottie the Body, Baby Scruggs, Miss Topsy, and so many others were brought to my attention by the research of burlesque performers and academics like Chicava HoneyChild, who did a master's thesis on women of color in burlesque, and Dr. Ginger Snapz. Yes, she really is a Ph.D. I am so grateful to them because most burlesque history books and documentaries gloss over the existence of these women. There were many black, Latina, and Asian performers in demand during burlesque's heyday.

Abiola: What an impactful history. What do you bring to this art form that is unique?

Essence: Me. I'm an exhibitionist ecdysiast nerd who is a bit socially weird yet can brazenly embrace and express sexual energy onstage.

Abiola: Tell it, goddess. Let's talk about body love and body acceptance. A woman must feel good in her skin to bodaciously rule the stage like you do in her real "big girl panties."

Essence: When I started stripping there was nothing much to hide once down to a G-string. I learned to accept every dip, curve, dimple, and jiggle. I stood on stage, unrestrained by clothing, dancing to music I loved. I was surrounded by so many different types of bodies. I could be next to a woman who was the same weight [as] me and see how differently our frames carry the pounds. Body acceptance eventually happened. I never worked so much as an actor as when I had natural hair. I think I was able to walk into casting rooms feeling most confident and it showed. Hair acceptance happened.

When I walk down the street in my sweats sans makeup, I get very little attention. When I have on makeup and am dressed more "traditionally" feminine, I can't get three steps without street harassment. So, I like to have pics online with me in burlesque drag and fresh faced so women can see that anyone can be glamazon with good lighting and makeup.

Abiola: Yes! What does the sacred feminine and yoni power mean to you?

Essence: If more women got the power of the P, man, we'd move mountains! As a dancer I saw what a motivation just even the potential of the P is for men. We create life through this vessel. It is powerful. It is valuable. It is also ours to do with what we choose. Choice is the key word here.

I hear adult women say things like, "I felt like I had to sleep with him because he bought me dinner and a movie." Huh? What? Is that what you feel your value is? The price of a dinner and movie is all the currency you're worth? Your worth is incalculable, beyond any monetary limitation. A dinner and a movie does not even compute on the scale of your worth. But women get fed so much about our worthlessness and some women buy into it.

I don't go to church but when I am performing on stage I am as close to Spirit as ever. It's like the strongest group meditation to me. Sacred feminine could be replaced with sacred humanity. On my best days, I remember that I am deserving and worthy for no reason other than being sprung from the sperm that made it to the egg. You know how few sperm make it to the egg? So just being born makes us worthy.

As women, we are given other qualities that make us uniquely valuable. We are the nurturers, the caregivers, the empaths, and the mothers. We are connected to the moon and gifted with intuition in a very real way if we allow ourselves to tap into it. I expect to be valued. I expect to be treated well. I expect respect. I also, in turn, give it.

Abiola: Many women might respond to that with an, "Easy for her to say. She's beautiful and educated." How do you get out of a funk on days you feel challenged to get out of bed?

Essence: Honestly, some days none of that matters and I just don't make it out of bed. Sometimes, depression or dysthymia wins. It's not a fun thing to deal with because so many people are not comfortable talking about mental illness. People are more empathetic about asthma or cancer. So, often, I'd rather hide out and take care of myself than have to "put on a happy face" and pretend to be okay. I allow myself time to feel and be human. Because I also have awareness of what is going on with me, I have support. I have close friends that "get it" and won't say hurtful things like "just snap out of it," "just think positive," or "but you're too xyz to be depressed."

Self-care has to come first no matter what. I spent time figuring out what I need to do to take care of myself. It's going to be different for everybody. So, spend the time to figure out what pampering means for you.

Abiola: How did you learn to love yourself?

Essence: I learned to love myself through therapy, self-help books, seminars, writing, and knowing that the voices in my head that tell me most of the negative things about me are not my voice. I was determined to reprogram myself and have self-love be my default.

One of the biggest steps was when I stopped putting more value on others' opinions of me than I did on how I feel about me. Once you stop caring about what "they" will think, life gets so much better. It is ongoing work. But I just got over wanting everyone to understand me. Now, if I'm misunderstood? Oh, well. If I can't call you when I'm having a hard day, then your opinion has no value to me.

Abiola: Essence, you are truly a woman who owns her power. As a professional seductress, what secrets can you share with other women looking to embrace their inner courtesan?

Essence: Know your worth! Confidence is the ultimate in sexy. Do whatever work you have to do to feel the best about you. Accept only the best in treatment. I was blessed enough to grow up seeing my father treat my mother way too well for anybody I date to ever get over on me by treating me subpar. Even if this wasn't your experience, that intuition I spoke of will whisper to you when things aren't correct.

I have a male friend who is the ultimate cougar magnet. It saddens me how insecure these super-uber-successful women are. They're willing to have him or any man on their arm even after he tells them he's in a happy relationship with the woman he lives with. Desperation-to-get-a-man behavior breeds ill treatment.

Allow men to be men – but only in the best traits of manhood. Praise the good ones. It's a fine balance. I am fiercely independent so it took a while for me to accept that it's okay for me to feel like I just want to be the girl. I chased many a man away because he didn't feel like I needed him. Well, I may not have needed him but I sure did want him. (laughs)

If you have a good mate, praise them as much as you critique them. I had many men as club customers who got tired of only getting the "we're outta juice" calls instead of the "I'm getting juicy for you" calls. They'd come into the club for a "fix." Reserve the good treatment for the good ones. Everyone is not spoil-worthy.

Expect love. I know I've had moments where I felt like because I'd been hurt so much, I'd expect the worst. That way, I'd be braced for the tragedy and "protect" myself from further hurt. Guess what that attracted? Expect better and remain open. It may take being hurt several times from going into new relationships totally open with no walls up before finding a good relationship. However, if we go into relationships on guard or on the lookout for all the failures of past mates, love will surely be repelled from you.

Abiola: In *Goddess City* you were known as the Goddess of Truth while I was known as the Goddess of Nerve. What makes you a bombshell — and a goddess?

Essence: The older I get the less I care about what other people think about me. Man, was that a long journey. Actually, it's an ongoing journey. But it feels so, so powerfully good!

Bombshell Takeaways:

- Self-care has to come first, no matter what.
- It really doesn't matter what others think of you; your opinion of yourself is all that counts.
- You are deserving and worthy for no other reason than being sprung from the sperm that made it to the egg!

Secret of Fullness Resources

1. *Eat Mangoes Naked: Finding Pleasure Everywhere* by SARK
2. Mama Gena's School of Womanly Arts by Regena Thomashauer (program)
3. *Unbreakable Spirit* by Lisa Nichols
4. "African Goddess Affirmations" by Abiola Abrams (cards)
5. *TranscenDance* by Michael Bernard Beckwith (audio)

Fullness Affirmations

1. I am fully open to bold, new experiences.
2. I have a right to exquisite pleasure.
3. I love life and life loves me.
4. I am courageous and filled with joy.
5. I am fully passionate about all that I do.

Seven

The Secret of Authenticity: Being True to Yourself

The Sacred Feminine Law of Authenticity

The Sacred Bombshell knows that life loves her and her authentic uniqueness. She is not her persona, mask, or the story of how she has lived up this point. She is inherently worthy and deserving of all good. The more she becomes herself, the greater the rewards. She is enough. She has full authority over her life. She claims her power by unapologetically being herself. This is sacred self-love.

Historical Bombshell Mentor: Celia Cruz 1925-2003

Superstar Úrsula Hilaria Celia de la Caridad Cruz Alfonso de la Santísima Trinidad was all about living authentically. The Cuban bella exuded guts and vulnerability. Her colorful costumes and wigs could only belong to the "Queen of Salsa." Her shoes were custom-made to look like she could fly. Some said that she was a Santeria priestess in addition to being a devout Catholic because she sang in the Yoruba-derived language of Lucumi. Celia's famous battle cry was in tribute to the slaves that worked the sugar plantations: *Azucar!*

The Authenticity Declaration

I am the daughter of all there is and today I accept my authentic Self. I am a miracle, perfect in my imperfections. If that which made me accepts me, who am I to reject myself? I accept myself completely and live authentically.

Previously I was bound up in my fears and perceived imperfections, mishaps, and missteps. I flagellated myself daily for not yet being perfect. Now I know the truth, that I am a daughter of the Universe. I am free from this tired self-critique.

I accept me. I am worthy of love and acceptance. I have faith in this authentic truth and deny all evidence to the contrary as lies. I need not approval of man nor woman. I am more than this earthly body. I am free. I may not be where I planned to be but I am exactly where I need to be. I am that I am, a co-creator with my Source.

I release doubt and banish anxiety. I know that I am not an island but a part of something greater than human understanding. I am a gift of love and I live true to that which I am. I no longer participate in limiting untruths or lies. There is power in being me and I realize this today. I am free at last.

I will no longer wait until I am rich enough, popular enough, or perfect enough to be great. I step into my glory today, perfect in my imperfections. I will be a great me today so that the even greater me of tomorrow can arrive. My choices are her red carpet. Today I accept the truth: that I am a miracle as is. For this I am so grateful.

And so it is.

The Story You Tell

The Chinese philosopher Lao Tzu said, "When I let go of who I am I become who I might be." Stop any woman on the street and there's a story that she leads with. We use these stories to define and separate ourselves. For some of us it's a visible or cultural story such as: I am a black woman, white woman, Latina, Asian, foreigner, tall or short, pretty or ugly. Maybe the story is your education, social background or career, like: I am an Ivy League grad, drop out, dancer, latchkey kid, trust fund baby, failed lawyer, or jaded doctor. For many of us it is our relationship or mothering status: I am divorced, never married, I have twins, I'm child-free, I had an abortion, I am a single parent, or I can't have kids. Some of our stories are righteous: I am an abuse survivor, cancer survivor, incest survivor, adoptee, child of an alcoholic. Others are a complex or condition: I have ADD, OCD, abandonment issues, disabilities, depression, or anxiety.

Sacred Bombshell, let me ask you this: Who might you be without that story to hide behind? What if you woke up tomorrow and couldn't tell those stories anymore, especially to yourself? Many of these stories are hereditary or cultural. What if no one around you knew your story or indulged you in it? What if those puny self-definitions simply did not exist? (I mean puny in the sense of all of the wonderful things waiting for you, not to belittle your experience.) What if you couldn't wear these stories as badges of honor?

What if you could respond "so what" to all of the excuses you make as to why you can't be who you want, do what you want, have what you want, and love who and how you want? "You're too old." So what? "You're too young." So what? "You're the wrong color." So what? "You don't have enough money." So what? "You're too single." So what? "You're too fat." So what? "You are not enough." So what?! It's not that you dream too big, bombshell; it's that you don't dream big enough. Allow yourself to be you.

Bombshell Challenge: Go the next seven days without trotting out the negatives in your story. The can'ts. The won'ts. The excuses. The "they won't let me," "I'm not enough," or "I am too much" stories.

The Sacred Feminine Power of Authenticity

"The privilege of a lifetime is to become who you truly are."
—Carl Jung

In 1896, poet Paul Laurence Dunbar wrote, "We wear the mask that grins and lies." Today, many women can relate. We are Stressed, Depressed, and Well-Dressed. We present the perfect face at social engagements, at work, and at PTA meetings while killing ourselves softly on the inside. You could be worried about a family member's health, stressed about your under-employment, and jilted by the lover you thought might be the one. Nonetheless, when it comes time to pretend to shine, you put on the face and plaster on the smile.

Have you ever thought that a couple was the picture of happiness and then been shocked by their breakup? We have no idea what is going with anyone else. With social media it's easy to wear the mask both personally and professionally. People used to have to wait for holiday cards or annual family newsletters to see the happy peer pictures. Now you only need to sign into Facebook for "Death by LOL." It's not healthy to compare your day-to-day life to someone else's glossy highlight reel.

Single women are lusting over the lives of married women; married women are envying single women. We're all forgetting to be grateful for our authentic own lives. Whatever is going on in your life right now, you created it. You have the power and the choice to create something different.

One way to tap into your femergy is by re-learning how to be authentic. What does inauthenticity look like? If you feel like you are an impostor, have to wear a mask, are not fulfilling your purpose, must keep up with the Joneses, or need to ignore your morality to move ahead, you are not being your authentic self.

"Keep it real" has long been a rallying cry. It even spawns humor-based memes like "when keeping it real goes wrong." However, this is not the realness that I mean when I say "keep it authentic" instead. People have shouted "keep it real" while upholding a credit card lifestyle based on someone else's value system. This limiting concept doesn't allow for different worldviews.

Lack of authenticity is at its core a self-love crisis, although it doesn't appear to be so on the surface. You may have power at work but you lack authentic power if you're not being true to you. An authenticity gap occurs when we live a lie in any way. In a world where "reality" shows are scripted and "keeping it real" refers to someone else's vision, it makes sense that we'd be confused.

Girls on Fire: Hunger for Ourselves

*"I found god in myself and I loved her
fiercely."*
—Ntozake Shange

One of the programs that I offer is called "Superwoman Anonymous." It's for successful women who are burned dry by living and still hungry for life.

Around 2001, I started holding private Goddess Circles in my East Harlem apartment with friends and acquaintances. I was in the process of birthing *Ophelia's Opera*, a short, experimental, domestic violence revenge film. At one gathering, we passed around a rock as a talking stick, meaning whoever had the rock had the floor. It was a Saturday afternoon and beauties like the light worker Yolanda "Shoshi" Shoshana were present. A woman confessed that she was "sick of feeling dead inside." Another co-signed. Each told a different version of the superwoman syndrome story: burning the candle at both ends, never feeling like you're enough, caught up in trying to get "there" and then feeling lonely and like an impostor when you achieve success.

I felt all of this then, in my 20s, and it only became more intense. I grew up believing that the only way to be loved was through achievement. Many of my friends also thought that the only way to be accepted is by having the right picture of perfection. We women have come a long way, baby, over the past forty to fifty years, right? So it would stand to reason that with all the choices we have at our fingertips that we're happier than ever, right? Wrong! Studies show that American women are more dissatisfied than ever before. Add to that the seeping guilt for being unhappy and you've got a generation of women who are not feeling the joy that every yogurt commercial says we should have.

We are the generational beneficiaries of women who sacrificed presumably so that we wouldn't have to. The majority of women reading this have always had the right to attend school, access to birth control and reproductive choice, the ability to get student loans and credit cards, voting rights, and the option of not sitting at the back of the bus. Yet so many of us are love-starved and hungry for ourselves. So we're unhappy and then guilty for being unhappy. Oy vey!

As a young teacher, my mother left everything she knew to find a better life in New York City. I've always felt that if previous generations made such huge sacrifices for me, I'd damn well better be happy and successful. Take my coaching client Dina. She's a successful accountant based in Manhattan. Her African-American mother was a daughter of the civil rights movement. Her Jewish father came from the tough public housing projects in the Bronx. Her privileged life is made possible in part by the hard times her parents experienced. As a result, she feels uncomfortable even expressing discomfort. Questing for "happy-happy, joy-joy" success is making her miserable.

Dina goes to work in her high-powered office, socializes with her educated friends, and then cries herself to sleep, feeling that she has no right to her pain. Betty Friedan, author of *The Feminine Mystique*, called this "the problem that has no name" all the way back in 1963. At the time she was talking only about middle-class white women who were unhappy despite their affluence. I call this a Dry Life Crisis, and I'm referring to any woman who has ever looked around and thought, "This is not the life I want." When we feel like that, there can be a general feeling of "stuckness." Feeling paralyzed and then not taking action causes even more anxiety.

So why are we having the same issue with joy deprivation that women had before the feminist movement forty plus years after the fact? Thankfully, the feminist movement did a masterful job of enabling us to rock the educational arena and the workplace. We adopted masculine energy qualities as our own and can outgun any man. Aside from much-needed equal pay for equal work, we are making strides in the workplace. This is awesome – but there's another r/evolution necessary. Feminine energy qualities were undervalued, deemed less than, and took a backseat. This left us hungry – hungry for our very selves, our sacred Selves.

The entire planet is starved for the balance of rich, feminine power. Is losing ourselves the price of having it all? It doesn't have to be. It starts with us as individuals taking action to make our own lives more harmonious.

Bombshell Exploration: Your Passion Statement

A Passion Statement is a statement of purpose that sums up your aims and values. For example, every mom has the mission of being a great mother. A good passion statement details how you plan to do this and how you plan to express your personal power in the rest of your life. You can't figure out where you're going without knowing (1) where you are and (2) where you want to go. Lucky for us, where you've been is the least important part of the equation.

I recommend having a Personal Passion Statement and a Professional Passion Statement. It should be at least a paragraph but under a page and a half. Print it and hang where you can see daily. Answer these questions in detail to create your Passion Statement.

- Who am I currently?
- Who do I want to be?
- What do I value?
- What do I enjoy?
- What do I need?
- What matters to me?
- What legacy do I want to leave?

Bombshell Playbook Exercise

Answer these questions in your Bombshell Playbook. Take five deep, cleansing breaths to get centered and begin.

1. How would I describe myself?
2. If I didn't hold back, who would I be?
3. If time and money were no object, how would I express myself?
4. What do I believe about: love, family, creativity, money, and

pleasure?

5. What are my biggest secrets and why are they still secrets?

My Big Fat Bombshell Diary: My Summer of Misery

*"Once you are Real you can't be ugly, except
to people who don't understand."*
—The Velveteen Rabbit

June 2005 kicked off my official Summer of Misery. I moved partially into my husband's bachelor pad (which he had kept as a rental property), unsure of what the future was for us as a couple. I spent half the week at the "work" apartment and the other half at home. "I just need a *pied-à-terre*, a place to quietly work for half the week," I told my high school girlfriends as they looked at me cross-eyed over mimosas.

As far as everyone else was concerned, Henry was the perfect man and I was the crazy bitch who moved out after a 10-year relationship to find herself. I could deal with them thinking I was "off." I could not bear the thought of my loved ones not liking Henry. It was battered woman syndrome, although I was not physically abused. I had protected him for so long that it was hard to stop doing so. Henry cemented my sorrows when he explained that he needed to go on a solo one-month sabbatical to Costa Rica to "sort himself out."

"Don't worry. When I get back everything will be okay. Unfortunately I'm going to miss either your birthday, your graduation, or our anniversary," he said. "You pick which one." I picked our first wedding anniversary since it obviously meant so little to him. I spent Monday, August 29 with my sister and my mother in a cheap Caribbean eatery. "Happy anniversary," my mom sang. I looked at her like she was crazy. Henry sent me a text message the next day from Costa Rica "in remembrance." I went home and cried until I vomited. That had become my daily routine. Every morning, I could only make an agreement with myself to get through the next

24 hours.

I turned on the TV that night and the newscaster explained that the hurricane down south had become a "near catastrophic event." The next day all hell broke loose, for me and for the country. Hurricane Katrina had destroyed the levees that were supposed to protect the people of the Big Easy. I watched as the newscasters described my fellow displaced Americans in New Orleans as "refugees." I finally had permission to be as devastated as I had been feeling all year. I was no longer grieving alone. I felt connected to the families trying to survive the devastation in the Superdome, to the ordeal of feeling evicted from your own life. I was in the Biblical flood with them, praying for a life raft, surrounded by water but thirsty. Then I felt guilty for my petty relationship problems when people were losing lives and family members.

My sadness moved to anger. I was able to feel rage at the situation in New Orleans that I was unable to feel about my own life. I was pissed off and helpless, burnt and brittle. I started to phase through all the stages of grief on an hourly basis, sometimes all at the same time. I was drinking cups of resentment for breakfast. The water slammed the Gulf Coast and ripped me open. Loving Henry was a habit that I was too broken to break. FEMA abandoned my brothers and sisters. Love had abandoned me. I was adrift with no paddle and thirsty for myself. I was drowning in the midst of a raging Dry Life Crisis.

I called everyone close to me and told them a truth that I had not been able to speak. I was not hanging out in a fun apartment-turned-office. My life was a lie and my marriage was in shambles. I confessed that Henry had cheated and I was alone. I didn't know how I could make it work, but I wanted to try because I took my vows seriously and I was in love with my husband. Submerged under the weight of my choices, I could no longer breathe. My loved ones were angry at him but I wasn't there yet. I was furious only at myself.

"He's doing his best," I told PJ, my soul sister and maid of honor.

"Then I would hate to see his worst," she said.

Trying to fix our relationship at that point was building on swampland. My own ego was keeping me stuck. I felt too stupid to admit that I had made a mistake. I remember saying to PJ a couple of months before the wedding, "I don't know if we should be doing this."

"We already bought our tickets," she said. And I would have said the same to her. The four violet gowns were standing by; the tea party was planned; and Nicola, the best wedding planner in the world, was on the case.

We were already a powder keg. The blunt edge of the truth just ignited our demise.

Surviving a Dry Life Crisis

A Dry Life Crisis or dark night of the soul is the sudden realization that the bottom has fallen out. Everything could have been fine yesterday, then you wake up and realize that you desperately need to make changes to survive. It's like a functional nervous break-down.

There are standard transition periods like puberty, quarter-life, midlife, menopause, or empty nesting, but a Dry Life Crisis can strike at any time. You suddenly feel hollow. You may try to fill yourself up with work, drugs, food, or alcohol. None of those things will satiate you because you are hungering for you. I call it a Dry Life Crisis because you are thirsty for yourself.

In nature, plants or fruits are dry when they are no longer viable. Youth and vitality are dewy, wet, and juicy. The only one way out of a Dry Life Crisis is to become juicy again, by starting a love affair with yourself. There are no shortcuts. As with a burning building, the only way out it is through it. None of this can happen until you are honest with yourself about where you are. So how do you start a love affair with yourself?

1. **Get to know the real you.** People say "be yourself" and we wonder, "Which self do they mean?" Mother, friend, daughter, employer, employee, sister, lover? Make a list of your core values. What do you respect and require for a whole,

happy, healthy life?

2. **Invest in yourself.** We women tend be focused on everyone else's happiness, putting ourselves last on the to-do list. What can you do daily to show your love and appreciation for the real you?

3. **Feel your feelings.** Do you find yourself saying yes when you mean no and vice versa? Who would you be if you allowed yourself to feel all of the joy and pain? Instead of numbing or avoiding, practice opening up to what you really feel as a part of your journey to authenticity.

4. **Value your own opinion.** What "they" think of you isn't your business. How can you care more for what *you* think than the opinions of others?

5. **Aim toward bliss, like a plant pointing toward the sun.** Make small shifts to acknowledge your value and worth. If you're facing an authenticity crisis you are disconnected from your Source. "Am I operating from love or fear?" This is a good question to ask anytime you feel like you may be betraying yourself.

People Pleasing Is Killing You

Like most women, I was never taught to address my own needs or to be authentic. After all, authenticity means that some days we're giddy and gleeful and other days we're grumpy and grouchy. It ain't always pretty. "Good girls" are taught that no matter what kind of anguish we are going through, we show perfection to the outside world. So I learned to bury my feelings with food and achievement. My story is common. We're taught to make everyone happy but ourselves. We take this behavior into our adult lives and wonder why we're unhappy and our relationships don't work.

As a highly sensitive person I am acutely aware of my energy and the energy of others, and being an empath was draining before I knew how to ground and center myself. We are all communicating with each other on a subconscious, energetic level. That's the lesson of Dr. Jill Bolte Taylor. She learned about energy and feelings firsthand when she lay in a hospital bed unable to process thoughts and emotions as we know them. Without understanding words, she was able to feel every single person's loving or fearful energy.

If you are happy, you want to be able to dance, and if you're angry you should also feel comfortable enough to say, "I am upset and here's why." Here are four reasons to let go of your people-pleasing ways:

People Pleasing Is an Intimacy Killer

When you're people pleasing, which is living inauthentically, you're not able to be intimate. If you are not being real, others won't feel like they can be genuine with you. When you are honest about your ups and downs, then others know that you are comfortable with them bringing their whole selves to your interactions and relationships, too.

The most powerful feeling of love is when you know that someone completely sees and gets you and loves you anyway. You cheat yourself of that if you present a mask. True intimacy comes from vulnerability. Vulnerability comes from authenticity, not people pleasing.

People Pleasing Is Passive-Aggressive

People pleasing leads to passive-aggressive behavior and outbursts. People pleasing *looks* like it's about making other people happy, but the reality is people pleasing is selfish and manipulative. Not only do you rob your loved ones of knowing you, but you also may have a martyr complex. This "poor me" mentality leads to passive-aggressiveness. "Poor me, look at all I've done for you." You then end up criticizing the people around you rather than appreciating them.

People Pleasing Is a Receptivity Blocker

People pleasing doesn't allow you to receive. Yes, we're discussing receiving again. Feminine energy traits like being receptive and intuitive are often trained out of us. Sure you want to please your loved ones, but are you leaving room to be pleased in return? If you're the one usually responsible for making things tick and holding everyone else together, you may be giving off an "I don't need anything from anybody" vibe. Have you ever tried to give anything to someone who's not receptive?

People Pleasing Is Codependent

People pleasing leads to the codependency/counter-dependency paradox. Being codependent means that you only experience the world as it relates to others. This is not a healthy way to get your needs met. It's depleting and your energy will eventually read as desperate. When a woman is desperate, she attracts narcissists and spiritual vampires seeking to feed on her lack of strength. You will draw users to you who will suck you dry of all you have – and it still won't be enough for them.

As a people pleaser you may fear not being enough. Your relationships are a mirror, reflecting to you what you believe about yourself. For every passive-aggressive codependent there is an aggressive counter-dependent waiting in the wings. Having clear boundaries will allow you to feel safe enough to be genuine. The genuine you will attract healthier friends and suitors than the faux perfect you.

The opposite of people pleasing is being authentic, standing in your power, embracing your emotions, and expressing them. Yes, you should cater to those you love and they should cater to you in return. But Little Miss Perfect is a lie and your true soul mates don't want her anyway. Let down the façade. With a wall up, you may not let anyone get close enough to hurt you but you won't let them get close enough to love you either. Anyone worthy of being in your big bombshell life wants you to be yourself, not superwoman.

People who judge themselves harshly will find any reason to rip other people to shreds. Self-acceptance will allow you to be a fully expressed woman who lives authentically. Put you first. You can't give from an empty cup and pretending through your tears makes your life drier.

Bombshell Playbook Exercise

Complete these exercises in your Bombshell Playbook. Take five deep, cleansing breaths to get centered and begin.

1. Here's a list of 100 sensational things about me...

2. Here's a list of the 100 awe-inspiring experiences that I have been responsible for...

3. Here's a love letter to my phenomenal Sacred Bombshell self...

Bombshell Confidential: "It's Just About to Get Good"

I started to think about living more authentically in earnest a few years ago when having drinks with tastemaker and fashion maven Bevy Smith at Tillman's in Manhattan. I met Bevy, the host of Bravo's hilarious *Fashion Queens*, when we hosted sister shows for BET back in the day. As a voluptuous, mocha brown, multi-platform personality, Bevy Smith cleared a path for me and others to do the same.

Over cocktails, Bevy asked how old I was. I told her my phony TV birthdate, then immediately explained my real age. I had been taught since one of my very first media internships at the ripe old age of 22 that aging in media would hold me back, so I'd subtracted from my age at that point and rolled with it.

"Really? Who cares how old you are? You're still young. It's just about to get good," Bevy said. I explained to her that I had always been warned that being too old could prevent one from being hired in television – even as a lifestyle journalist. "I just keep it authentic," Bevy said. "And people hire me for being me."

Bevy then offered gentle advice on being genuinely me, explaining how if I tried to give what she called "Sister Girl," it obviously would not work because that's not who I am. Of course I knew this but I was not living it. Heck, I was teaching it, but it was mean-

ingful to have a talented role model and big sister affirm that it is
about walking in your truth. It's not what you know intellectually.
It's what you are living. Living authentically means being in tune
with your Source, tapping into who you came to this planet to be.
There is no competition when you are living authentically because
no one can be a better you than you.

Inauthenticity and Impostor Syndrome

As Sheryl Sandberg discusses in her business advice tome **Lean
In**, men feel more confident speaking up for themselves at work
and asking for raises and promotions even when they are not as
qualified as their female associates. For women, this comes back to
self-worth. When you feel worthy and are living with authenticity,
you know that you deserve success. You operate with wholehearted
courage. You know that you are enough. To be living beyond what
your ancestors, your family or even you yourself imagined is not
being an imposter. Playing small and imagining yourself to be less
than the bombshell woman you are, is.

War survivors often have survivor guilt as do those of us who
have "made it out" of less privileged backgrounds. This is the
guilty feeling that you are betraying your group or tribe by leaving them behind. Survivors commit acts of self-sabotage or keep
themselves small in order to remain connected to the larger tribe.
Survivor guilt leads us to become enablers to others who may feel
entitled to a "piece of the pie" of success although they may have
had the same opportunities and not taken advantage of them. People around successful women play into this because it serves them
to reinforce the idea that you got lucky.

This is inauthenticity, and it leads to shallow and unfulfilling
relationships. Real relationships require vulnerability. This is
complicated for superwomen because we forget that we're human. Unfortunately, so do the people in our lives. When we avoid
our humanity, we are left ravenous, brittle, and hollow. There's a
saying that we don't find ourselves but create ourselves. We also
reveal ourselves. How lucky are those that get to experience the
real you! You rock and it's about time that the world knows it. The

authentic you is a gift, to yourself and to the planet. Have the courage to share that gift.

Who Are You?

You can't find your voice, express yourself, or live your passion if you don't first know who you are. If you've come this far, you're willing to trade the persona, daily performance, and mask you've been wearing for juicy self-acceptance. Consider this your Come as You Are Party; an unmasking. Getting to know our beautiful selves should be a succulent unfolding and lifelong pursuit as we keep evolving and growing.

Ever since I was a kid I would make friends with people who revealed a "Major Problem They Had Never Told Anyone Else." I would then end up drained and depleted as I spent all of my mental and physical resources trying to cheerlead, empower, and yes, coach the person. It wasn't fair to them because they needed a professional coach, counselor, or therapist, not an untrained kid, and it wasn't fair to me because I wasn't fully empowered myself!

My mom and sister would say, "Why do you always attract these situations?" I bonded with these individuals because I was a vibrational match. Someone I was dating asked me to take a standardized personality test with him. Apparently he did this with every girlfriend. Among other traits and qualities, my personality type was determined to be "The Counselor." It turns out that I was trying to do what I was born to do.

This revelation helped me to put much of my life in perspective. Clearly, as someone who has used words and media in the practice of empowering women I have always felt that I had a mission. When I was 16, I was in a rap group called Females Beyond Control. I've always been doing the same exact thing. This information helped me to clarify my mission, get the necessary skills, and crystallize it! Being authentically you builds self-integrity and self-trust because you are saying, "I am worthy just as I am." Take off the mask and stop pretending.

Bombshell Playbook Exercise

Answer these questions in your Bombshell Playbook. Take five deep, cleansing breaths to get centered and begin.

1. Who am I "supposed" to be and why?

2. What role do expectations play in my life?

3. When is the last time I said no but wish I had said yes?

4. When is the last time I said yes but wish I had said no?

5. Is there a difference between my public persona and the real me?

6. When do I put on my mask?

7. If I let go of my mask, what would happen?

8. How have the expectations of my group (ethnic, religious, gender, sexuality, education level, social class, etc.) or family of origin held me back or limited my full self-expression?

9. What choices created my present life and situation?

10. Were these choices based on my desires or outside pressure? Are these pressures real or imagined?

Bombshell Dialogue with Tamar Braxton: How to Love Your Authentic Self

"Girl, get your life!" When we think about living, laughing, and loving authentically, the vivacious Tamar Braxton is one of the first to come to mind. The youngest Braxton sister has two reality shows, **Braxton Family Values** and **Tamar & Vince**. Tamar is also a co-host on the FOX daytime talk show **The Real**. Her musical single "Love and War" hit number one on iTunes.

Tamar is a larger-than-life woman who bears the first name of my powerful paternal great-grandma. When I was playing small, loud and brassy women like Tamar used to annoy me. My feeling was, "Stop being so over the top." In other words, stop playing so big. Their shine only made me uncomfortable because I was uncomfortable with my own. Luckily I cleared that drama for myself by the time the opportunity to dialogue with Ms. Braxton arose. I didn't know that she was pregnant during our interview. Her loving hubby, Vincent Herbert, sweetly lurked outside the door, clearly her biggest supporter. Their son is named Logan.

Abiola: Tamar, you look absolutely gorgeous.

Tamar: Thank you. I guess it's in the room because you are too!

Abiola: Beauty knows beauty. (laughs) So, what do you think is your cross-generational appeal?

Tamar: I feel like there's a Tamar in everybody's family. You know, I think I kind of identify my character with somebody you actually know in your life.

Abiola: That makes sense because when you say "there's a Tamar in every family" we know what that means! You have so much going on.

Tamar: Isn't that amazing? It's so crazy. "Love and War" is pretty much the soundtrack to my life and it's just about having a relationship with someone that you're not only in love with but that you're passionate about.

Abiola: I always say, "You'd better live like you mean it." Tamar, you are living like you mean it. Now, is all really fair in love and war?

Tamar: Not all the time. But there's something called compromise that I did pick up along the way that definitely works for me.

Abiola: That's the number one thing, right? The compromising in relationships?

Tamar: Definitely! I had to learn about that one. Because at first I was all about me and what I thought and what I felt. When you get married and when you decide you're going to spend your life with someone, it's not just about you. You're one [together] for a reason. Half of you leaves so the other half can come back in.

Abiola: Wait, we need to write that down! Your show *Tamar and Vince* is one of the positive representations of marriage on television. How did you know Vince was the one?

Tamar: I knew when he had a girlfriend because at first we were friends. And I just looked at him as my friend. So when I found out that he had a girlfriend and I was like, "What? What are you talking about?" That's when I knew.

Abiola: When you talk about Vince, the energy shifts. You're madly in love with your husband.

Tamar: Yeah! I'm madly in love with him and he's my best friend. And you know, we almost lost him and I don't even know where I would be without him.

Abiola: Is it hard, Tamar, to share so much of yourself?

Tamar: Well, no, not really. I just look at it as a testimony. We have to learn from something. And if it's not something positive then it's [something] negative. So, why not learn from something that's completely positive and apply it to your life?

Abiola: You and Vince look pretty steamy in love. How do you keep the passion going?

Tamar: With every other relationship – failed relationship – I've gotten into, I've experienced love, I've experienced getting my feelings hurt. But I never experienced passion until I got with Vince. It's the level of love and the respect and the trust that we have for each other. And we don't ever want that to go away.

Abiola: And the way you keep it going is by waking up and choosing to still be in love every day.

Tamar: Definitely, definitely. Yes. I don't even think it's a choice anymore. It's just what it is. He's my family.

Abiola: You've been in this game a long time but people look at you and say, "Wow, overnight success!" They don't realize it takes a long time.

Tamar: It takes all your life. You know, a lot of people weren't checking for me and thought that maybe I had missed my time. And I didn't give up on me and certainly God didn't give up on me. As long as I had those two people, myself and God, I knew I had a chance.

Abiola: What inspires you to keep going?

Tamar: When you have a dream that is set in your heart and in your mind you should never let it go. It's there for a reason.

Abiola: Thank you for being beautiful and passionate and being yourself. When people see you being yourself, it gives them the permission to be themselves.

Tamar: Everybody should be themselves. It took a while to figure out that this is what I'm supposed to do. I tried making everybody else happy. But I only win when I am myself. That works for me and works for everybody else too.

Bombshell Takeaways:

- You only win when you are yourself.

- When you appreciate and accept yourself at face value you can do the same for others.

- Being authentic means being vulnerable enough to fall publicly and keep shining.

Bombshell Dialogue with Jackie Collins: How to Be Your Own Goddess

Pop culture celebrates the beauty of young hotties, but a culture is only possible because of those who laid its foundations. The older woman has been devalued in our recent past. Thankfully, this is a new age, where wise, bodacious, and brazen senior bombshells like Diahann Carroll, Diana Ross, Joan Rivers, Betty White, Tina Turner, and Jane Fonda are refusing to go gently into the night. These women are showing us how to age with verve, sass, smarts, and sex appeal. I call them the OGs: the Original Goddesses. For this reason, I love having conversations with Jackie Collins. The word diva seems too small for the best-selling author. Jackie is legendary. She became internationally successful by weaving tales of intrigue with strong and authentic female characters.

Abiola: You say that "Reform School to Hollywood" will be the Jackie Collins memoir if you ever write one?

Jackie: Yes. I was thrown out of school, and my parents burnt my clothes. I was a punk way before punks and they said, "We can't take this any longer." This was back in London. We lived in a basement apartment and I would go out the window every night from thirteen until I was fifteen. My parents said, "Your sister is a movie star in Hollywood, so it's reform school or Hollywood. Which would you prefer?" And I went, "I think I'll take Hollywood." (laughing) And they put me on the plane.

Abiola: You must have been a handful of trouble.

Jackie: If I do my memoir I can't write the truth about what I used to do when I was thirteen, fourteen, and fifteen.

Abiola: Oh you have to, you must!

Jackie: I was too bad without going all the way, so use your imagination.

Abiola: What are your bad girl tips for recovering good girls? I consider myself a "recovering good girl." So many women are raised to be people pleasers, to be the nice girl, to be the good girl – to the detriment of ourselves.

Jackie: Well, so many people want everybody to like them. You can't go through life that way because everybody is not always going to like you. I'm on Twitter, so sometimes I get a really hateful tweet. I just get rid of them. I don't let it bother me because I realize that not everybody is going to like me.

My main character, Lucky Santangelo, when she first meets her husband, Lenny, she thinks, "He's cute." So she says, "Come up to my room." He comes up and she says, "We're going to have sex now," and he goes, "Huh?" She does things like a man does and she's like, "Don't call me; I'll call you." She's a single bachelor girl and for singular bachelor girls, trust me, that's how you should behave with men.

Abiola: A single bachelor girl – I love it. Very different from being a bachelorette.

Jackie: Exactly. Bachelorette, you get this picture of six girls in miniskirts that aren't even covering their bums lurking through Vegas.

Abiola: That's not true empowered sexuality.

Jackie: Exactly. I mean look at [your maxi dress]. You look fabulous today. Now if that was a really short skirt, you wouldn't look so fabulous because it would be cheesy. You look beautiful because you've got something out, something covered – and that's the secret.

Abiola: Well, I knew you would give a little bit of cleavage today, so I said, you know, we'll have a boobie-licious interview.

Jackie: Well, you look beautiful.

Abiola: Thank you, Jackie. I'm a lot of woman. I say I'm a life-sized woman.

Jackie: I went to a fashion show this week and all the girls looked like they were on heroin. They were "this size" and they were so drawn. I have this passion to photograph you because you look so great. I love that.

Abiola: I... (speechless)

Jackie: Pictures, photos... (makes flash sound)

Abiola: Now, you of course, are the queen of drop-dead beauty. What do you do to stay your Jackie Collins drop-dead beautiful self?

Jackie: You know, I was playing ping pong with Nate Berkus; that's one of my hobbies. Ping pong and swimming and I don't do anything else. My girlfriends and I go shopping on Saturday afternoons for all the lovely new creams. I can't be with the needles. I've seen all these women in Hollywood with the frozen faces. Creams don't cover everything, but so what? I like getting older. I love having experience on my face. I like my laugh lines

Abiola: You're stunning.

Jackie: Well, thank you. You should see me in the morning. (laughs) I just did something I shouldn't do, because I always tell my girlfriends when they receive a compliment, you just say, "thank you."

Abiola: Yes. Own it. Okay. We'll try it again.

Jackie: We'll do it again!

Abiola: Let's do a take two. Jackie?

Jackie: Yes?

Abiola: You look absolutely gorgeous.

Jackie: Thank you, so much! (laughs)

Abiola: See, ladies. That's how it's done.

Jackie: That's how it's done – yes.

Abiola: In the beginning men were furious about your work. They felt like you were...

Jackie: Attacking them personally! I know. When *The World is Full of Married Men* came out where the guy cheated on his wife for nine years, and then finally she did it back to him – with a rock star. After all, this was a Jackie Collins book. And he goes to his beautiful girlfriend and he says, "Claudia, I'm going to marry you because I'm leaving my wife." And she said, "I don't want to marry you. I just like sleeping with married men."

Abiola: Some men reacted like you killed someone.

Jackie: They were furious. There was one guy that took a half page in an English newspaper. He said, "This is the most shocking book I've ever read." All because I threw the double standard on its head. And I've been doing it ever since.

Abiola: Jackie, how do you define the word bombshell?

Jackie: Let's see, a bombshell … well, I had tea just before I left Beverly Hills with Raquel Welch. There is a bombshell. She looks amazing and she's so much fun. And she is a bombshell.

Abiola: There's a bombshell. And you are a bombshell. What do you think makes you a bombshell?

Jackie: I speak my mind. I'm not sitting here with you thinking, "What should I say next?" I'm just me. I think that's good for a woman to have confidence and be able to speak her mind.

Bombshell Takeaways:

- Living authentically means paving your own path.
- When someone gives you a compliment, accept with a gracious "thank you."
- The story of your life is written on your body – celebrate it!

Secret of Authenticity Resources

1. *Wreck This Journal* by Keri Smith

2. *Wild Feminine* by Tami Lynn Kent

3. *Share My Insanity: It Improves Everything* by Francesca De Grandis

4. "Questions I Ask When I Want to Talk About Myself" by Mindy Kaling (cards)

5. OwningPink.com, run by Dr. Lissa Rankin

Authenticity Affirmations

1. I am enough.

2. It feels good to be me.

3. I honor myself and rise into my shine.

4. I am worthy and deserving just the way I am.

5. I dare to dream bigger.

Eight

The Secret of Nizhoni: Beauty as a Spiritual Practice

The Sacred Feminine Law of Nizhoni

The Sacred Bombshell embraces beauty as a spiritual practice. She knows that at any moment she can make the decision to be beautiful or to enjoy beauty. This is Nizhoni. The bombshell need only rise to her true magnificence and step into her greatness. All beautifulness or ugliness she sees shines forth from her. The beauty she admires in others is the reflection of her own divine light. This is sacred self-love.

Historical Bombshell Mentor: Dr. Maya Angelou, born 1928

Author Maya Angelou has been a calypso singer, dancer, civil rights activist, filmmaker, and composer. She has been awarded the Presidential Medal of Arts and three Grammy awards. A true artiste, her work is not limited by societal expectations or labels. She teaches, "We delight in the beauty of the butterfly, but rarely admit the changes it has gone through to achieve that beauty." Well, Marguerite Ann Johnson went through changes to become Maya Angelou and her life is an example of beauty as a spiritual practice. The "caged bird" sings because it must. It would be depriving us all of too much beauty if it did otherwise.

The Nizhoni Declaration

I thought that I was seeking beauty but she was seeking me. I was convinced that pretty hid among the jars and potions on my dressing table but I was wrong. I thought that loveliness would appear on the scale and good looks in expensive labels, but I was mistaken.

I feared that beauty had forgotten my address but lo and behold! Beauty was here all along: riding the wave of my giggles, the curve of my hip, and the crinkle of my hair. Beauty embraces me; in the fleshy green of kiwis, in the vivid pinks of poppies, in the splashing azure of the waves. She was always with me because beauty is me.

This is a Sacred Bombshell's trip through the looking glass: I am a beautiful woman. I am the beloved mirror and the face who winks back. I am the rose and she who admires it. I respect my body temple. Being a noticer of beauty makes me more beautiful.

I awake to infinite possibilities, surrounded by beauty and the wealth of nature. I feel this beauty coursing through every cell of my being and I surround myself with her gifts. My abode reflects beauty's smile as do my dress and my actions. Pretty is as pretty does.

I thought that I was chasing beauty but she was chasing me. Waiting for me to open my eyes and embrace her. My beauty bursts forth and shines and she is everywhere. My skin glows; my curls blow; my words flow; my eyes know. I am a rare treasure and I treasure this beauty-filled planet. There is no need for conceit. My knowing attracts all I need. It feels good to embrace the beauty of the world. For this I am so grateful.

And so it is.

Beautiful Like You

In my woman-power, all-girls, liberal arts education, we were taught that physical beauty was frivolous. We were women of books and letters. Beauty was irrelevant. This led us to rebel by hiking our uniform skirts up as high as we could, peroxide-bleaching our hair, and wearing makeup like it was going out of style. Whatever you forbid a child, the child will most likely fetishize.

For me this meant trying to emulate some combo of Janet Jackson and Madonna. It also meant entering scholarship-based beauty pageants as soon as I could. Apparently I not only wanted to be pretty – I wanted to be named the most beautiful in all the land. And I was; I actually won a few titles in my day. I even used the lines from a Maya Angelou poem "Pretty woman wonder where my secret lies / cause I'm not cute or built to suit a fashion model size" in the talent portion of metropolitan Miss New York City in the Miss America pageant system circa 1995. I didn't win talent but I did win "Best Interview." That's because I am better at speaking than standing around being beautiful for the sake of it.

It doesn't matter what physical attributes you have, only that you know that you are beautiful. Play up what works for you – the things that make your beauty unique – and release the rest. Wear what beguiles you. Your beauty, although commodified, is not a commodity; it's an entity. Nature's own force. Roses don't shrink or play the background and neither should you. Enjoying our beauty has been dismissed as manipulative bewitchery or trickery because that's just how dynamite you are. Boom.

True feminine wiles are not about plastic beauty. Charm and charisma come from a sense of enjoying yourself and enjoying other people. Our beauty doesn't live in jars or salons. Beauty is not pre-packaged sexiness, designer vaginas, or self-hate rebranded as thinspiration. Even as a self-love coach, I would never say that there's only internal beauty and that external beauty doesn't matter or exist. External beauty, shine, glow is real. Look at how Mother Nature shows off outward beauty! What I am saying is that you are much more beautiful than you think you are.

Your beauty is exquisite in its uniqueness. Consider the way that fabulous drag queens revel in the play and power of beauty. How magnificent that you have been gifted with your unique face, body, scars, marks, and lines that say here I am, I have lived, I am living! Inhale the beauty and exhale the ugliness. Revel in your own beauty and the beauty of the Universe. Beauty is as beauty does so live as a testament to the wondrous beauty all around you.

The Sacred Feminine Power of Nizhoni

When an opportunity to visit the Grand Canyon arose I was indignant. This was not something I wanted to do. "It's grand and it's a freaking canyon," I argued. "What's to see?" As a "city girl," I would even need to buy jeans and sneakers to go because that was not a part of my skirts and stilettos repertoire.

I arrived at the Grand Canyon the next day, jonesing for the opportunity to be proven right about what a waste of time it was. Instantly, I was stopped in my tracks. The canyon that the Pueblo people call "Ongtupqa" in the Hopi language envelops you before you even get close. The air changes. The sound of the sky is new. A nature-made miracle stared back at me in mostly shades of red but also glints of green, gold, brown, violet, and blue. I started weeping uncontrollably.

"What's wrong?" my travel partner asked.

"It's the face of God," I said, still unable to stop crying. I was seduced and overwhelmed by its beauty.

Alice Walker explores the concept of Nizhoni in *The Color Purple* when she writes, "I think it pisses God off if you walk by the color purple in a field somewhere and don't notice it. People think pleasing God is all God cares about. But any fool living in the world can see It always trying to please us back." Yes, the force that created us has a vested interest in beauty and in our reverence and enjoyment of it. Nature's beauty is seductive as part of the evolutionary process. Beauty is in art, faces, places, and fields of purple flowers.

You deserve to drink in beauty as a spiritual practice on a daily basis. Make your living and work spaces lovely to behold. The way you prepare your food should be an act of beauty. Adorn your body with garments that make you feel divine. Visit libraries and museums that enrich you and let cultural beauty seep into your skin. Go hiking and admire the bold elegance of Mother Nature's beauteous creatures. Enjoy lush flora and sunsets. Gaze upon the still surface of a lake and see your own unique visage and one-of-a-kind beauty. This beauty, my Sacred Bombshell, is a living force. This is Nizhoni, the full love of all things beautiful. Beauty is truly divine.

You are beautiful. How can I say that without even seeing you? Because I have yet to meet an ugly woman who is turned on and tuned in to her radiance. Each of us has the capacity to be our most bombshell beautiful at any moment.

Bombshell Challenge: Go on a beauty-finding expedition in your neighborhood. Collect beautiful objects like stones, acorns, and fallen ribbons. Leave the walkway more beautiful than you found it by disposing of garbage that others have carelessly left strewn about. Turn the "garbage" into found art if the beauty muses strike!

Bombshell Confidential: Pimp Your Pretty

Jackie Collins taught me one of the most important lessons I've ever learned about physical beauty. Women in business are told to embrace our brains and forget our beauty. Jackie warned me not to leave my beauty behind. She said, "You're very beautiful. You are also very smart but be sure you take full advantage of that beauty!" This was shocking, raw, taboo – and great advice. In other words, enjoy your beauty as a tool in your arsenal. If you don't think that men enjoy their charisma as a part of their toolbox, think again.

My Big Fat Bombshell Diary: Beauty Acts of Stupidity

A beauty act of a stupidity stems from the idea that you have to suffer for beauty. I was taught this as a kid sitting in Miss Headley's kitchen getting my hair straightened with a hot comb. The combs were heated in the flames of her gas stove. I watched the fires lick the angry teeth, then she would pick up the sizzling comb and test the heat by singeing a paper towel. She would then pull the iron comb through my hair, often burning the edges of my ears and the nape of my neck.

"You have to suffer for beauty," she would say as she pressed my fluffy, curly, coily locks into limp, relaxed submission. We even made up a song in her Queens, New York, kitchen back in the 80s about how "when I'm finished you'll be able to shake it like your father is white!" After she straightened my hair she gave me more acceptable curls than the ones I had been born with – Shirley Temple curls. Then we would sing, "shake it like my father is whi–ite!" as I shook my new straighter, bouncier curls from side to side.

Know this: Even self-love coaches are prone to committing beauty acts of stupidity. Last year I got "permanent" eyelash extensions done at a chic downtown salon. I lay back like I was receiving a facial and the practitioner taped my eyes shut. If that wasn't a clue that this was a terrible idea, I don't know what could have been. She then glued long, lush movie star-worthy lashes onto my eyelids. The next morning and every morning for the next three or four weeks, my eyes were swollen, puffy, and somewhat glued shut when I awoke, although I've had temporary lashes done for photo shoots and TV many times with no issues.

Did my Inner Wise Woman shout that semi-permanent lashes might be a bad idea for someone who wears contacts lenses and has severe allergies, carpets, and a Sacred Bombshell kitty cat named Miss Anabelle? Of course. But who wants to listen to that boring, cautious old biddy? I wanted fluttering butterfly lashes.

It is a woman's right to do what she wishes with her own body. So if super-glued lashes work for you, go for it! It was just a beauty act of stupidity for me. And yes, it turns out that they actually do use a form of super glue. I ended up with fewer natural lashes than I started with!

You Are Never "Too Fat for Love"

"What is fundamentally beautiful is compassion for yourself and for those around you. That kind of beauty enflames the heart and enchants the soul."
—Lupita Nyong'o

At my highest weight I was racked with food allergies, pre-diabetic, no longer fitting into my clothes, and extremely unhappy with my lethargic body. I believe in bi-individuality, meaning that there are women who can be healthy at every size. Unfortunately, I am not one of them and my body rebelled. Nonetheless, I was beautiful and 1,000% worthy of being loved.

My Afro-Caribbean culture prefers a more zaftig female form. I've had more friends and family members comment on my weight now than when I was using food as a drug, seriously overweight, and compromising my health. They say, "Don't lose another pound. Do you eat? You look malnourished." I love my healthy body and can't "weight" for people to learn that the bodies of women, no matter the size, are not on display for public commentary.

I was watching a **Roseanne** rerun recently, and there was a touching scene between the comic and the over-the-top actress who played her mother. The mom talked about how she taught Roseanne to "feel better" about her problems by eating. "Did you teach me any other ways to feel better, Mom?" Roseanne asked. The character, and maybe the actress herself, was an emotional eater. I am intimately familiar.

The last "acceptable" prejudice is fat hatred. It's been a while since supermodel Tyra Banks instructed her detractors to "Kiss [her] fat ass." Since that time, Howard Stern insulted the body size of lovely, Oscar-worthy actress Gabby Sidibe. Model Kate Upton also felt the effects of bullying from women bloggers for not being a size zero. Some fashion mags reportedly hire skinny models and accentuate their bodies with Photoshopped curves.

Voluptuous Kirstie Alley admitted to feeling too fat for love, sex, and a relationship. After dancing her way into a more fit body on ABC's **Dancing with the Stars**, the actress revealed that she had been celibate because she "did not want to have fat sex." Kirstie told **People Magazine** that she is finally ready to find love because now she likes what she sees in the mirror.

In my coaching practice, I find that many women feel the same way. We all want to feel our best when we're naked with a partner but to deprive yourself of joy, pleasure, and love because of your body image issues is self-neglect. Just because your body is not your ideal does not mean that you don't deserve a relationship or to feel sexual or sensual. Any partner you're with should love you through the body's changes and fluctuations.

Let's focus on saluting our real beauty instead of the pre-packaged, one-size-fits-all generic look that is forced upon us. Whether you are a size two or a size thirty-two, you are a living, breathing human being worthy of loving and being loved.

Bombshell Exploration: Five Ways to Live Nizhoni

1. **Make your environment sing with Nizhoni.** Your home should be a place where you see love, peace, and beauty reflected in every corner. **Make a Nizhoni board that** reflects everything beautiful you encounter from that fading and imperfect daisy to that picture of a perfect pirouette.

2. **Makeup-free Mondays.** In the book *Mirror Mirror Off the Wall*, author Kjerstin Gruys went without looking into a mirror for a year and also enacted "Makeup-free Mondays." Do you dare? There is nothing inherently wrong with makeup, hair extensions, and other adornment. I love them! Dressing up is fun self-expression. However, if you can't appear publicly and feel good in your skin without these extras, this is something to think about. Revel in your natural beauty. Make a collage of your most beautiful moments.

3. **Inner beauty makeover.** Beliefs like "I am ugly" and "Others aren't attracted to women like me" have to be dissolved on a core level. Try a thought-interrupting method such as EFT to dismantle negative beliefs about yourself. Good self-care is not just manicures, pedicures, and massages. It's getting help for yourself if you need it. It's reminding yourself that you are worthy. That's how to be a good girlfriend to yourself.

4. **Spread the love.** Share your beautiful thoughts about yourself and other women instead of your scornful ones. Criticism is an act of violence against the self and others. Make your body a criticism-free zone and refrain from critiquing other women's bodies.

5. **An ode to your own beauty.** Write a self-praise poem about your physical beauty. I'm not talking about how pretty you are or the way other people see you. Pay tribute to the way you see you. If you're not "there" yet, write about how you would like

to see yourself. Don't get caught up in iambic pentameter or trying to rhyme. Seeing yourself the way that the Universe sees you is inherently poetic.

Bombshell Tool: The Body Map

The Body Map is a healing tool that I use with women to find the beauty in our bodies. Begin by writing an autobiography of your body – the history of each of your body parts. Then create a life-sized self-portrait traced around your body that includes collaged items that represent the memories your body holds and how you feel about your body parts. Find full instructions at SacredBombshell.com.

My Big Fat Bombshell Diary: My Beautiful Body

"Make your future dream a present fact by assuming the feeling of a wish fulfilled."
—Neville Goddard

A few years ago I started setting intentions instead of resolutions. My main "New Year's Intention" one year was to finally gift myself with the strong, healthy, and fit body that I deserve. I improved my cardio fitness by 70%. I shed unhealthy fat and released 55 pounds and eight sizes. I am on a healthy nutritional journey and working out almost every day.

In late 2008, after I was cancelled out of hosting my BET show *The Best Shorts* (a short film competition), I received an offer to be a participant in the first season of a reality matchmaker show. Simon & Schuster had published my popular debut novel *Dare*. I had already directed my award-winning feminist art films *Stranded*, *Knives in My Throat*, and *Afrodite Superstar*. I even had a national advice column in the weekly urban newspaper *Rolling Out*. So why would I go on reality TV? A number of reasons. Sure, I'd hosted shows and been a lifestyle correspondent for HBO and NBC, but the reality TV gig seemed like a good way to publicize my book and empowerment work to a greater audience. It sounded fun and at worst like possible fodder for a future book about love.

One of the few genuine "reality TV" experiences happened on my first day shooting, booting me right out of the self-created character that I was excited to play. Behind the scenes I was bragging to my castmates that I was a "life-sized woman" and proud of it. I was at least 170 pounds at the time. Our first assignment was to parade around a pool while three average-looking guys gave their first impressions. To paraphrase, all of the guys basically said that I was fat – cute, but fat. The character full of bravado and moxie that I was focused on portraying went right out the window!

Fat?! I was definitely bigger than all of the other cast members, but I had never, ever had a man consider me FAT and therefore undesirable before. Despite the matchmaker theme of the show, I had a boyfriend waiting for me at home – and so did almost all of my castmates. Yes, I was bigger than my usual size, but my motto was, "I am proud to take up space in the world." For the beauty challenge on the same show, I even posed with cupcakes to represent the fact that alluring women come in all sizes.

So what happened next? I burst out crying! I felt awful and humiliated, but why? I was not fat. So why was I crying? I realized that somewhere inside I had to believe what they were saying – that I was not good enough. The fact is that even if I *was* fat, which is subjective, I didn't deserve to be judged by a group of random men. But that's exactly what I'd signed up for and subjected myself to!

The last time I had felt so judged and uncomfortable in my own skin was when I was one of a handful of black girls in a predominantly white all-girls school at a time before certain celebrities made my "bootylicious" body type desirable in the mainstream. The experience reminded me of seventh or eighth grade when my friends attempted to create a dating club with our neighboring all-boys school. We sent them a folder of profiles and descriptions of ourselves and awaited their responses. This was pre-Internet! When we received the package back, one boy had written under dislikes "brown nipples." Even though no one was getting near my nipples for years to come I felt deeply flawed and humiliated.

Months later when the reality show aired, African-American women on message boards were up in arms that I would dare cry in response to feeling hurt. "She should have punched them in the face," they said. "Why would she cry?" How easily we pigeonhole each other based on race and gender as to what "appropriate" reactions should be!

I didn't care about the jackasses on the show, but I repeat: The fact that I was crying means that subconsciously I agreed with their low thoughts of me – that I was unworthy. As adults, no one can belittle us EVER without our agreement and permission.

Your body size has nothing to do with your happiness or desirability. No matter what, you deserve to be happy. I dropped 20 pounds easily while at the reality TV house, mostly because we weren't allowed to have alcohol. Yes, those weekly cocktails add up. In addition, my food allergies were raging at the time so I couldn't eat dairy or food from my local takeout spots when I came home without breaking out in hives.

Fast-forward two years. I had regained that 20 pounds and much more. This time, I was just back from taping the MTV series *MADE*. I was on the show as a Teen Dating Empowerment Coach, transforming a sweet, insecure high school kid into a positive and confident "ladies man." For the six weeks that I was alone in Atlanta, I sat in my hotel room between shoots eating fattening Chinese food and pre-packaged diet program meals. I wasn't dashing around and burning calories naturally like I did in NYC because in Georgia I had to be driven everywhere. My body read the new and unfamiliar situation as an emotionally unsafe experience and I packed on a wall of protection.

When I came home, I was clearly fat and I spent the year getting fatter. I have a sugar addiction plus I'm a desk potato – a detrimental combination. I also have the body type that, for better or worse, hides weight well. As I taped episodes of my web series, it became harder for Kristal, my producer and soul sister, to shoot and edit around my body image issues. In addition to my growing health issues, I had a double chin, pudgy arms, and a belly – things that I wanted hidden through camera angles, creative distraction, fashion choices, and editing.

One summer day we shot three webisodes: an interview with *Cosby* actor Doug E. Doug, an overview of my Goddess Year Program for single women, and a wine tasting. It was a great day until I saw the footage. I hated how I looked as a tried to hide my girth in a sleeveless fur jacket. Did I mention that it was summer? I couldn't lie to myself anymore. Still, I continued to gain weight. The issue felt beyond my control as my worry caused me to eat even more.

Because I had long ago declared that "I love myself unconditionally" and "I enjoy who I am," I had fallen into denial about my weight gain and my emotional eating. In other words, my healthy positive thoughts of myself were actually blocking me from acknowledging how unhealthy my weight gain was. I was in fat denial. Someone asked me, "Have you ever been fat-fat?" (Whatever that means.) You don't have to be morbidly obese to be at an unhealthy weight for your height and body type, and I have a number of conditions in my immediate gene pool – from diabetes to joint issues to hypertension – that I need to head off at the healthy pass.

I'm a beautiful woman, as are you. Beauty had nothing to do with it the fact that my body was rebelling. I had constant outbreaks from food allergies and was ridiculously out of breath walking to the subway. I had gotten to the point where I couldn't comfortably wear my clothes. Sure, wearing a bigger size and being cute made it easy to dismiss the problem, but I deserve perfect health. I also had sleep apnea and acid reflux and had to come to terms with the fact that I had always been an emotional eater. This was an undiagnosed eating disorder. Let me repeat: Emotional eating is an eating disorder, and a form of self-mutilation. You are escaping into the plate. It is an act of violence against the self to eat unhealthy foods until you feel comfortably numb. Bingeing into a food coma will get you out of feeling angry, scared, and sad. Unfortunately, it will also keep you from feeling blissful, relaxed, and confident.

How much did I love me if I didn't permit myself the basic

human function of feeling? How much love was I giving myself if I wasn't feeding myself with healthy, homemade food instead of emotional carb-loading? How much was I loving myself if I wouldn't work out? As my father always says, "The body is our temple on earth and we only get one. We have to take care of it." We don't have to be perfect; we just have to love ourselves inside and out.

I now knew I had a problem and I promised myself every day to make changes. I tried a well-known diet and gained weight. I worked with a wellness coach and took none of her advice. The evidence that my situation was dire was mounting. A jarring wake-up call came when my doctor told me that she couldn't properly examine my abdomen because I had too much belly fat. Then there I was in *ESSENCE* magazine with a double chin. In the shower, I now had an underbelly to wash. My very sweet producer on a TV talk show told me confidentially that my tummy was poking out on camera. I had dressed thinking I was going to be sitting on the show but I was standing. My outfit that would have looked great with my legs crossed to hide my tummy made me look pregnant when I was standing.

This was all compounded by the fact that in my culture it is acceptable to stay stuck in an unhealthy body. A recent survey revealed that black women weigh more but have higher self-esteem than other groups. We also carry body fat differently as per another study in *ESSENCE*. This is not a judgment on anyone else. I am talking about what was unhealthy for me. If my lifestyle of eating junk and being sedentary was working, I would have had a fit, strong, healthy body.

Years earlier I had accompanied a friend to an overeater's recovery group. Although I could relate and shared the issues discussed, the program wasn't for me at the time. I was not ready yet, but the biggest moment for me was the meeting leader saying, "Your own best thinking got you here." I had been able to achieve success on my timetable in many other areas. It was time to rise and shine – for me. My own best thinking had gotten me there and as I had been telling other women, "How you do anything is how you do everything."

What if there was something else to believe? What if I could see this differently? I refused to diet again because I had regained and lost 20 pounds repeatedly with that method. Diets don't work. Instead, I began my recovery with intuitive eating, did research on nutrition, developed a self-love fitness program, made lifestyle changes, and started a wellness journey.

So much changed after I released the pounds in a healthy way. I no longer get out of breath going down the stairs. I don't feel sick after every meal anymore. I eat clean and plant-based, mostly vegan with about 20% vegetarian, raw in the summertime. We all deserve our healthiest bodies. My physical insides – heart, lungs, stomach, and kidneys – deserve to live beautifully, too.

Bombshell Exploration: Make Your Bedroom a Beautiful Boudoir

Practice Nizhoni by making your bedchamber a place of loveliness. This is the place where you dream, relax, are physically and emotionally naked, make love, and reflect. Your bedroom is a reflection of your self-devotion. Walking into your sacred space should feel like a treat for the senses of smell, sight, and sound.

Your boudoir should be a clean and clutter-free sanctuary. If your bedroom doesn't make you feel enchanted then you've got work to do. Are you welcomed by art when you enter? Does the color scheme make you feel enveloped, warm, and safe? Are your sheets soft to the touch? Are your walls and windows wrapped with beauty? How many memories, good and bad, are lurking under your bed and in the corners? Clear the old to make room for the new. Perhaps add an altar and soul-nourishing books.

Are electronics beeping digital energy at every turn? Remove the TV hub and computer center. If you live in a studio space, cover your TV and computer with sumptuous fabric and create sacred zones.

Whether you are coupled up or single and wanting a relationship, your bedroom is not a boudoir until it seems welcoming for a twosome. Singlistas, if "the one" showed up tomorrow, do you have room? Be sure that everything from the pillow and end tables to the artwork reflects twoness. Your boudoir should feel inviting to both yin and yang energy.

Bombshell Dialogue with Amel Larrieux: How to Face What You've Been Running From

"In the miracle that is this / Beautiful emotion / Life is breathing with us." So sings "Bravebird" Amel Larrieux. Audiences have long been passionate about the songstress's expressive and natural style. The poetic performer burst onto the scene as one half of the neo-soul group Groove Theory in the 90s and music has not been the same since. Amel's latest album is called *Ice Cream Everyday*. I spoke to her in the summertime in NYC, on stage at the magnificent Highline Ballroom. Amel was ethereal and had her yoga mat in tow, ready to share her favorite moves and photos of her lovely daughters. Behind the scenes, her supportive husband orchestrated everything for her comfort. Amel says that you know the fire has begun when gems fall from your tongue. There goes another sapphire…

Abiola: Amel, I'm so excited that you're here.

Amel: I am too and it's not every day where you get to have this kind of exchange. I believe in sisterhood. I am already feeling it. I just met you and I feel it.

Abiola: I do too and sisterhood is so important. We are a reflection and you can't love yourself if you are outwardly criticizing and hating others.

Amel: The thing that I remember hearing and it not really clicking until I became an adult and started to experience stuff: the idea that if you don't love yourself, you can't really love someone else. It means that it will be a dysfunctional love if you don't get right with yourself. It's a big reason why I had to start a serious meditation practice. Because here I am, forty, but in my thirties the whole trip had been like all those things I spent my life running away from. It hit me because of my daughters and that kind of experience, whoa, the catharsis there is another story. It makes you either look at yourself really hard or run the other way and mess up their lives. So you kind of have to deal with it.

Abiola: We're the same age and I feel like that's one of the gifts of aging: being able to look at your life in a very real way and find solutions. Your mother Brenda Dixon Gottschild is a scholar in her own right; an author and a dance critic. How was it growing up in a family of artists?

Amel: Well, she was a single mom pretty much and in my early childhood, getting her Ph.D. and my pubescent and teen years, doing it all. She's taught yoga for over twenty years. It wasn't part of my experience with her because she was just trying to always provide for me. I grew up in a very artsy community. I danced for the first twelve years of my life and everybody thought that I was going to be a ballerina.

Abiola: How did you find your voice?

Amel: I'd always written and sung songs. My mom spent a lot of time recording me and she has recordings of me like when I'm eighteen months old, [creating] songs.

Abiola: What a gift to you; that your mother honored your work in that way. Groove Theory was such a juggernaut and in many ways you were innovators.

Amel: We were not even aware of it. And I still feel like "Oh, I don't know if you should say that." I'm still learning to honor what I do. That's probably a bit of a habitual thing. Like, to put myself down, to say, "Oh no…" But I also feel like I'm such a product of these incredible artists that I was influenced by. I know that there is a piece of Amel that's within my creative expression. But I feel like so much of it is just an amalgamation of Stevie [Wonder] and Jimi [Hendrix] and John Lennon and Joni

[Mitchell] and [John] Coltrane and Ella [Fitzgerald] and all the people that were so great.

Abiola: Understood; but we are about owning it because right now a young woman is saying: "I'm an amalgamation of Amel Larrieux and Erykah Badu and Lauryn Hill."

Amel: I get it. (smiles)

Abiola: How do you juggle life as a creative person who also owns her own business?

Amel: Well fortunately for me I'm married to a person who can do that really well. I don't have that gene. But Laru, my husband, who produced the music on all the solo albums I've done and is my manager ... he runs the business side of Blisslife. It's kind of lovely the way our positions have kind of fallen together that way. We make an effort to be a team.

Abiola: And you're raising daughters together, which is the most important job on the planet.

Amel: I don't understand how people say that mothers who decide to stay at home, that it's not career, that it's not a job.

Abiola: That is the most important job.

Amel: And the hardest. When you clock out, that's when stuff happens. In one hour you can be completely filled with joy and pride, which is another story altogether, cause it's all just ego and you don't need that but these high, high emotions and then be brought right down to complete anger, sadness, or all this other stuff. It's all about knowing how to be in that gracefully.

Abiola: Can you share what yoga has meant to you?

Amel: My firstborn is eighteen now, almost nineteen. Two years after I had her, I started having episodes that were panic attacks. I thought I was dying, having heart attacks. Then I started having episodes of vomiting. And what I was diagnosed with is a medical condition and I would have these episodes and they would all be connected. First a panic attack and later on I'd be sick all night. And after I had my second child, four years later, and they continued on and I just knew I could not be a parent to two kids and be literally falling apart every time something scary happened with one of them. I would just start shaking and then have an attack.

I had an amazing OB/GYN with my second birth who said to me, "We can put you on medication or I can teach you pranayama." And that's how I came into the world of yoga. I started out with breathing and I started a meditation practice. Very devoted. And I started cultivating a yoga practice around trying to balance my nerves and my stress and my anxiety and my panic and so I came to the physical part of it later on.

And that's maybe why yoga feels like something so precious and personal to me. Because it really had to do with me getting better. In the last five months I started Emotional Freedom Technique – tapping. I have a tapping therapist and I work with her. That was the next level of transformation. It saved me, it saved my life, literally.

Abiola: Thank you so much for sharing that. These techniques have saved my life as well.

Amel: I think it all starts with a breath. Every day I practice Kundalini yoga and it is centered around the breath of fire which does amazing things for your hormone balance, for your blood pressure, for clearing out toxicity from drug abuse. It helps with lower back pain. Oxygen aids the blood flow. So this is something that I do also when I'm tired and I need energy. It's like a cup of coffee. The breath of fire is very basic. But you can do it in your car when you're feeling tired or before you go into a meeting.

So it's all about on the inhale you expand and on the exhale you blow out. It's all through your nose with your mouth closed. And you can do it slowly and you progress into quicker breaths. We'll do an inhale and we'll do an exhale about a third of the way out. It's noisy breathing, so you can make noise.

Abiola: There's power in just awareness. Once we're able to just be aware; even just being able to observe ourselves and observe our behavior, in that by itself there is just so much.

Amel: When I learned that, then it made my meditation practice the best. I didn't master meditation, but that's when it made it get really good and juicy. First I was trying for something. The whole idea that the practice of yoga and meditation isn't the doing. It's the balance of being and not doing.

Abiola: Yes! What makes you a bombshell, Amel?

Amel: Well I would say this: I am a woman on the road to owning herself. And that I have been able to give myself. I think I can honor myself in saying that I want desperately to own myself and love myself. And I am aware of that … and aware of that journey. So there are little places where I catch myself and I never did that before. So that's all part of it; baby steps.

Bombshell Takeaways:

- Be open to exploring healing modalities that you might not have considered.
- There is power and responsibility in choosing to be a mother and a wife.
- Learning to love ourselves is a process.

Bombshell Dialogue with Sheena LaShay: How to Take Back the Night and Your Voice

Aim your smile at the sun. We're in for a beauty-filled soul empowerment class with Sheena LaShay. Sheena is a "pole activist," keynote speaker, writer, creative artist, and portrait and boudoir photographer. She is also a member of the Rape, Abuse, and Incest National Network (RAINN) Speakers Bureau. Before this conversation, I came across her name three times. I first encountered her byline on the Owning Pink website. Then I was researching the Sanskrit word and principal *bodhicitta* and found her kickass blog. The third "coincidence" was that I was invited to cover Match.com's Single in America event and couldn't go because of a deadline. I did a search to see how it went, and there Sheena was. Clearly it was time for us to talk.

Abiola: Sheena, if I didn't know your personal history I would think, "This empowered woman obviously had a great life the whole time that she's been alive." Please share your story.

Sheena: I am the survivor of childhood sexual abuse that began when I was seven years old, and it continued for seven years by my ex-stepfather. So while I had on one hand a pretty normal childhood – school, playing Barbie, and friends – for most of my childhood I was also being sexually abused. This was within the bubble of a church that knew about it and demanded my silence. Once I went into high school I tried to pursue a court case. He confessed and never served a day in jail. That made things even worse because I had trust issues with family, with church, and with the justice system.

By the time I went to college I was depressed, suicidal. I had an eating disorder. I couldn't emotionally connect with people. I was very controlling and manipulative and had PTSD and I was paranoid. After I graduated from college I realized I was either going to die because of alcoholism or depression or I could try something different. I reached rock bottom. I'd gone even further than bottom and I went on a personal journey to change myself.

Abiola: In the direct aftermath of this abuse, during your teen years, did you have any adult advocates?

Sheena: When my mother found out about the abuse she stood by me. She never questioned the validity of my story. When things were at their worst and we were shunned by our community, my mother packed up me and my other siblings. She didn't have a dollar to her name because she was a stay-at-home mom. She left him and we were living in someone's one-room attic until she could get back on her feet.

Abiola: All power to great mothers. Why was the church so adamant about protecting your stepfather?

Sheena: He was a deacon. He was also my Sunday School teacher. He was a leader in a number of different ministries. I found out years later that I wasn't the only one where the church kind of kept all the bad things that were happening quiet.

Abiola: When you were trying to just lean toward the light, how did you do that, Sheena?

Sheena: I believe, whether it's the small voice inside of you or whatever it is, it's something in your gut, your intuition. Sometimes that voice is very, very tiny and it's like when a kitten can't fully meow because it's such a baby versus a lion that can growl. That voice within us, for each person, is at a different level. At that point when I was at my worst, it was barely there. But it was still there.

I went to a conservative religious school. After graduation was the first time I could make all of my choices. Even at school, I had to sign a covenant which outlined behavior and what I believed about the world. This was the first real time I could make decisions [about] what I wanted to believe. I could choose what I wanted to think.

The other part was that around that time my ex-stepfather had bought a house. And he'd gone on vacation. He was living his life. And it pissed me off that I was at bars every night hovering over Jack Daniels, sobbing and depressed, and he was in Jamaica on the beach having a great time. I was so sick of crying and giving him the responsibility for my life. Yes, he victimized me as a child but at this point I was choosing to stay a victim. And I just didn't want to do that anymore.

I knew that it wasn't going to be one thing that would "fix me." I also knew it was going to be painful. I think sometimes people believe "when I get my empowerment and claim my life again, it's going to be amazing. I'm going to feel good." First, to remove whatever it is that harmed you, there's going to be some pain in that process. When you heal from a crash and you're going through rehabilitation, it's painful, too. But the difference is that it's a healing thing, and it's not a dying thing. I went to therapy. I would journal. I found support groups online and in person. Whatever felt good, whatever made me feel more alive, I moved more toward it.

Abiola: That's such beautiful advice. It's not like suddenly you wake and up feel great, because you don't have access to that. It's trying to feel a just a smidge better than you felt yesterday. Sometimes it's in five-minute increments, feeling a little bit better than you just felt. What does it mean to be a pole activist?

Sheena: I moved to New York about four years ago, and I wanted to meet people and try new things. So I was always on Groupon looking for activities and events. And there was one for a pole dancing class. I said, "I'll go by myself and see if I like it. If I don't, I can leave after five minutes." I went and loved it, and it's four years later. Now, along with calling myself a pole dancer, I am a pole activist. And by that I mean I believe that movement and dance is a huge part of being human.

We have bodies and they work in motion. I believe that movement and dance, to be engaged with your senses, can help us find our truth. It can help set us free. Things that are locked within the body can be touched and healed through movement and specifically with pole because it has a connotation of sensuality and sexuality. For some people that's a negative thing but for me, that's a great thing because that's inherent to being human.

Abiola: Somatic therapy – body-oriented therapy – is critical because we have this separation from our bodies. Like the mind is up here and the body is down there. There's so much power in just physically inhabiting our bodies. There's cellular memory, memories we are unaware of that we hold in our bodies. How do you define spiritual eroticism?

Sheena: You can be sensual, which is at its base engaging your senses and just being present and aware. And your movements can also be sexual and suggestive. But I think there is also this deeper level that connects us to whether you believe in God or whatever your Higher Power is or just knowing that everything is comprised of energy and we're all connected. It's just the juicy bits of life, that energy, that inner siren, that erotic creature that's in you and gives life to everything.

To add that into your spirituality and your daily living practice, to use that energy and breathe it in and out – that's important to me. Especially considering [how] we've repressed this, especially in women. Growing up in a church, in a conservative home, it was like, "Don't you dare think about your body. Don't you dare think about men or sex. And don't you dare think that this connects to your higher purpose in life." It actually is all connected.

Abiola: Yes, life force energy! Do you feel that pole dancing can be an empowering and healing practice for other survivors of different kinds of abuse?

Sheena: It definitely can. It's not just pole dancing. It's sensual movement. So sometimes in a class I don't even touch a pole, but maybe I'm on the floor and rolling around. It helped me get even more in touch with my body and to find the joy there. Because we feel like our bodies are these broken things, and we're ashamed of what happened to them or maybe you have physical scars.

I was in this room and the lights were low and there were no mirrors. And the teacher was just telling me to do what felt good to me. I had two hours to just focus on what pleased me. No one was watching me and telling me how I needed to behave. I wasn't broken. I was just this gorgeous woman simmering in her pleasure. That was such a huge thing for me even just having the safety in that room. Because a lot of people don't have a safe place to go. And it was so important for me, knowing that I have this sanctuary with other like-minded people encouraging me.

Abiola: The power of community. Let's talk *bodhicitta*.

Sheena: Well, I first came upon this term reading a Pema Chodron book. What I've taken is that it's about being present, about having focus, about learning to breathe in the darkness and breathe out light. It was so freeing.

Abiola: I first encountered *bodhicitta* writing about beauty as a spiritual practice, which relates to ***When Things Fall Apart*** and what Pema Chodron writes about. But beauty as a spiritual practice is how I would describe your work as well. Would you find that to be an accurate term?

Sheena: I would and it's so funny. I think a year ago I would have balked at that because I used to have such a problem with the word "beauty" whereas now I think that is very accurate to my life and the work that I do.

Abiola: It's so interesting that you say you would have balked at that because you capture other women's beauty as a photographer and you are emanating your own beauty. Why was that word was so charged for you?

Sheena: I think because I was being immature. When I heard the word "beauty," I would think fashion and makeup and pretty dresses and while I love those things, they're just things. The other part was because I think the value in beauty can be assigned however you want it to be. I think it's very deep-rooted and ingrained and it emanates from within you, but it's also however you assign that value to it. A lot of the people I encounter have so many hang ups about beauty like, "I don't feel beautiful." I'm like, "Because you're choosing that." So the word was so hard for me to even take in because so many other people had such a hard time seeing it in themselves.

Abiola: Well, do you now feel comfortable with your own beauty? Do you know now how beautiful you are?

Sheena: Oh, I could – see I'm blushing a little. But yes. I have to get used to the word. It's not something I would say [in] my everyday life, but I do agree with you! (giggles)

Abiola: All it takes is a willingness. Sheena, what makes you a bombshell?

Sheena: Oh, my goodness, because I'm awesome.

Abiola: Yeah!

Sheena: Well, I don't apologize when I walk into a room. I understand my power and I understand my beauty and my potency. I live in it and I exude it and I don't downplay myself. I understand my worth and my value and I believe in it. Because of that, it emanates in every part of my life. I just revel in what pleases me. I love exploring passion and just engaging sensually in the world and being present. It just stirs up some wonderfulness. That's what makes me a bombshell. And because I'm sexy and awesome. That's important, too.

Abiola: Yay! New affirmation: "I am sexy and awesome."

Bombshell Takeaways:

- Even when you can't find your voice, it's there.
- Engage the body as well as the mind to awaken the spirit and find your truth.
- Joy is a choice, as is suffering.

Secret of Nizhoni Resources

1. *A Gift of Love* by Deepak Chopra (audio)
2. *The Beauty Blueprint* by Michelle Phillips
3. *The Rosary* by Immaculée Ilibagiza
4. *The Body Book* by Cameron Diaz
5. Afrobella.com, run by Patrice Grell Yursik

Nizhoni Affirmations

1. All the beauty I see is a reflection of me.
2. It feels good being so beautiful.
3. I notice nature's beauty wherever I am.
4. Life is beautiful.
5. I create beauty; every day in every way.

Nine

The Secret of Releasing: Setting Yourself Free

The Sacred Feminine Law of Releasing

The Sacred Bombshell liberates herself by letting go. She lives in an abundant world so she feels no desperation to clutch. She is unattached to expectations and traveling light. She has the courage to slough off the old in exchange for the power of possibilities. She releases the past, lets go of what does not work, and sheds the excess. She is free. This is sacred self-love.

Historical Bombshell Mentor: Jane Fonda, born 1937

Septuagenarian Jane Fonda is showing women how to age un-apologetically. She writes and speaks out about letting go of what others think of her and releasing what no longer serves her. Born Lady Jayne and raised as Hollywood royalty, she made her own mark. Besides being an acclaimed actress, the activist and author tells Britain's **Hello! Magazine** that she is having the sexiest time in her life. She has also become more spiritual, saying on her site, "Religion and feminism are different expressions of the same impulse toward making life more just and whole." Staying on the leading edge, Fonda has created an online community to connect to her tribe.

The Releasing Declaration

Today, I release all things I no longer need. I release what is for what might be. Letting go is part of the cycle of life. I travel lighter, baggage-free. I no longer clutch desperately to what is defunct because I have faith in the abundance of the Universe. I am excited to see how the vacuum left behind is filled when I release old energy, things, people, and resentments.

Harmony is the song of my life played with the instrument of balance and heard on the notes of synchronicity. I reap and sow. I ebb and flow. I receive and release. I fast and I feast. I play and I work. I awake each day and go to bed each night with a clear picture of myself: vibrant, healthy, and well-nourished. And when the time comes I easily let go.

I let go. I shed, detoxify, de-clutter, and empty to make room for me. I will crawl until I can walk. I will walk until I can run. I will run until I can leap. I will leap until I can fly, and I will release that which no longer serves me.

As I release I will feed my soul and nourish my spirit. I listen to my aches, pains, and whispers rather than trying to silence them. When I listen carefully, I know what is needed. I feel peaceful and harmonious when I treasure myself. For this I am so grateful.

And so it is.

My Big Fat Bombshell Diary: Letting Go

A few years ago, I had the most grace-filled letting go experience. My ex, Henry, and I had become great platonic friends and on a summer's day he invited me to the park and asked my "permission" to marry his girlfriend. It was such a beautiful and healing gesture. Of course he didn't need my permission to do anything. We were separate citizens leading separate lives with the care that people reserve for once-close relatives. I wanted him to be in love and happy. He wanted the same for me. His graciousness was kind and heart-mending because it reminded me that I was not temporarily insane when I chose to marry him. He is a good and decent man. I told him I was happy for him and said a silent prayer for his joy and marital success.

He then asked me how my love life was going and, confession, I lied through my teeth. I just couldn't bring myself to admit while he was sharing his happy ending that I was still creating mine. A year later, unfortunately, we had a big disagreement over his apartment. I was still renting his bachelor pad and, NYC real estate being what it is, had no immediate plans to move. I suggested that we meet to chat and resolve the issue and he coldly responded that his new wife wouldn't appreciate that. He also said that I was "mistaking his kindness for weakness." There had never been any illicit ex trysts or post-breakup sexy energy between us; we were like brother and sister at that point. Now this dude I grew up with, shared air with since sixth grade was no longer allowed to be around me?!

Even though we were no longer close, in that moment I felt I'd lost my friend. The volatility and meanness of the exchange devastated me. The next morning was a Wednesday and I felt the 9-1-1 calling to run to somebody's church somewhere, ASAP. I hadn't been to services in years, so I Googled and found a Unity Church in session near Columbus Circle and headed there. My guidance told me that I needed to get out of his space. Just being there was a toxic environment. Fabulous one-bedroom or not, it was my past.

My closest friends were pissed because they viewed the apartment as my alimony. The fact is, it was his apartment, not mine, and he was within his rights to do as he wished with it. Sentiment aside, no one "owes" us anything. End of story. How was I coaching women about moving on or the bad feng shui of keeping an ex's jewelry if I lived in my ex's apartment? I needed to walk my talk. It was time to let my beloved space go. It took a few more months but I packed up and left, bawling the whole way.

Apparently, Henry was under intense personal pressure at the time. After that experience, he mailed me a heartfelt letter of support, championing my victories that I didn't even know he was aware of. How beautiful that this division led me to find unity. The mysteries of life being what they are, that fight was exactly what I needed for my personal evolution.

The Sacred Feminine Power of Releasing

"Sometimes you've got to let everything go –
purge yourself. Whatever is bringing you down,
get rid of it."
—*Tina Turner*

Earlier we examined the power of the Secret of Receptivity. The other half of the cycle of receiving is releasing. You can't have one without the other. Well, actually you can – but that will throw you out of balance. If you are receiving without releasing, you are on overload or hoarding. If you are releasing without receiving, you are starving, dry, and depleted.

The day-to-day grind can begin to feel like a spiritual or even moral malaise. Be thankful for where you are. This is a great opportunity. The more clear we are about what we do not want, the closer we get to what we do want. The catalyst for a Dry Life Crisis could be a devastating breakup, unplanned changes at work, inner circle betrayals, financial challenges, or all of the above. Whatever the trigger, sometimes we wake up and realize that we are not where we wanted to be. At that point it's time for new thinking.

What might you need to let go of? How about: toxic anger, physical clutter, excess body weight, poisonous relationships, unhealed drama, exes, defunct friendships, limiting beliefs, expectations, grudges, beefs, and family feuds. My "28-Day Love-Body-Spirit Detox Program" is an intensive online coaching program about releasing everything that doesn't serve us. We know that we need to detoxify our bodies of unhealthy foods, but we also need mental, emotional, and spiritual detoxing.

Bombshell Challenge: I once had the honor of being in a creative workshop led by master dancer Bill T. Jones. He told me, "Baby girl, if you don't have a fight song, get one, because life is hard." I don't know if he meant it literally but I took it that way. Music is a part of my therapy. My fight songs range from Pharrell Williams's "Happy," Christina Aguilera's "Beautiful," and The Black Eyed Peas's "Let's Get It Started," to John Coltrane's "My Favorite Things," Ludwig van Beethoven's "Für Elise," and "Empire State of Mind" by Jay-Z and Alicia Keys. Create an uplifting Fight Song Playlist that inspires you to release the old and savor this moment.

Reset Yourself with a One-Week Bombshell Detox

Consider this mini-detox release a reset button. Cleaning up your stale beliefs and stagnant behaviors in one area will affect every other area of your life. You may want to begin on a Sunday with a soothing bath and sweetgrass, sage, or cedar incense for energy clearing.

Day 1: Define, define, define.

Use this day to become comfortable with life as you want it to be.

If you aren't specific about where you're going, then don't be surprised when you never arrive. Are you behaving, dressing, eating, and socializing like the person you want to be? What do you need to let go of to become that woman?

We've discussed getting clear about what we want in previous chapters. Hopefully you have created a Big Brave Bombshell Bliss Board (yeah!) and Passion Statement. If you have, review them today. If not, get to it. Today is about specifying what you want life to feel like and look like. You can also work in just one area, such as finance or romance.

Define and describe in detail what you want. Being clear about what we do want helps us to release what we don't want. Let go of the story of who you are for who you are becoming.

Day 2: De-clutter your environment.

Use this day to release the physical things you're attached to that don't enrich you.

Some people live a minimalist existence. They have nothing in storage, no personal tchotchkes, excess files, or memorabilia. Then, there are the rest of us – who keep everything. We can easily identify the hoarding in other people's lives, but don't see it our own when we hold on to furniture, clothes, electronics, books, relationships, and online profile "friends" that no longer enrich us. Just because you have the physical room to store more stuff doesn't mean you should.

Hoarding, whether a little or a lot, blocks our blessings. At the base of any thought of holding on to anything that has outlived its clear and current use is a belief in scarcity and an acknowledgement that you are not yet the person you wish to be. For example, holding on to clothes or shoes that don't fit (in size or style) indicates that you don't feel abundant enough that you could purchase something similar if needed in the future. Keeping old goodies from defunct relationships says that you could never acquire something even greater from yourself or another relationship. This clutter is often a blocker to getting the love you deserve.

The poverty mindset of holding on to old stuff doesn't leave room for new things and relationships to flow into our lives. Ask, "What is the most self-loving choice I can make right now?" and let it go.

Day 3: Detoxify your bombshell temple.

Use this day to clear your mind and body.

The way you treat your body directly reflects how you feel about yourself. If our bodies aren't clear, our minds won't be either. If we treat ourselves poorly by ingesting junky foods, then how do we expect other people to treat us?

Detox your body from the inside today by eating only raw fruits and vegetables or doing a fresh juice fast. This will allow your body to cleanse itself. Be sure to check with your medical practitioner to know what's right for you. You can detoxify the outside by doing a dry brushing to exfoliate and slough off old skin. The ancient Ayurvedic practice of oil pulling – swishing coconut oil in your mouth for about 20 minutes on an empty stomach – is also said to help with detoxification.

Day 4: Deserve, deserve, deserve.

Use this day to release your feelings of unworthiness.

What do you deserve? Do you feel worthy of wealth, friendships, leisure time, and love? For example, look at your most recent romantic relationship. Was it a mutually loving situation? Were you in communion with someone worthy of your time and energy? Did the relationship feed and enrich your mind, body, and spirit? Was this person completely in favor of your well-being? If not, you have beliefs to release.

Commit to free-writing in your Bombshell Playbook for 45 minutes. The topic? Whatever comes to mind when you say, "I deserve." The task is to purge and examine your subconscious babble. Free-writing helps your mind-gunk to come out. What others think of you is none of your business but what you think of yourself is everything.

Day 5: Desist and let go.

Use this day to release relationships with people who do not enrich your life.

We are hereby decreed to cease and desist from any non-working or defunct relationships. If there are people in your phone or mental rolodex that are taking up space, delete them. This means removing the deceased from your phone. (Most challenging for me!) This also means cutting off dead conversations and communication with people who drain you.

Make a list of everyone you interact with on a weekly basis. Do these people reflect who you are as a person? Do your interactions leave you feeling energized or vampirized? Limit contact with energy drainers and release "people clutter."

Day 6: Defy the electronic norm.

Use this day to go against the status quo of being plugged in.

Our environments can be a constant assault of minutia and gossip, and a barrage of bad news. Take a media time-out. No news, no web, and no TV. If something big happens in the world, don't worry. Someone will tell you. If you cannot spend even one day without gossip, violence, and negativity then you're not placing enough value on your mind. While you're clearing your body and physical surroundings of gunk, this is the time to do the same for your mind. You are not a magnet for what you want; you are a magnet for what you are.

Day 7: Decompress.

Use this day to nurture, de-stress, and restore yourself.

You have been through six days of releasing. Today is about building yourself up. Spend time with people who make you feel full and happy. Enjoy activities that revitalize you. Nourish your body with nutritious meals and positive entertainment. Ways to relax include: sauna, massage, working out, soothing music, being in nature, reading, and aromatherapy.

Treat yourself like you want to be treated because you are a queen. Living by default can leave us filled up with everything that we don't want so it's time to let go of the things that aren't working to make room for greatness. You deserve to live proactively rather than reactively. Release dead energy for a life that is simultaneously divine, delectable, and alive!

Bombshell Tool: De-Cording Visualization

When you were born, they cut the umbilical cord that attached you to your mother. This signified that you are an individual and separate entity. De-cording is an energetic process of cutting the cords between you and another person.

It's not always as easy as "let go and move on" after your relationship with a loved one, friend, or romantic partner has come to a close. In fact, it almost never is. Our minds and mouths may say it's over, but our hearts hold on.

Just as we were once physically attached to our mothers, we form temporary energetic cord attachments all the time. When we are in any kind of relationship with another person we are energetically connected and engaged. This connection continues even after your brain, heart, or circumstances cause the situation to end. Imagine your energy as cords attaching you to wherever your focus goes. Now imagine trying to move forward with dozens or hundreds of these old energy cables, like tangled extension cords, attaching you to everyone you've ever cared for. All of those old, dead, emotionally charged, and unnecessary cords would make it pretty hard to move forward, right?

Sometimes this "procedure" is simple. You de-cord and never feel the person's energy again. With others, your bond may have been so strong that you feel the person's energy all the time. Interactions can reattach you. You can de-cord as much as you need to. There is no harmful energy or intention toward the other person, ever. You don't even have to have been in a relationship to have someone's energy stuck to you. De-cording is helpful after dealing with energy vampires who sap your energy as well.

Think of cord releasing as an energy cleanse. You can use this releasing exercise to de-cord from a parent, mate, boss – anyone! Or you can de-cord the energy of a specific situation with another person. This process doesn't have to mean that you're no longer in each other's lives. It just means that you are not feeding from each other's energy.

Your Bombshell Power Hour at the end of the day is a great time to let go of draining connections. Here's how:

1. Sit comfortably and close your eyes.

2. Visualize the cords attaching you and the person or people you wish to release.

3. See yourself unplugging each cord from you. You can visualize handing the cord back to the other person. You can also see the cord being pulled back over to them as soon as you release it. For persistent or strongly attached cords, you can see yourself cutting them with huge scissors.

4. Replace the energy with your own soothing light. Picture a spinning vortex of golden, yellow light – like a ball of sunshine surrounding you and refilling you with positive, good-feeling energy.

5. In your vision, you may want to clearly tell the other person, "It is over. You are released from my life. We are complete. Goodbye."

6. Sit quietly until you see yourself whole, loving, and loved.

Say a prayer for the person's highest and best good. Repeat to yourself, "It is safe to let this go. It is safe to let this person go. I am safe."

Don't be surprised if the person feels the energy shift and suddenly contacts you. Sometimes, we're the ones who keep reattaching ourselves to a defunct relationship. Be aware of your own grieving and healing processes.

The Wisdom of Our Ancestresses: Full Moon Releasing Power

Yes, once again we're about to get all woo-woo up in here. I am a girl who believes in magic and miracles. I am not narcissistic enough to think that we understand all that is. It wasn't too long ago that atoms and iPads seemed mystical and fantastical. I believe in the wisdom of the Universe. I trust that the Source of Everything that created me has a divine perfect order at work and I believe that we are a part of that sacred order.

We feel displaced and ungrounded in part because we have lost our rites of passage. First we say, "Boy that year flew by. Where did the time go?" Then suddenly five years have flown by. This. Is. Your. Life.

Rituals mark the passage of time. Rites of passage ground us and anchor us in the rhythms of our life and the life that is expanding around us. Let's refuse to let the wisdom of our ancestresses be lost one more moment.

We get scared of the word "ritual" but we have plenty of rites and rituals in our "modern" culture. Christmas trees, Thanksgiving feasting, dressing up for Halloween, and New Year's resolutions are rituals. Singing anthems before games, blowing out candles and wishing, kneeling to propose, and saying "bless you" when we sneeze are rituals, too. Sweet 16 and bachelorette parties are rites of passage. Today's religious holidays like Passover and Easter are based on solar and lunar calendars. Every ancient culture, calendar, religion, and spiritual tradition had moon rites and rituals.

A part of loving and respecting ourselves as women is loving and respecting the Great Mother Earth that feeds and nourishes us all. The farmers in my family knew that animals react differently during the full moon and the planting and harvesting of crops is also often done in accordance with the moon. Just like the moon controls the waters of the earth, she affects our cycles. After all, we're made mostly of water. The moon affects our sleep and productivity cycles even though we don't all menstruate in alignment with Mama Moon anymore.

New moon time and full moon time, just like the moontimes of our bodies, are powerful. In the next chapter we have a New Moon Ceremony which is about going inward and manifesting our desires. The full moon, however, is a time for shedding what no longer works, releasing negativity, and letting go. It's literally the time of bringing light to the darkness. If the new moon is about drawing inward, the full moon is about reveling unabashedly and boldly in our kick-ass womanhood. Some people also do love and abundance rituals at this time. Supposedly, full moon lovemaking is otherworldly and leaves you knowing "this is the one" or "I need to go." Pow.

Bombshell Tool: Full Moon Releasing Ritual

This is a simple, positive-energy full moon ritual of letting go. Feel free to embellish or adapt it. Call in your best girlfriends, Sacred Bombshell Sister, or your Bomb Squad for a circle of sisters. Wear skirts and dresses or loose pants to aid your femergy flow. Three days before and three days after the full moon is the window for this celebration. Here's what to do:

- If you can, go to nature. A beach, backyard, park, or somewhere your bare feet can touch the ground is ideal. If you're a city-dweller, your fire escape or patio can work just as well. If you're indoors, you can purify the space by burning the incense of your choice.

- Ask everyone to bring an offering for the group. This can mean a song or poem. It can also be meaningful trinkets.

Other possible gift offerings include flowers, essential oils, stones, and bath salts.

🔮 This is about letting go and reveling in the joy of release, so begin by releasing what you no longer need. One approach is to sit in a circle and pass a "talking stick" to indicate each person's turn to speak. You can also shout your goodbyes into the air as a cacophony of endings. Another approach is for each woman to call out, "Good bye to _____" in quick succession going around the circle. You fill in the blank each time with what you want to release. This can turn into a fevered frenzy; let it!

The full moon is not about holding back your emotions. Laugh, cry, scream, react however feels most freeing. Grief is a patient mo fo. If you've been numbing or avoiding dealing with sorrow or anger, the ignored grief won't dissolve. It will wait. The way we release emotions trapped in our bodies is with tears, voice, and motion. That's why you see people even in the most reserved religions crying, swaying, singing, or shouting when they feel connected to their Source.

🔮 Call out the names of those you wish to honor. If you can have open flames in your location, you can each hold a lit white or silver candle. Start with female ancestors. Name the women in your family who have transitioned and thank them for being. In my play *Goddess City*, my co-writer Antoy Grant, the Goddess of Fever, and I spoke the names of our mothers and grandmothers in acknowledgement. Do the same by visualizing the women who came before you freed from whatever suffering they experienced. You can also call out cultural ancestors who are not related to you. Then thank your living elders and your sisters in the journey. You can thank your brothers as well if you choose. It's your decision whether to include the names of men in this celebration.

🔮 Hand out paper and pens. I like the energy of purple ink. Pencils are not needed because there are no wrong answers. Invite the women to journal for a set amount of time, like 10 minutes. If someone feels more comfortable drawing pictures than words, she can do that.

Consider these full moon intention questions: *What would you like to release? What beliefs no longer serve you? Are there relationships that no longer feed your soul? What stories do you no longer need? What beliefs do you hold on to because they make you feel righteous? If you were brave what would you do next? Are you courageous enough to welcome the void that will result from releasing people, behaviors, and beliefs?*

- If you're in an environment where you can burn these journal pages, do. You can also rip them up and stomp-dance on them. If you're at the ocean you can speak the words into a shell or something else natural to the ocean and release it into the water. Always be eco-friendly.

- After all of that emotion, it is feast and gift-giving time. Leave your candles to burn all the way down. Share your poems, songs, and offerings. Indulge in great food and drinks. Pour libations if that's a practice you follow. Music and dance works throughout. Close with a gratitude shout-out in present tense. For example, "I give thanks for my abundance," "I give thanks for my healthy, magnificent self," "I give thanks for my loving and steamy relationship." Amen!

Forgive Everything

"Near your breastbone there is an open flower.
Drink the honey that is all around that flower."
—Kabir Das

When you are looking at things from a place of ego, the thought of forgiveness just feels wrong. "Revenge is a dish best served cold." "What's in it for me?" "I'm right and she's wrong." "You mean, someone does something wrong to me and I release them from blame? And why would I want to do that, again?" Once I watched a woman on a talk show explain how she forgave the man who killed her child. I thought, "Jeez. I am struggling to forgive the guy who bumped into me on the subway."

Forgiveness forces us to fly. Listen to the scholars. Nelson

Mandela, who served 27 years in prison for fighting for human rights under apartheid said, "Resentment is like drinking poison and hoping that it will kill your enemies." Spiritual life coach Iyanla Vanzant teaches, "Forgive everything! Forgiveness does not erase the memory of an experience, it neutralizes its impact." Author Mark Twain put it poetically when he said, "Forgiveness is the fragrance that the violet sheds on the heel that has crushed it." Iconoclastic feminist bell hooks says, "For me, forgiveness and compassion are always linked." A Chinese proverb prophesies, "He who seeks vengeance must dig two graves: one for his enemy and one for himself." And then of course, there's the classic wisdom of Oscar Wilde: "Always forgive your enemies; nothing annoys them so much."

Consider forgiving for selfish reasons. Stress can shorten your life expectancy. Do you want to be right or do you want to be at peace? There is no way you can be happy and hold grudges. Maybe there is someone that you need to ask for forgiveness. Most often we need to learn how to forgive ourselves.

It bears noting that forgiveness doesn't always mean that you are yucking it up over mojitos. The person doesn't even have to be sorry for you to forgive them. Forgiving just means that you are willing to release you both from the binding turmoil of grudge, guilt, and blame. The person you're forgiving could have already been out of your life for 10 years. Forgiveness is a dish that is right on time whenever it's served.

Bombshell Tool: Forgiveness with Ho'oponopono

Ho'oponopono is the traditional Hawaiian practice of seeking forgiveness and attempting to remove ego from the process of reconciliation. The mantra, repeated to another party or as a prayer, follows different versions of: "I am sorry. Please forgive me. I love you. Thank you."

When you're having a hard time forgiving, remind yourself of your own follies, foibles, mistakes, and missteps. Drop the judgment and self-righteousness because none of us is perfect.

Remember why you were close to the person to begin with. Whatever your spiritual beliefs, try to see the other person as your higher power (as you understand it) sees the person and their behavior. This is true compassion.

If you're trying to forgive someone and your frame of reference becomes only the terrible things that they did, you won't be able to move forward. Try seeing the situation from the other person's point of view, if only for a moment. This empathetic approach may help you answer the question, "What were they thinking?" Then decide whether you can move past it or if you need to walk away. Why stay in a situation that tortures you and the other person? When it comes to family members, you are allowed to love them from afar.

When you're ready, think of the person you want or need to forgive and begin chanting: "I'm sorry. Please forgive me. I love you. Thank you."

Harnessing the Soul-Cleansing Power of Water

Water is the symbol of life. All major religions use water in worship. This parallels the cleansing power of the planet's natural waters. Christians use baptism as a sacrament. Jewish people go to the mikveh as a bath of purification. Muslims wash for prayers in ritual purification. My father's Spiritual Baptist church does baptisms in the ocean. Many earth religions also bathe in the rain. Japanese researcher Masaru Emoto reveals in his groundbreaking work **Messages from Water** that water crystals can be affected by prayer, positive words, and even music. To harness the power of water, you can go to the beach or use your daily shower as a mental cleansing.

A spiritual bath is soul-cleansing. It helps to get rid of emotional energy that you pick up from life's stresses and your environment. I spent my 38th birthday bathing in Berbice Beach near the border of Suriname. It was three days after the full moon and the moon was more than 90% visible. I was born three days after the full moon in Brooklyn, New York, so make of that what you will!

That week, I had joined my family for a full moon bonfire at the 170th anniversary of my family village of Buxton. In 1840, the British Guiana (as it was known then) village was purchased by a group of freed African slaves. In 1862, a group of irate Buxton women protested unfair taxation and confiscation of land by literally stopping a train. Clearly, these were the wrong women to mess with. They stood on the tracks in front of the Bajan governor's train until their men could arrive from the fields. Talk about leaning into your power! Take that.

At the bonfire we sang songs about love, freedom, betrayals, sexuality, and relationships while friends, family, and strangers drummed and danced. The combination of the full moon ritual and birthday rebirth sea bath made me feel connected to myself, grounded, and whole. The ocean bath was especially healing as I'd just had a "nobody cares about me so I'm flying home" meltdown less than 24 hours before. It was hard to sell myself on the mantra of being unloved or unlovable after being filled with so much self-celebration and reverence for the majesty of my big, brave, bombshell life.

Bombshell Tool: Cleansing Spiritual Bath

Like altars, I am blessed to say that this is a tool that I was raised around. In African cultures, bathing in spiritual water helps you to release and set intentions for a prosperous new beginning. The Mayans supposedly used this practice as well. Like my great-grandma, who used homeopathy for her ailments, my sister Damali is a master herbalist. See SacredBombshell.com for sacred herbal bath recipes and how to boil and properly prepare them.

You may want to take a regular shower first as this bath is about energy, not daily skin grime. An Epsom or sea salt bath is a purifying salve. Depending on your intentions, herbs and oils you may add include: sweet rose, balancing basil, healing hibiscus, protective plantain, restorative mugwort, soothing lavender, wild yam, and spicy cinnamon. Coconut milk also enriches a spiritual bath.

Use soothing beats, candlelight, flowers, crystals, and incense to make this a multi-sensory experience. You can meditate, pray, visualize, and give thanks. Just the fact that you think you don't have time to do this means that you should. Hug yourself and speak love into every part of your body. See beauty in every fold, bend, and stretch mark.

Conjure feelings of luxury, prosperity, gratitude, and deservability as you indulge in this basic but potent ritual. Use self-love declarations to reinforce how good it feels to be you. Read sacred poetry or your preferred spiritual texts, like psalms, that make you feel empowered. You should come out focused, aligned, clearer – and energetically clean! Give yourself this gift at least once a season.

Bombshell Playbook Exercise

Complete these sentences in your Bombshell Playbook. Take five deep, cleansing breaths to get centered and begin.

1. The love traumas I still carry make me a victim of...

2. If these things never happened I would be...

3. Because it is too painful I avoid feeling...

4. If I released this victimhood I might...

5. I need to forgive myself for...

Post Traumatic Love Disorder: It All Went to Hell – Now What?

"ever since i realized there waz someone calli
/ a colored girl an evil woman a bitch or a nag /
i been tryin not to be that & leave bitterness / in
somebody else's cup"
—*Ntozake Shange*

"You sure didn't get that angry black woman gene!" he said, grinning.

"Angry black woman gene?" I repeated. He was bold for a first date. I moved my silver stilettos into "go" position under the table.

"Yeah," he explained. "All the black women I meet seem pissed."

Of course, everyone reading this is asking, "How dare he?!" but unfortunately, this man was not alone. I have heard versions of this same story (often) from coaching clients.

Homeboy didn't see me a few years earlier. He didn't know me when I was woeful, grieving – and mad as hell. He missed me when my heart was shattered. During that time, I was in real emotional pain and saw no way out. It felt like me against the world. I didn't go as far as declaring that I didn't need a man, but I proceeded as if "I could do bad by myself" and ended up hurting others. So, hell yes, I was angry. I am also black, a woman, and human.

So what happens when we are angry and bitter women of any background? We heap hurt on top of pain on top of heartbreak. We lead with our righteous scars, unable to let love out – or in. Our Heart Ceiling is locked, we are brittle, and our lives are dry. We either attract only people who are vibrating at the same low level of energy or we can't accept those coming to us with something different. When anger is your shield it becomes a wall. This looks different depending on who's experiencing it. Some women are pissed at the world. Others turn the anger inward as depression. We live it as chronic stress and anxiety or try to stuff it down with everything from pizza to religion.

After I noticed this very real trauma in enough of my coaching clients I gave it a name: post-traumatic love disorder (PTLD). Soldiers – as well as assault and rape victims – experience PTSD, a normal reaction after surviving the devastating, traumatic ravages of life-changing war. PTLD occurs after a devastating love event, an incident that may trigger childhood issues. We feel betrayed, broken, or abandoned. Then we take this energy forward, living and dating like love zombies and the walking wounded. When in the midst of suffering from PTLD we may feel like fractured or broken shells of who we once were. As the saying goes, pain is inevitable but suffering is optional. When you're in the middle of PTLD, though, it sure doesn't seem like it!

These incidents can shatter our self-worth, if we let them. A devastating love challenge or revelation can leave us feeling unsettled, scared, or out of control. Your situation may have triggered old feelings of rejection, abandonment, or trust issues. You may be calling your deservability into question and wondering if you are unlovable.

When you are in love and physically intimate with another person, your brain, body, and soul are engaged. Your heart collaborates with your brain's connecting chemicals to create a bond that feels unbreakable ... until it is. It seems like you're crazy when it's over because "withdrawal" from a person is the same as withdrawing from an opioid, like heroin. You can easily become a love addict, going from relationship to relationship without ever healing.

You will be tempted to numb or distract yourself, but the only way to heal is to go through it. It's important to allow yourself to feel heartbreak and cry it out. After a love loss, you have suffered a death — the death of a dream. If you don't deal with your grief honestly, it will pop up when you least expect it. Be honest with yourself about where you are emotionally. Surrender the illusion you had of being in control.

Write this down in your Bombshell Playbook: There is nothing wrong with me. I am enough. In fact, I am more than enough. I am too much, and that is a good thing.

How to Move On

You're going along, minding your business when it all comes crashing down. It happens to all of us. So what should we do when faced with a dark night of the soul? Cry. Scream. Scream again. Curse. Bawl. Lather, rinse, repeat.

Get Grounded

When things fall apart it's hard to think. Your mind, body, and spirit go into survival mode in a crisis. Your brain is thinking fight, freeze, or flight. It is impossible to be your "normal" self. The only way to move forward is to ground yourself. What does that mean?

Start with the breath. Breathe. Get the air in and out of your lungs. Be still and breathe. In moments of extreme duress, go back to the basics. When everything else feels like it's gone, what could be more basic than breathing?

Feel Your Pain

This is not the time to have a stiff upper lip. It's not about being a strong woman. We are human. We bleed; we hurt; we cry. Your tears are not a sign of weakness. Your tears are a sign of your humanity. You have to feel the grief of a loss or you don't heal. Allow yourself to feel your pain. Cry, stomp and scream. When depressing things happen it is natural to feel sad.

When my doctor heard that I was leaving my newlywed home, she offered a prescription for antidepressants. There is nothing wrong with taking something recommended by your physician if you have severe long-term emotional issues, but my depression was situational. I needed hugs not drugs. Who wouldn't be sad at the conclusion of a marriage? So cry. Cry like our mothers and fathers have cried before us. Grief is a process and it is not optional.

Tell the Truth

This is the time for radical truth-telling. Don't sell yourself short. If there are people in your circle who will judge you for your problems then these are not people you need around you. It is better to have a couple of supportive, stable friends than a group of judgmental jerks. Be honest about where you are and what you need to get where you're going.

Get Support

When my marriage completed itself my loved ones were grieving the unexpected deaths of two of my mom's sisters so I could only lean on them so much. I joined a support group and found solace in the security of strangers who became friends. Check a message board like Craigslist or Meetup.com to find people dealing with similar issues to yours. Your local hospital, women's group, or house of worship may know of a group you can join. You are no less strong because you need support.

Remember that if someone pokes you and venom comes out, it's not because they poked you. It's because that's what was inside of you. Find one-on-one coaching or therapy with a knowledgeable and caring counselor if that's what you need. Heal this hurt so that you can have a healthy, love-filled life.

Be Gentle with Yourself

Soothe yourself. You have experienced a trauma. You need to get grounded, connected, and back into your body. Remember, it takes time before a bombed out shell can be a bombshell again. Work on your meditation or yoga practice. Practice self-compassion with healthy eating or a new dance class. Give yourself closure. Re-parent yourself with healthy self-devotion. Say goodbye if you need to in a letter you never send. Toss everything that makes you think of your loss. It is "bad juju" to have your past taking room away from your future.

Become Aware of Your Thoughts

If you're rolling around the "what ifs" or repeatedly wondering "why me," you can't move forward. Why not you? Terrible things happen to awesome people every day. Get a hold on the negative self-talk. When you're most vulnerable, your Inner Bully can go ballistic on you. Wake up every morning and freestyle journal in your Bombshell Playbook. Write it out.

Take Responsibility

Outside of physical illness, very few things just "happen" to us without our participation. If you make someone else fully responsible for your situation that means that only someone else can get you out of it. Learn the lessons of the situation. If you hope to have the skill of commitment, you have to take responsibility for your part in the close of each relationship. Even if your lost love was emotionally unavailable, a cheater, or a liar, you chose him or her.

Choose Connection over Isolation

PTLD can feel like you're in the middle of a tornado. If you focus only on your problems, you will keep going around in the tornado. You have to see the outside to free yourself. Sadness causes many of us to retreat. We stay alone with our sorrows and then lash out. Don't retreat. Of course you don't want to weigh down those around you, but your loved ones want to have your back.

Use Healing Tools

Talk therapy and journaling are great for emotional purging, but try a mind interrupting process like the Lefkoe Method, acupressure, eye movement desensitization and reprocessing, Acupuncture Moxibustion, EFT, or even hypnosis. These are techniques that help the mind to break repetitive thought patterns and beliefs (see SacredBombshell.com for more info). Visualization can also be helpful. See yourself looking back at the situation a year from now and realizing how much happier you are.

Find Your Joy

This is the time for something new. Break old patterns with new activities. Don't let your mind get the best of you. Instead of imagining that your dysfunctional man has suddenly morphed into a prince and some other woman is reaping the benefits, realize that he is over there being exactly the same with her as he was with you. Date – several people. They say the best way to get over an old love is with a new love. This doesn't mean that you jump into bed with the next person at the bus stop. It's also not about jumping into another relationship. Either of these choices could be detrimental. Just meet people and have a great time.

Give Yourself Closure

Healing takes time. You may not ever understand why a situation took place. It's not your job to interpret someone else's behavior. Your objective is getting back to being the best you. For your mental health, you will (eventually) need to forgive anyone else involved. However, you need to first take responsibility for your choices in the situation and forgive yourself. You can't move forward unless you are able to forgive yourself and the other parties.

True forgiveness may take months or years. In that case, even being *willing* to forgive can soften the "stuck" energy and allow progress. Let go of the wish that the past could have been different. Your blessed future is your gift for having the courage to love like you've never been hurt — again. I see you filled with more love than you ever thought possible.

Reach for Gratitude

As always, give thanks.

Bombshell Dialogue with Jill Scott: How to Move Forward Triumphantly

I had the pleasure of interviewing chanteuse and poet Jill Scott about her project *The Light of the Sun*. The album was a labor of love born after a difficult divorce and other personal struggles including a broken engagement. Jill's labor includes plenty of joy, too, which can be seen in her music video for "Shame." I was thrilled after so much strife to find Jill happy. She was open and honest in our conversation. An actress as well as a singer-songwriter, Jill is set to play James Brown's wife in a biopic. Her son is named Jett and she recently released 60 pounds.

Abiola: You are our own Poet Laureate, singer, actress, and all-around goddess.

Jill: Thank you! *The Light of the Sun* was my fourth studio album. It is refreshing, warm, and revealing. There is some jazz, some funk, and definitely some old-school hip-hop. Some poetry, some sexiness, some vulnerability, bravado. The entire record is a journey, a trip. "Shame" was a song that happened by accident. I love that. We were in the studio, a couple of friends and I and we were chilling, just free-styling. You know, I'm still called to the cypher. So, we were having a cypher. And "The Magnificent" beat came on and I just sang and those are the words that I sang. And the guys that I was hanging out with were singing background. You know, I get a chance to get a little aggression off. You know, make people want to do the Kid 'N Play.

Abiola: You are taking it back. So Jill, you mean to tell me that we can still find Jill Scott, Peabody Award Winner, in a Philly street cypher?

Jill: Absolutely. I love hip-hop and I love to hear MCs think out loud.

Abiola: One of the wonderful things about you, Miss Storyteller, mic controller, is that you are also a beauty icon. From the range of natural, textured, and straight hairstyles to your wonderful curves – you always seem to exude such confidence. You designed a line of intimates for Ashley Stewart.

Jill: Well, the Butterfly Bra came about because big boobs are heavy and they need support. It is simple. I needed a bra that gave me support as well as didn't dig into my shoulders. Because the older you get the more the indent is there.

As far as beauty is concerned, [it's] better when I feel better on the inside, internally, when I have peace of mind, when I have had enough rest, when I surround myself with people that really care for me and I care for them as well. When I feel good, that is when beauty comes. There is a glow from within.

Externally, I have been riding my bike, swimming, taking long walks, doing kickboxing, and doing some things that are good for my body. I am getting older, as we all are, and I have a two-year-old son. And I would like to have another child maybe so I just was watching what I eat, when I eat – and not in some crazed, deranged way. I do eat what I want. I just mind my portions and I make sure I get up and do something. It is a little process. So far so good. And just try not to worry so much.

Abiola: You went through a challenging divorce a few years ago. How did you heal and come back from that?

Jill: It took me a while because you have to forgive yourself. So I did, and I definitely had to ask God for forgiveness because it bothered me making a vow to God and not keeping it. It bothered my ex-husband too. We are still friends. He is a good guy and I love him but we just … I don't know. Life works the way it does and I ended up here. I guess all of that to have this baby. All that to be in this place now. But, yeah, first I had to forgive him, forgive myself, and I asked God for forgiveness as well.

Abiola: Forgiveness is the key component of any kind of healing.

Jill: We talk a lot, and try to understand what happened to us. Because [my ex-husband] Lyzel and I were great friends. We were really – we are good friends now. It takes time but we were the best of friends. That was my homey.

Abiola: What does it mean for you for you to be a mother?

Jill: I am loving motherhood. Love it, love it so much. I love it – with help. It is definitely a job, but it is so rewarding because you can see your work. I love when my son says "please" and "no, thank you." I love seeing him count and tell me what color things are and spell dog. I am teaching him how to be nice.

Abiola: With you as a mother, he can't go wrong.

Jill: They can all go wrong. Believe me.

Abiola: Well, he has a good foundation.

Jill: That's true; and prayer.

Abiola: Prayer is definitely important. You met another pair of phenomenal parents, President and Michelle Obama. How was that experience?

Jill: It was incredible. I loved being in their house, first off. I never expected the White House to be warm and the artwork on the walls was extraordinary. I am a fan of the Louvre, but being there it was just as good on a smaller scale. I cannot imagine being surrounded by that kind of art on a daily basis. It was great. [The Obamas] are very loving toward each other. I enjoyed watching them together. I am very, very proud of their relationship. Just two human beings loving each other. It is beautiful to see. And being invited to perform and read poetry, it was a memory that I will hold deeply in my heart forever.

Bombshell Takeaways:

- Appreciate the difficult times for the blessings they bring.
- Forgiveness is the key to healing.
- Letting go nurtures the spirit.

Bombshell Dialogue with Meg Batterson: How to Let Go When You Can't

Just lie back on the comfy velvet sofa … for this self-love class on healing from trauma and learning to let go with my friend Meg Batterson. Meg is a licensed psychotherapist in private practice in the Flatiron District of New York City. Currently, Meg works with both couples and individuals. She's been practicing in NYC since 2009 and did her clinical social work training at Columbia University. Then she went on to The Relational Center in Los Angeles. We met at a nationally syndicated talk show, where Meg provided guests with after care and I was a recurring life coach.

Abiola: Meg, how do you describe your work?

Meg: I'm a relationally oriented therapist. I'm always curious about how we as humans impact each other and how our environment impacts our well-being. I seek to help people live out their potential by supporting them where they are. I want to help my clients be present with their feelings and not get stuck in the past or worry too much about the future.

Abiola: That's so important. Although we are talking specifically about therapy, starting from where you are and dealing with the present is what I call "self-being." It's a higher principle. It's mindfulness.

Meg: That's definitely an area of expertise for me, helping individuals live out their potential and be present. Also with couples, helping them be more present with each other, and then thus be more vulnerable with each other and able to create a more intimate bond.

Abiola: What made you initially want to become a therapist?

Meg: Really my own experience and life trauma and a strong desire to have my life work line up with my lived experience and my values. I always felt like the social, [the] personal, and the professional could not be compartmentalized. I feel like as a therapist I can work with my own issues in the context of therapy.

Abiola: I coined the phrase "post-traumatic love disorder" because I feel like so many women and men, but women in particular, are like the walking wounded. Either with primal love wounds from their families of origin or dealing with breakup issues that then trigger those primal wounds. I hear from women, "I know it should be over but I can't let it go. I keep going back." In your professional opinion, why can't people walk away?

Meg: Letting go is a really tricky lesson to learn in life [and] in the context of a relationship. Attachment is such a powerful bond. In the beginning of a relationship we release those intense chemicals like oxytocin that make us bond together. That's really important for survival because it's about procreation and we need to bond together in order to have a child.

It's my impression that something in us biologically feels compelled to stay even just for survival reasons. We need to stay connected as human beings in order to survive. That's a definite truth. Even though psychologically we're caught up in a relationship that we know isn't good for us, there's something biological (and it must also be somewhat psychological) that compels us to stay. Even if there's a situation of abuse …. There are lots of women in those situations and people often wonder, why do they stay? Well part of the reason that they stay is because of this biological need to stay together no matter what.

Abiola: So if you're dealing with a situation like that, what should you do in order to be able to break away?

Meg: This is really an important question and one that we all need to really think about and actually teach. One of the keys to that is the body. We have our mind, our brain that's usually caught up in some obsessive thinking about the person or the relationship. You're chewing it over and over, and you're going over everything you did together, all the good memories. Maybe even minimizing some of the bad memories.

But if you are able to just sit quietly with your body, maybe you get into some kind of meditation practice, or yoga practice, or even just sitting on your couch and dropping into and checking into your body and not focusing so much on what your brain is telling you. The brain is rationalizing, "I should stay in this bad situation" or "I need to stay connected to this person; I can't let go."

If you drop into your body you allow yourself to drop into that grief process and you make contact with "What is my heart feeling? What am I feeling in my stomach?" and then you maybe start to get new information that you didn't have access to when you were obsessing over the old story. People often just want to avoid pain, to stay away from the body. They don't want to drop into that grief process and loss because it's scary.

Abiola: That's where we get into trouble because like you said our instinct is to naturally run from pain. We think, "I'm going to close my heart," but the healing comes from opening your heart not from shutting down.

Meg: And oftentimes we shut down when we don't have a bridge. We don't have relationships. Relationships are another really important factor that plays into this concept of learning how to let go. We need each other. We can't do things alone.

It's a fallacy to think that you're this independent being roaming around out there. Most Americans like to think of themselves as individualists. Yes, you can be an individual but we also need to be connected and we need each other in order to heal. Reaching out to your friends and family, and going into yourself but then going back to others and talking about your story is also really important.

And it goes back to what we already started to talk about, going into your body and being able to grieve by being present with your feelings. People get hijacked by their thoughts. About the what ifs, the should haves, could haves, would haves – these are all regrets. You're living in the past and [those thoughts] come up because we're just doing what we know.

It can be so hard to drop into the painful feelings that you have in your body but it's so necessary in order to heal. This isn't a perfect recipe but a combination of being by yourself and dropping into those feelings. Whether it's sitting or being with a therapist in psychotherapy, in treatment, and then bridging this idea of having your pain and experiencing it but also reaching out to others. Processing what happened to you by talking about it with other people.

You could get feedback from them and then you can create a new story. The old story is like, "Something was wrong with me" or "Why didn't he love me?" or "I'm not attractive enough." Instead of going into all your old insecurities, reaching out to others gives you a different way of processing letting go.

Abiola: Being honest with yourself about what you're experiencing is important as well. The grief that happens when a relationships ends; we think sometimes we can avoid that grief, or skip over it. But as you said, we have to go into it and feel it because grief is patient and grief will wait.

Meg: The direction to go to is to be able to stay present with that grief. Maybe you need someone to hold your hand while you're doing it, sitting right beside you. Being able to tap into your vulnerability.

What happens to you didn't just happen to your brain. It happened to your whole being. It happened to your soul. It happened to your body. Your body has to go through a process of feeling. People are so caught up in their heads, decapitated.

They're just like a body walking around without a head but it's all connected.

We have to stay present with that vulnerability and those feelings because they'll come back around again. You can go out and party and sleep with a million people, but that grief will still be waiting. You need to engage it and have a relationship with the grief.

Abiola: That it's a very poetic way of putting it. For many women, love traumas are only the most recent manifestation of pain that they've experienced before. Some have experienced violent traumas and are trying to have relationships without dealing with those issues. Do you think that it is possible for women to have healthy relationships after abuse, rape, or other forms of violent trauma?

Meg: The brain is malleable and the trauma doesn't have to be fixed. We know this from the research. It may still influence you. It may still flare up in the next relationship, but if you're able to process it with somebody who's trained to do it there's a potential for you to heal.

Abiola: Thankfully there's almost no stigma left around therapy. It's healthy to take care of yourself emotionally and mentally. How can people heal from "mommy issues," "daddy issues," or those basic family of origin issues?

Meg: Engaging in an awareness practice or some form of body work that can bring the issues into awareness. It's one part building your own awareness but then also having the practice of bringing that awareness into relationships.

I know it sounds strange but you need to have a relationship in order to know what you actually worked out on your own. It's like the test. "Okay, I've meditated, I've gone to therapy but then I need to bring what I've learned back into contact with somebody."

People can learn to be more aware of what their issues are but they're going to flare up. I don't think they're going to entirely go away but the awareness is the healing. You may be triggered in your relationship by something that happened in the past with somebody in your family of origin but you need to know when you're triggered. When you're taken by surprise by it, it overwhelms you and it devours the relationship and then the relationship usually dissipates or ends.

Abiola: Often my clients are successful women who feel like, "I don't need a man and I don't want to need a man." But then the men say to me, "Well, the problem is that I don't feel like she needs me." And so there's no understanding of interdependence, that once you are in a relationship it is healthy to want and need your partner. Not in a life or death kind of way; because of course you don't need someone in that way. You can survive without them. It's a tricky dance.

Meg: Yes, and there's something called "healthy dependency needs." I see it a lot in my practice as well. When I use the word "need," people freak out. They kind of panic a little bit. This goes back to adolescence; how everyone says to be cool and not be needy. We have healthy dependency needs. We all need something from another. We need more than something – we need a lot from another human being. It's about being open to the fact that you are vulnerable and you can't do everything by yourself.

Abiola: Let's talk about abusive relationships. When we think of abused women we immediately think of the PSAs of a physically battered woman but there are also people who are verbally and emotionally abused. What is your advice for women who are in abusive relationships of any kind?

Meg: Leave. Seriously, I know it's not that easy. Get connected up with people in your community who are there to help you. Talk to friends; talk to family. Really, if you're isolated you're in the worst position – you're really not in a position that you can feel like you can leave. But once you start bridging, once you start talking ... it will make the transition a little bit easier. Don't try to put on a brave face or make it feel like everything is okay when it's not.

Abiola: Really great advice, Meg. What makes you a bombshell?

Meg: I try to listen to my instincts and make my own decisions based on conversations I have with people in my life that are important to me. I've tried to build my own career so I don't have to rely on anyone. Ironically enough, along the way I have learned that I do need people. Being open to the fact that I know that about myself makes me a bombshell. I'm open to my vulnerabilities.

For me, a bombshell would have to be someone who's in touch with their own vulnerability. Anyone who's displaying like a false sense of confidence, trying to stay away from that kind of stuff.... You know how people go into, "I'm a confident woman" and they're kind of just telling themselves that? There's confidence in vulnerability.

Bombshell Takeaways:

- We all need healthy relationships with other human beings.
- Being open and vulnerable makes us stronger, not weaker.
- Everything that happens to you happens to your whole being; drop down into your body to heal.

Secret of Releasing Resources

1. *Forgiveness* by Iyanla Vanzant

2. *The Dark Side of the Light Chasers* by Debbie Ford

3. *You Can Heal Your Heart* by Louise Hay and David Kessler

4. "The Love-Body-Spirit 28-Day Detox" by Abiola Abrams (e-course)

5. "Conscious Uncoupling" by Katherine Woodward Thomas (e-course)

Releasing Affirmations

1. Every day in every way things are working out for me.

2. I am safe. It is safe to feel safe.

3. I am worthy and deserving of all good things.

4. I may bend but I will not break.

5. This too shall pass.

Ten

The Secret of Abundance; Prosperity & Riches

The Sacred Feminine Law of Abundance

The Sacred Bombshell knows that she is worthy of living an abundant life. She acknowledges that we live on a bountiful, prosperous, and affluent planet. Giving and receiving her riches makes her a part of earth's flow where there is no such thing as scarcity. She respects the power of manifesting her own abundance. This is sacred self-love.

Historical Bombshell Mentor:
Elizabeth Taylor 1932-2011

Elizabeth Taylor was simultaneously the symbol of unapologetic opulence and a daring humanitarian. The former child star made no apologies for loving her rubies and diamonds. She also started the Elizabeth Taylor AIDS Foundation to raise funds and awareness. Taylor, a shrewd businesswoman, shared her financial and empowerment advice with other celebrities. Dame Elizabeth risked her glamorous reputation by being photographed with a shaved head after brain tumor surgery. When asked why, the survivor said she wanted others to feel, "Hey, if she can get through it, so can I."

The Abundance Declaration

Today, I claim my fortune. Prosperity and abundance are my inheritance. I am wealthy beyond measure. Add up the parts and systems that make up my precious body. Are they not priceless? Who can place a value on the sun and stars that I enjoy freely?

Previously, I was a prisoner of limiting beliefs and lies of lack. Today I am freed from those falsehoods. I know that I have more than I ever thought possible. The Universe is always generous and loving with me. In return, I am generous and loving even when I am afraid. Before today, I accepted the illusion of lack to fit in. Now I claim the truth of my wealth and others will see what is possible for them.

Every day is a thanksgiving and I am drunk with blessings because I am worthy. Prosperity and abundance are my inheritance. I deny all illusions of lack, for today I am full and complete. I am valuable beyond measure, rich with love, joy, faith, and hope. My coffers runneth over with these true jewels. Richly nourished, full, and humble, I am heiress to a world of wealth and today I claim my fortune. I give and I receive. This is karmic law. I am safe in the prosperity of love.

I am not happy because I am wealthy. Rather, I am wealthy because I am happy. I deserve happiness. I deserve wealth. I deserve love. I am worthy of all that my Creator has made for me and I now feel no guilt, shame, or embarrassment for these riches. The Universe is generous with me and I am generous with her children. I am wealthy beyond measure and more generous than I ever thought possible. For this I am so grateful.

And so it is.

My Big Fat Bombshell Diary: My Financial Limiting Beliefs

"There are people who have money and people who are rich."
—Coco Chanel

Last summer I attended an Ayurveda class with a teacher who had been a practicing holistic doctor in her native India before coming to the States. In her village she doled out cures to heal people of afflictions ranging from skin issues to cancers. Like my family in Guyana, she knew the homeopathic healing properties of herbs, plants, and spices. She built a thriving practice but experienced issues when she would give a simple prescription such as cinnamon, which has antibacterial and anti-inflammatory properties. The *Journal of the Academy of Nutrition and Dietetics* reports that the spice may even be used to treat type 2 diabetes. Nonetheless, when this healer prescribed cinnamon she encountered a problem.

Her patients refused to pay because the cure seemed so simple. They figured, "I have cinnamon in my cupboard. I don't need to pay someone to tell me to take cinnamon," even though the doctor had given her time to examine them, diagnose them, and offer her expertise. When she prescribed pills, she had no issues in collecting her fees because the patients saw pills and formal medications as something of value. Her solution to this issue of perceived worth was to give the patients placebos plus the cinnamon or whatever herb in unmarked packages. Then she received her payments and her patients received their healing agents.

I was shocked the other day to hear my mother say about a shamanistic healer, "People shouldn't charge for services like that anyway." Much of my family, including my mother, have had clairvoyant experiences with dreams, for instance. I believe that we all have the ability to be intuitive on different levels. Some of us are just more comfortable allowing inner guidance to come through and may have a stronger, better trained muscle in this area.

"Do you really believe that?" I asked.

"Yes," she went on. "These talents are gifts. They should share them for free." My mother was expressing a common belief that money and spirituality don't mix. In other words, if people have this sort of intuitive gift, then it is wrong for them to accept money for it.

"So a faith healer should work for free but a medical doctor should be paid? How do you expect them to make a living?"

My mom shrugged.

"What about the work I do with women, Mommy? Do you think that I don't deserve to make an income?"

"No. That," she said, "is different."

It was actually helpful to hear in plain language the source of some of my own financial limiting beliefs. It has been a longstanding issue for me to be paid what my work is worth. If I examine my own financial past I find that from hosting TV shows to writing columns, I have had issues collecting what was owed to me. If you believe that you are not worthy of payment, then you will always have issues "tracking down your money." This is the bane of freelance living. However, the statute of limitations on blaming my parents ran out at around age 21, so my belief system (BS) is my own responsibility!

Like my mother, we harbor beliefs about who is worthy of making money and who isn't. "Artists, musicians, creative, and spiritual people? Well, they shouldn't be compensated for their time or talent." This is a value judgment. How do we expect these people who provide the honey of life to survive? Somehow we believe that God wants them to starve, like the stereotype of the "starving artist" indicates.

There is a hidden belief system that money is bad or evil, that those who possess money are bad or evil. We then create a society where the very people responsible for molding and educating our kids are underpaid and (in my city at least) expected to buy school supplies from that pittance for their overcrowded classrooms with minimal reimbursement.

These beliefs are why there are so many broke yoga teachers, professors, coaches, therapists, artists, and healers. We believe that we either don't deserve to make money from a gift or that it's not spiritual to become wealthy. There is no inherent price tag on anything. Goods and services are worth what someone is willing to pay for them.

One of the greatest gifts my father has given me is an abundance mindset. Whenever I asked for a few dollars for school my dad would say, "Why are you even asking me? You see my wallet there, take it." I was shocked to learn as an adolescent when I went to prep school that I was not wealthy. I had all the food I could eat, my parents had a luscious garden, I had a kid's dream bedroom, lots of friends, and a mom who took me shopping whenever I wanted. How could I not be wealthy?

New friends are always fascinated by the humble neighborhood and home that I was raised in. At first this confused me, but then I realized that it's because the feeling of wealth that was instilled in my bones shines through. People have always thought that I was rich. As the granddaughter of farmers, alchemists who made nourishment grow from dirt, of course I should appear to be affluent. I have no designs on hoodwinking anyone. I am very proud of how hard my parents have worked to lay a foundation for me.

One of my earliest memories is at age five or six giving my toys away out the window. I started to tell this story to a friend and she commiserated, "It was your people pleasing!" As a people-pleaser today, I agreed. However, that's not what I felt at the time or where I was going with the memory. It felt odd to try to explain but there was no inkling of, "I want to make them like me" in it.

Sure the kids gathered outside to receive my toys may have been using me, but I had no concept of that. I just felt that they needed toys and so it wasn't a big deal. They could have some of mine. In my childhood mind I already felt prosperous enough to share. My parents were always taking people in, taking us out to dinner as a family, giving people food and money, and frankly, spoiling me, so I felt rich, even as a kid.

In high school my boyfriend's sister had a falling out with her mother and my parents "adopted" her for two years, buying her school clothes and everything. It wasn't until my first summer job that I realized how long it took to earn the $300 that I required for my fancy hair extensions and sneakers.

My dad also taught us a lesson about budgeting during a family trip to Disneyworld. We were given a budget to buy whatever we wanted but warned that the amount we had to spend on souvenirs and toys was finite. My brother, sister, and I bought up a storm when we stopped at a local attraction on the way called South of the Border. Imagine my surprise when we got to Disneyworld and were not able to buy any souvenirs besides T-shirts. We had spent our budget.

There were many holes in my financial education, but I value these life lessons. It's now up to me to educate myself about personal finance, savings, debt, multiple streams of income, passive income, investments, and the like. Yay money!

The Sacred Feminine Power of Abundance

What is your Self actually worth? What quality of life do you desire? How large do you want your life to be? When you see wealthy women basking in the lap of luxury, how do you feel? Jealous? Annoyed? Happy for them? Angry that some should have so much and others should have so little?

A mindset of lack can only manifest lack. As a creative writer and media producer creating content to empower women, I spent over 10 years thinking that being a starving artist made me superior. I secretly looked down on people with money, as if somehow they were less spiritual because they weren't down with "the struggle." I felt that my "Broke Down Buddy Club," with resumes and educational backgrounds full of accolades, were more in touch with true values than the miserable people we knew who were locked into material wealth's golden handcuffs.

Much like the belief system (BS) my mother expressed, I felt that money was not a part of the compensation package for my work. I never considered that there might be a middle ground between being poor in pocket but rich in world contributions, and being wealthy and shallow. My limiting BS left me bankrupt with a heap of consumer debt and unpaid student loans. I was overworked and underpaid – by me. I thought that my achievement was my self-worth.

When people asked me to work for huge media outlets for practically no money, I said "no problem." I figured that somehow all of the financial "stuff" would magically sort itself out. As we saw when the market crashed a few years ago, many other Americans were thinking like I did. It's easy to sit in judgment but I felt that my financial idiocy was somehow nobler than other people's financial idiocy because I was following my dream and finding marginal success.

Our attitudes about money and our beliefs about self-worth are linked. If I am being real with myself, I can admit that deep down I never felt that I deserved to make money. My limiting beliefs included the idea that men were the ones who made the real money.

I had a poverty mindset. It might have looked pretty because it was dressed up in the façade of being a successful creative person, but it was a poverty mindset nonetheless.

If you have a poverty mindset, not only will you not attract money to you, but you will actually repel it. You can be "temporarily out of funds" and have a mindset of abundance. You can also be wealthy and have a poverty mindset. Whether you surround yourself with poor-minded or prosperity-minded people, you will begin to think like them.

Self Worth and Abundance

Imagine this: Not so long ago, I was working 70+ hours a week but didn't allow myself to earn a fair market wage for my time. Because God has a sense of humor and our shadow will always be mirrored back to us, I became betrothed to someone who was literally the cheapest person I had ever met. In other words, if you have a belief that you are unworthy of being supported, then you will attract a partner who will prove that to you.

We have so much shame around money issues that I have found that it's much easier as a coach to get people to open up about their sex lives than their finances. I have a friend who was ashamed of being a secret heiress. My money point of view was challenging because I went to school with old-moneyed, wealthy women and some had the good fortune of being taken care of either by their fathers' or husbands' incomes. The men in their dating pool want and expect to step in and provide for them as women and partners. It was actually a very positive thing to witness in some cases. After all, who can place a monetary value on raising children and maintaining a household?

However, if your partner takes care of the bills and you both view him (or her) as a patron or sponsor, then you earn at the favor of your benefactor. If someone else is responsible for your financial life, you have positioned that person as daddy. This works if you're both in accordance with it. If not, how free are you? If you are unhappy, can you afford to leave? Women I know have made decisions on whether to stay or go in relationships based on income. Not being able to leave someone for financial reasons is a form of slavery.

To step up as a woman worthy of abundance, I stopped making up stories to myself about why I couldn't have what I wanted. I started charging fees that better reflect the hard work I put into everything that I do. I realized that I am worth it. I put my heart and soul into every offering I put out into the world to help women live their best lives. I deserve to be compensated for that and be able to make a living.

Full disclosure: I am still getting my financial life in order, but I am no longer ashamed to say that I love making money. Unless you're a rapper, this is a very controversial thing to say in some circles! Nonetheless, I welcome prosperity into my life. "I can't afford it" is no longer my mantra. Remember, whatever you keep repeating to yourself is what you will create. Your brain will make sure through your beliefs and actions that whatever you believe about you turns out to be true.

Developing a Prosperity Mindset

The reason why lottery winners seem to have such bad luck is that they win new money but have the same old poverty mindset. They have not adjusted their beliefs about value and self-worth. They have the same prosperity set-point of lack.

Spiritual and artistic are not the opposite of wealthy. The more money I have, the more I can help others and that feels great. I have separated myself from the camaraderie of poverty and "Sisterhood of Traveling Brokeness" point of view. In fact, abundance is proof of the wealth of the Creator. Look at the vast seas, the rich colors of flora and fauna, the prosperous selection of animals and insects, the abundance of ways that our very bodies are miraculous. Mother Nature herself is showing off every time you look at a bountiful garden. Step into your abundance. It is safe to be full, luscious and beautiful like our planet.

Money is not good or bad. Money is energy and it takes many

forms. Someone could look at my grandfathers, hard-working farmers in South America, and assume that they were poor. However, when I hear my parents speak of them, they sound incredibly rich. Their families never went hungry and they always had enough to give to those less fortunate. A farmer knows that a portion of the seeds must be returned to the soil to keep the blessings flowing. That is the definition of prosperity.

In **Fortune Magazine**, billionaire business maven Warren Buffett acknowledged that women hold tremendous power. He explains that "For most of our history, women – whatever their abilities – have been relegated to the sidelines. Only in recent years have we begun to correct that problem." Buffet insists that he is positive about America's future because women are feeling unleashed and coming into our true power. I agree.

No more waiting for the prince to daddy you into abundance. No one is coming to rescue you. To love you, yes. Take loving care of you, absolutely. Save you, no. Save yourself. Invest your femergetic talents in being a goal digger – a miner of your own strengths – rather than a gold digger. Ideally your partner will step up and be able to bring his or her own worth to the table, but this is not to be depended on.

We all grew up reading fairytales of Prince Charming swooping in to rescue Cinderella. We forget that our men were raised hearing these same fairytales. When they are unable to be that kind of man to us, it terrifies them and leaves them feeling inadequate. What do scared people do? They run.

A woman who knows her worth is abundant in health, friendships, opportunities, and creativity. Your wealth potential is greater than you can ever imagine. Let's do it together. Having a prosperity mindset is greater than lots of zeroes in the bank, although that's part of it too.

We buy into a story that prosperity is about goods; the labels on the clothes we wear, the car we drive, the neighborhood we live in. Nice things are fabulous. We should all consider ourselves worthy of only "the best of the best" as spiritual guru Deepak Chopra says. This means the best that we can acquire without going into debt, because debt is part of a poverty mindset. It also means that your worth is not locked into labels.

What we own owns us. We fear abandonment and then we end up abandoning ourselves by spending time, money, and energy on fad living. A designer could take turds from the toilet and slap an LV on them or a red sole and some of us would salivate. We don't even know what we like anymore. Instead, we know what a commercial, magazine, or celebrity told us we should like. We are literally label whores; whoring ourselves out to jobs we don't like to get more stuff to impress people we don't like.

"Follow your bliss," as Joseph Campbell said. Feeling good and being prosperous is your birthright. You do not need to do a single thing to make yourself worthy of wealth. You deserve to be abundantly full, rich, and happy. As I had to learn, an attitude of lack is not noble. Your poverty doesn't help the world and neither does money hoarding.

Until you are filled with you nothing else will ever fill you up. Not clothes, money, food, or anything. This is how people are rich and miserable. Being rich and miserly or miserable is not abundance.

You don't want money. Money is just paper with cool photos and symbols that we assign meaning to. You want peace of mind, joy, and wondrous experiences. You want to feel safe. You want to feel free and limitless. That's a prosperity mindset.

Bombshell Challenge: Bring your financial secrets to light by communing with others. There are a myriad of social and recovery groups concerning every money situation. Try Underearners Anonymous, Spenders Anonymous, or Debtors Anonymous. Perhaps start a "sou-sou" – a savings club where you pool a few hundred dollars – like my family members. Depending on your situation, maybe joining an investment club or Tiger 21, a support group for multimillionaires, is right for you. For education, begin with AbundanceTapestry.com, LearnVest.com, TheFrugalFeminista.com, or the DailyWorth.com.

Bombshell Explorations: 25 Ways to Call in Your Abundance

1. **Exploit your uniqueness.** What is unique about you in your chosen field? Are you the most caring accountant, the most fun tax attorney, the most bubbly sanitation specialist? Find your uniqueness and exploit it in the most positive sense of the word. If what you bring to the table is a dime a dozen, why should people come to you? How do you add value? My favorite laundry service is called Ladies Who Launder. They bring your clothes back smelling heavenly, folded in boxes with leopard tissue. They charge more because their uniqueness has value. Make it a pleasure to do business with you.

2. **Dress like the woman you want to be.** How does the woman who earns the money you want and lives the lifestyle you seek dress and speak? What is her attitude and outlook on the world?

3. **Look at the people you socialize with.** Your salary, wellness, and lifestyle often reflect the five people you spend the most time with. Of course you shouldn't dump all your friends, but open your circle up to people you can learn from.

4. **Receive everything.** I've said it a million times but it bears repeating: Work on receiving. Accept and allow good things and positive energy to flow.

5. **Acknowledge the wealth that is already around you.** Be vigilant about looking for the blessings, prosperity, and abundance in every facet of your life. If someone buys you dinner, that's abundance. Do you know that there are air mileage millionaires and coupon millionaires? Sure they may seem like fanatics, but these smart cookies are taking advantage of the everyday riches that surround us.

6. **Believe in miracles.** If you think that miracles only happened in Biblical times, think again. Be a miracle counter. Pay attention to the coincidences. Be an ardent noticer of serendipity.

As Albert Einstein said, "There are two ways to live. You can live as if nothing is a miracle or you can live as if everything is a miracle." Miracles happen every day. The miracle is in that "chance" elevator meeting with the investor, the childhood friend you were thinking of and there she suddenly is, and the simple beauty of a sunrise.

7. **Raise your vibration.** Find reasons to feel good and celebrate feeling good. Spend time with Mother Nature. Acknowledge her wealth and abundance.

8. **Change the conversation you have with yourself.** "I am valuable, worthy, and loveable" should be words you say each morning before your feet touch the ground. Instead of asking, "Why me?" ask with exultation, "Why was I chosen for so many riches and good things?" Yes!

9. **Use your gifts to give back.** There is always something to give. Time, caring, food, love, hugs – and money – are all currencies. Tithe monthly to a cause you believe in.

10. **Release your abundance blockers.** Negative people, old clothes, and broken things all equal stagnant, dull, and poor energy. Remember from physics class that an object at rest tends to stay at rest? Be an object in motion. Shed anything that brings you down like a lizard sheds old skin.

11. **Ask for help.** Ask, believe, receive starts with ASK. Ask for assistance if needed and step up and ask for what you want when it comes to financial compensation for your work. Check out my dialogue with media producer and philanthropist Tonya Lewis Lee in the upcoming supplemental e-book *The Sacred Bombshell Dialogues*. Tonya encourages wellness and abundant living on her blog HealthyYouNow.com. Find more about her at SacredBombshell.com.

12. **Visualize.** Use visualization as a tool to accept more prosperity. It turns out that science is proving the woo-woo, hippie dippy folks to be accurate in this area. One technique recommended by Professor Hal Hershfield of NYU Stern School of Business is to visualize our future selves.

Apparently, part of the reason we don't want to save or prepare our bodies for the future is that we see our future self as a stranger rather than a friend and loved one. If you can, get one of those age-progression photos done. Write a detailed bio of yourself in 20 years. Who is "she"? What do you need to do now to get her there? We have to go there in the mind before we go there in the body.

13. **Try pink bubble technique.** Play with visualization pioneer Shakti Gawain's fun pink bubble technique. Along with green, pink is the color of heart energy. Close your eyes, relax, and breathe deeply. See an unbreakable pink bubble that you fill with all of your desires, big and small. When the bubble is nice and full, see yourself throwing it into the air, where it floats away to help bring your dreams into fruition.

14. **Examine your BS.** What were you taught about money? Probably the same things you were taught about playing big or small. Maybe you learned that people with money were "greedy" or selfish. "No one person should rise against the group." "People with money are just lucky." "One person's success can cheat another person out of theirs." "Successful people should step aside and give others a chance." This is all poverty consciousness because the underlying belief is that there is not enough goodness to go around.

15. **Be happy when others succeed.** Every time you find yourself expressing a feeling of contempt, envy, or anger about someone else's riches, catch yourself and send love her way. Work on being genuinely happy for her abundance. You have no idea what someone else's personal struggles are.

16. **Be generous with yourself.** Being stingy reinforces an energy vibration of lack. Are your good plates, fluffiest towels, or best rooms saved for company? Do you ration how much of your favorite candle you'll burn? Love up on yourself and allow yourself the best. Treat yourself like a queen and the world will do the same. For more on this, see my Bombshell Dialogue with "Persian Pop Priestess" Asa on SacredBombshell.com.

17. **Bless your bills.** If you have to spend money in any way, shape, or form, do it with joy. Instead of cursing the money going out of your account, try to see the situation differently. How about understanding that the only reason you have bills is that someone trusted you enough to give you services or goods. That bill is a vote of confidence.

18. **Surround your money with joy.** Every time you put money in your wallet or take it out, have a moneygasm. This can be vocal or in your mind but enjoy the fact that the money is there. Woohoo! Create an AbunDance to go with it – your own high-energy, fun money dance. Listen to Summer Mc-Stravick's *Flowdreaming* podcast on iTunes to learn a joyful technique to get in the flow of abundance.

19. **Become cash-based.** Consumer credit debt steals your money. You are paying extra today for something you enjoyed two years ago. Save your money and buy what you want. Have credit cards for emergencies and to establish a positive credit rating. Make a list of your debts and create a plan for eradicating each one.

20. **Mentally release all debt and money owed to you.** I know, this is a tough one. It doesn't mean that you won't be paid back by people who owe you. You are just releasing the puny, tit-for-tat energy of debt. Release your focus on debt and focus on abundance instead. Freedom, which is what we want from money, begins with freeing others.

21. **Take action.** Don't over-hatch your eggs. That's what I call people who sit on a vision, tweaking and tweaking it until it's perfect. Of course nothing is ever perfect, so they never make the leap into action. Whether it's an invention, a screenplay, or the Big Idea, give birth to it already. Stop sitting on your riches.

22. **Live as if.** Practice how you will feel when you have the prosperity and abundance that you want. Play with that feeling. Get it into your body and your bones. Know that you are worthy and deserving of all things. Are there stores and

places you don't go because you feel too poor, unattractive, or unworthy? Step outside of your money boundaries. Are there things you feel like people from your neighborhood, type, or ethnic background don't do? It's a new day. Plan these excursions as a positive prosperity exercise.

23. **Hire a pro.** Consider hiring a personal finance coach, planner, or adviser like Kara Stevens. See our dialogue at the end of this chapter.

24. **Time is money.** How much is an hour of your time worth? Are the ways you spend your time worth this? Say you make $40 an hour. Are the four hours you spent watching TV last night worth the $160 of your time that you invested? Maybe they are, because leisure is important. Then again, maybe watching other people earn is not how you want to spend your time and money. Make sure that everything you do and everyone you spend time with is worth it.

25. **Develop a practice of gratitude.** Nothing new will come into your life until you appreciate fully what you already have. Remember that cosmically, the future never exists. It is always now. If you plan to be happy or feel rich ultimately, it's time to realize that ultimately will never come. Be grateful now. Ask your Sacred Bombshell Sister to gently let you know when you're being ungrateful for your riches.

Bombshell Dialogue with Kimora Lee Simmons: How to Feel Like You Deserve the Best

Kimora Lee Simmons is a mogul, mom, reality star, and entrepreneur. Recently, Kimora has been making exciting changes. She's saying goodbye to the past and hello to a glorious future with gorgeous children Aoki Lee, Ming Lee, and Kenzo. The life we create for ourselves reflects what we think of ourselves and Kimora obviously thinks well of herself. She could have been easily dismissible as a model who married well but she's clearly a brilliant woman in her own right. Her first husband was business magnate and yogi Russell Simmons, her second was a Hollywood hunk. She was still married to Djimon Hounsou at the time of our conversation. Her current husband is banker Tim Leissner.

Abiola: You are a working mother. You are a wife. You are an entrepreneur and a philanthropist. How do you juggle all of that, Kimora?

Kimora: I try to do everything that's in front of me one thing at a time. I prioritize and multi-task really well. And it's always important to have the support of family and friends around you to help with the kids or the house or whatever. I just try to get it done in that way but so many young people are getting it done in that same way. They have school. They have jobs. They have bills. They have responsibilities. They have kids. So we try to juggle it all and maintain our fabulosity while we do it.

Abiola: You have such a beautiful, multi-cultural family. You represent Africa, African-Americans, Asia, and all the beautiful blends in between. How do you celebrate that?

Kimora: Well, for me and my kids it's about really just expression. Your own self-expression, and enjoying being who you are and what you are. Nowadays, it's so much more accepted to be mixed and anything different. When I was growing up it was [you're] either white or black. I think that now the world is definitely changing and we're becoming a little more cultured and a little more tolerant of one another. I think you celebrate every day, every moment by being who you are, embracing who you are, and loving who you are.

Abiola: Yes, it always comes back to loving who you are. So Kimora, let's talk business!

Kimora: I'm moving on with Kouture and KLS Design Group which is under its umbrella. For example, Hello Kitty and KLS, which are higher-end contemporary lines. To get a great style or great look is not about compromising quality. In the world, people will charge you a lot of money for a lot of things, but you don't really quite know what you're getting or where it was made or where it came from or who was working for it. You don't really know what you're getting when it comes to quality. Even if you paid $500 for a handbag, it could be made of plastic. But you like it or it's fashionable or someone said it was hot at the moment. There are 200 reasons why you want that bag, but don't just think because you paid a lot of money for it that it's about the quality. You can pay a lot of money for something and it can be high-quality, but also, you can get things that are high-quality that don't cost a lot of money.

Abiola: We love that. Now, Kimora, there are a lot of men giving women advice…

Kimora: None of them know what the hell they are talking about! … Who are they giving advice to? Women or men?

Abiola: They are giving women advice so I want to know from you, what are the top Kimora relationship tips?

Kimora: I think one great tip is that you should always love yourself. If you don't love yourself, take care of yourself, cater to yourself and that little inner voice, you will really not be very worthy of being with someone else. Because you won't be the best version of you.

That's in any relationship – with your kids, with your parents, with your lover – always love and take care of yourself and don't feel guilty about taking a little, small moment, spare time, anything, for yourself. Do it for yourself so that you are in a good place to be able to do for others and participate with others.

Number two: it takes a special man to be with a certain kind of woman. I look for someone strong. Whatever it is that you like in a relationship, you should look for that. Don't accept less than what it is that you know that you want. Don't allow someone to be a jerk. Don't allow someone to disrespect you. Listen to the bigger voice in your head telling you that you deserve the best, whatever that is you decide for yourself. It may differ from what I like or what is ideal for me. But the bottom line is to never accept less than what you know you deserve.

You attract what you think you deserve, and I don't really think there's any such thing as being too selective or anything like that. At the same token, I know how to be a very supportive and loving partner. Everybody in different stages and times of the day has their own moment to shine.

Sometimes you're the one shining and sometimes you're the one supporting. I also know how to play my role and my responsibility very well. But at the same time, I don't think that any of my sisters are being too demanding. Let's assume we're all thinking rationally and reasonably, then I would say, "You should not settle for less."

Abiola: Can you leave us with a little Kimora inspiration and fabulosity!

Kimora: A word of advice I would have is to be fabulous. Believe in yourself. Do the best that you can. Live honestly to a higher note. Life is too short.

Bombshell Takeaways:

- Don't be afraid to build a distinctive brand by being unapologetically yourself.

- You attract what you think you deserve, and there's no such thing as being too selective.

- An abundance of love and prosperity are your birthright.

Bombshell Dialogue with Kara Stevens: How to Know Your Worth

Brilliant and beautiful, Kara Stevens is known as The Frugal Feminista. On her much-praised personal finance and lifestyle blog, Kara teaches women to be just as strong about our financial power as our girl power. The hard-working writer, speaker, and coach connects self-worth and net worth, having cleared $40,000 in debt. Unlike other financial freedom gurus, Kara believes that juicy living and financial empowerment are not radical self-love opposites. Kara's belief in the sacredness of sisterhood is evident in all she does. I don't usually identify my coaching clients, but Kara generously made a video singing the praises of the work we did together. It was an honor to be her Bombshell Breakthrough Business Coach. Kara boldly declares that there is an abundant and badass frugal feminist in each of us.

Abiola: What kind of money blog is TheFrugalFeminista.com, Kara?

Kara: There is a branch of finance called behavioral finance, which studies how human emotions and experiences impact spending behaviors and patterns. However, we don't need the fancy name to explain what we do with our money when we are sad, mad, frustrated, or even joyful – just check your closet, garage, wrists, and your neck.

The Frugal Feminista believes that self-awareness, and by extension financial self-awareness, sits at the core of all financial decisions. The more self-aware we are, the better equipped we will be to seek support, create structures, and change behaviors to bring about financial well-being.

Abiola: This is an important conversation because many people have the harmful belief (as I did) that money is somehow negative. People also misquote the Bible and see wealthy people as inherently evil. If you have those beliefs, there's no way that you will hold on to money. Who wants to be evil? (laughs) Now I know that money is not good or bad, it's just energy. In your opinion, is making money anti-spiritual?

Kara: Absolutely not. More money allows you to be more of who you are. If you are generous, thoughtful, and abundantly living and loving with little money, chances are that your generosity and goodness will expand exponentially with a bucket-load of money. On the other hand, if you are stingy, unkind, and thoughtless, having more money will allow you to be that way on a larger scale.

Rejecting money is definitely a "blocking your blessings" move. If you are uncomfortable about being wealthy because you fear being selfish, consider how much good you could bring to the world if you view money as a tool for social change.

Abiola: Why do you feel people are so fearful when it comes to cash and personal finance?

Kara: Personal finance is fraught with fear because we do not openly talk about money. It's cloaked in secrecy, which leads many of us to fill in the gaps with misinformation. On a deeper level, we don't talk about money because it reveals who we are at the core. Humans express our identities, deepest desires, and wants through our purchases. As a result, we often fear judgment and rejection from those that we love when it comes to revealing who we are through our financial priorities.

Abiola: Did you always feel comfortable regarding money, Kara, or was this something you developed?

Kara: My mother always called me "sensible." I was a levelheaded child and a mama's girl, so I emulated some of her money habits – which included a love of saving, wholesale shopping, side hustles, and coin rolling. I have strong sense of financial acumen that waned in college but was restored after a financial rude awakening. I realized that I was messing with my credit by not attending to my student loans and other debts.

Abiola: What a blessing that you learned that lesson much sooner than many of us. What did the rest of your family and culture teach you about money?

Kara: I am first-generation American, meaning that my cultural paradigm and by extension financial influences come from at least three cultures: Antiguan, American, and immigrant. I had the fortune of being surrounded by professionals and business people in my family that illuminated the possibility of entrepreneurship for me.

When I would visit my grandparents in Antigua as a little girl, I would look forward to when my grandfather would come home because he would allow me to help him count the money that he earned from the pharmacy that day. He had a serious briefcase – the kind you saw in *Men in Black* movies. I remember looking at his money so neatly organized and pretty (Eastern Caribbean currency is colorful) and feeling very happy.

To this day, I speak with my favorite uncle, a business owner, about my ideas for taking over the world and he supports me. My brother, who is one of the smartest dudes I know, also works for himself and tells me to quit my job and pursue my passion – with a plan.

Abiola: What a knowledgeable family, Kara!

Kara: Growing up Antiguan in America, I learned about the immigrant hustle. My mother who was a registered nurse sold clothes on the side. There was a strong belief in hard work and saving aggressively. My father left my mother, brother, and me when I was young – so I felt that no matter how much money was saved, there would never be enough.

Money was to be used on necessities and not on frivolous things.

In other words, no name-brand sneakers. The only thing name brand you could get was an Ivy League education!

Abiola: I love that. How do you define an abundance mentality?

Kara: Wow. An abundance mentality is the belief that you are entitled to feel at the center of your world, that goodness and possibility are just as much yours as someone else's. When things are going well, you experience abundance when you align who you are to what you do, creating a sense of peace, inner knowing, and flow. When you have an abundance mentality, you also encourage others to find their sweet spots. You know that you have an abundance mentality when things are not going your way as well. You still have hope, you employ your resourcefulness, and you create inroads to return yourself to alignment.

Abiola: Important point. Your abundance mentality doesn't go away when life ebbs and flows. Money is cited as one of the biggest reasons for divorce. What can a Sacred Bombshell do to safeguard in this area?

Kara: Money isn't "just money" for everyone. Money is a proxy for love, status, power, freedom, and identity. Based on the messages that we internalize from our parents, peers, and media, and based on your gender, money serves to either bolster your femininity and masculinity or to strip you of it. In any relationship where there is a struggle over money, dig a little deeper and listen between the lines. The conversation has more to do with a person protecting their power, status, freedom, femininity, masculinity, or the like.

Conversations where you openly talk about childhood memories around money can help you uncover you and your partner's relationship with money and the value that it carries for each of you.

Abiola: Many women are afraid of the idea of frugality because they think being frugal means having a miserable, austere life.

Kara: I coined the phrase "saving for a sunny day" because all you hear financial pundits talk about is that we need to save for an emergency – as if money is only to be used to rescue and repair. Money is also a tool to fund your wildest and not-so-wildest dreams. Money is a tool that can help you create joy and happiness.

I have used money to achieve some of the things on my [beach] bucket list: running a half marathon in Panama, starting my blog, treating my mother to whatever she wants, giving to causes I believe in, and splurging on spa treatments.

Abiola: That's truly the American dream, Kara. What makes you a bombshell?

Kara: I am a bombshell because I know that I am not perfect but I am trying my best to live with authenticity and purpose. I believe in the power of sisterhood and collaborative energy. There is a lot of room at the top and I am not afraid to share what I have.

Bombshell Takeaways:

- You block your blessings when you reject abundance.
- An abundance mentality doesn't change if your bank account decreases.
- Your sacred self-worth and your net worth are linked.

Secret of Abundance Resources

1. **Creating Affluence** by Deepak Chopra
2. **True Abundance** by Michael Bernard Beckwith (audio)
3. **The Law of Divine Compensation** by Marianne Williamson
4. **A Plentiful Harvest** by Terrie Williams
5. **Money: A Love Story** by Kate Northrup

Abundance Affirmations

1. My generosity multiplies my wealth.
2. Abundance flows every day in surprising and miraculous ways.
3. My investments are flourishing and I am my best investment.
4. I love being paid well for the work I do.
5. I am grateful for the prosperity I experience daily.

Eleven

The Secret of Ubuntu: Community & the Tribe

The Sacred Feminine Law of Ubuntu

The Sacred Bombshell knows that togetherness is the key to the evolution of human beings as a species. Educate a mother and you begin to liberate a village. Diplomatic communication, mutual respect, valuing the team, and process-oriented approaches are the yin feminine energy keys to leadership, community, and the global tribe. Power does not come from a rejection of yang masculine energy leadership but rather from yin and yang partnership. This is sacred self-love.

Historical Bombshell Mentor: Rita Moreno, born 1931

Rita Moreno, born Rosa Dolores Alverio, fully embraces how important she is to her diverse Latin community. The Puerto Rican beauty is one of the rare stars who has won every major Hollywood award. Anita, her *West Side Story* character, was the "strong Hispanic woman" she wanted to become, she says in *Variety*. Rita declared that the birth of her daughter turned her into a lioness. This community leader and civil rights activist still speaks out against sexism, racism, and ageism. She is Rita, hear her roar.

The Ubuntu Declaration

I am a leader and my community is me. Giving my time, knowledge, and energy means that I will leave the world better than I found it. Previously I lived a life of meager generosity, helping only when it was comfortable in order to stroke my own ego. Today I realize a new truth. My giving back is not about me. My treasures are the dominion of my universal source.

The riches bestowed upon me are directly proportional to the riches I share. I give not from duty or the obligation of tithing. I give from my soul. I tithe from my heart to my brothers and sisters because they are me. If I cannot give knowledge I will give coins. If I cannot give coins I will give time. If I cannot give time I will give prayers.

Charity begins at home. I treat myself with benevolence and good will, just as I treat the members of my tribe. With the same energy that I share alms and tithe, I care for my Self.

Previously, I believed in the illusions of lack and limited resources. Today I am clear that there are unlimited resources. The Universe is generous with me and I am generous with her children. I give more than the asker seeks. My tithing is multiplied tenfold as are my blessings. For this I am so grateful.

And so it is.

Mistress of Two Worlds: An Ending and a Beginning

Wow. It's been quite a journey, hasn't it?

If you've read the lessons, utilized the tools, taken the challenges, studied the Bombshell Dialogues, and jumped into your Bombshell Explorations and Playbook Exercises, you've made peace with and slayed many dragons during our time together. You have faced your fears on this self-love quest, some reluctantly and others with blisspower and blissipline. You've challenged long-held beliefs, made decisions about the way you want to live, and you may be looking at things a bit differently.

You've learned that you not only have the answers – you *are* the answer.

Although you have gained many juicy ways to love yourself more, things around you may seem the same. As you look at your old world with self-loving glasses, you may seem different to those around you. This is part of the process.

You will now make choices about what and whom to keep and where to let go. Everyone will not continue this journey with you. That's right. The journey continues. You will do this again and again as you climb ever higher on your own platinum staircase, reaching new levels of consciousness. This is your own r/evolution.

You, my dearest bombshell, are now a mistress of two worlds. Surely, you have mastered your old world with your new ability to see beyond the illusions of lack and small thinking. The wondrous miracle is that with your higher level of thinking you have created a new world. The magical action of choosing to see things differently indeed changes your world. You are the mistress of this new world of your creation.

The sacred feminine energy secrets of Creation, Radical Self-Being, Receptivity, Emotions, Unconditional Self-Devotion, Fullness, Authenticity, Nizhoni, Releasing, Abundance, and Ubuntu give you all you need to click your ruby stilettos and say, "Yes, I was a bombshell all along — and now I know it. I have bombed that shell."

But wait … there's more.

Before you go, I hold one more secret key out to you. Please take it. It is the final secret and it is a tricky one. A central lesson of this book has been that you have the right to be selfish and that your world will only thrive if you take care of yourself first. From that charged up vantage point, I urge you to see further.

The Sacred Feminine Power of Ubuntu

Ubuntu, which I use to mean community, includes giving back, operating with integrity, having compassion, and being focused on solutions rather than problems for the greater good of all involved.

Great-Aunt Irene, who raised my mother, was a practitioner in the Bantu philosophy of Ubuntu even though she may have never heard the word. Auntie's home was known as "The White House." Her way station on the Greater Georgetown Railroad line provided a hot meal and a respite for anyone who wandered in.

When South African journalist Tim Modise asked Nelson Mandela to describe the sensibility of Ubuntu, he said: "In the old days when we were young, a traveler through our country would stop at a village. He didn't have to ask for food or water, once he stops the people give him food at the table." Auntie, as she was known by all, would surely have approved. Mandela went on to clarify, "It does not mean that people should not address themselves. The question therefore is, are you going to do so in order to enable the community around you to be able to improve."

The word "Ubuntu" roughly translated means human kindness and community. It has also come to represent an inclusive, humanist point of view: "I am because we are." This reminds me of the Brazilian expression *é minha cara* or "that's my face" that Issa Rae and I discussed in Chapter 6. Filmmaker Thomas Allen Harris found in his documentary of the same name that the way young Afro-Brazilians pointed out that someone was cool was to say, "That's my face." In other words, "I see myself in you."

I Am Because We Are

"We may never be together in this configuration again but know that we walk with you. That energy that you carry with us from tonight is us, nudging you forward and whispering in your ear."
–Rha Goddess

Like everyone else, there are reunions I don't attend. People who "knew me when" that I no longer see. Family members I run into every few years. Places where I used to wedge my triangular puzzle piece into a square game that I just never fit. Community is more than where you happen to be parked, or as rapper Rakim says, "It ain't where you're from; it's where you're at."

Rha Goddess, whom we dialoged with in Chapter 1, is the tribal leader of a heart-centered community called Move the Crowd, where the mantra is, "True. Paid. Good." This is a community of spirit-led entrepreneurs who have shrugged off the old paradigm of broke artists and activists. At South Oxford Space, a Brooklyn theater, I sat in a room with Rha and key members of her tribe – including authors J. Love Calderon and Meggan Watterson – this past February as Mother Nature raged one of the worst winters we've ever seen.

We discussed our big goals and how to create breakthroughs, much like the system I work through with my coaching clients. We talked about value and worth and making a difference and then Meggan led us in prayer to close the evening. I teared up as the self-described "freelance mystic" said that life would be so much easier if her ministry looked like a recognizable church. I think this sometimes as I pray for my clients before and after every coaching session, and with the ones that request it.

At the beginning of the evening, Anurag Gupta, a handsome and glowing lawyer-turned-yogi/social activist emphasized the value of community as a refuge: the place you plant yourself to thrive. This, I thought, looking around the room at women and men of every race, orientation, style, career, religion, and station – this is my tribe; this is my community. There was no uniform other than our smiles and a need to leave the planet better than we found it – and to be sustained while doing so.

Here, I am not the weirdo I imagine myself to be when I look through the eyes of former classmates and certain extended family members. Here, I am a "squircle" in a room that welcomes all shapes with no puzzle to fit in because fitting in is not on the agenda. I am because they are.

There is no reason for us to feel alone in our present time. If your tribe is Lego-obsessed line dancers, I believe fully that you can connect with "Builders who Boogie" on the world wide web. So seek out your tribe; find your community. Somewhere there is a Facebook page, podcast, meet-up group, or a blog that speaks to you. This is the blessing of our age. You used to only have the tribe you were born into. Now you can have the tribe and family of your own making, wherever two or more are gathered.

For that reason I am creating a new community for us. Go to SacredBombshell.com and introduce yourself!

Girlfriends, Interrupted

"Thank you for not tap dancing on my misery;
even when I wasn't always returning the favor."
—Gabrielle Union

A few years ago I attended the wedding of a Caribbean groom and a Nigerian-American bride. The groom was a lawyer and the bride was a doctor and the ceremony celebrated all of their cultures. The minister admonished us, the celebratory audience, about the lack of community around love.

"As you're all dressed up and present to witness this coming together, you are now partially responsible for this couple's success," he commanded. He went on to say, "Support them because if this doesn't work out you are all required to return here together and explain why."

This was such a holy covenant that it brought me to tears. They were my friends and I was obligated to be the keeper of my brother – and especially my sister. So when the marriage crumbled did I show up anywhere, question the situation, offer my support as the preacher instructed? Nope. Sadly, I was too knee-deep in my own dramas to even notice. Come to think of it, the preacher (my dad) said the same at my own first wedding and no one showed up when that completed itself either.

How would our men treat us if we really walked the talk of sisterhood? What if we adhered to a strict policy of no sister left behind? What kind of difference would it make if we truly had each other's backs? How would our own lives reflect the positivity we put out toward others? What if you celebrated the success of other women rather than reveling in their dramas?

Actor Gabrielle Union has been speaking out courageously about the way women treat other women. At the **ESSENCE** Black Women in Hollywood Awards she boldly proclaimed, "I used to revel in gossip and rumors, and I lived for the negativity inflicted upon my sister actresses or anyone I felt whose shine diminished my own."

Most of us are not Hollywood superstars, but we can all relate to backbiting and backstabbing. Women are taught to hate other women; people of color are taught to hate other people of color. We witness it time and time again, people who are hurt hurting others. It starts on the playgrounds when we try to diminish each other's shine with, "She thinks she's cute!" Then as adults we use the excuse of being "straight up" or "honest" to carelessly brutalize each other. We think, "Well, I don't know her so it's not my fault if her man wants me."

If you have been intimate with a man you knew had someone else at home, you were wounding another woman. If you had a chance to support or promote a qualified woman and you didn't, you were only keeping yourself small. If you saw a bombshell sister going down a heart-rending path and didn't at least ask questions, you were not doing your job. If you know things about a friend's relationship and you don't tell her, you need to look up the definition of friendship. If you participate in lowest common denominator gossip behind the backs of people you claim to care for, you are losing.

We hear women say things like, "That's why I only hang out with men." Perhaps we ourselves feel this way. Like all of you, I have felt deeply betrayed by other women. I have been hurt and disappointed by friends. I have had terrible women bosses. However, the next level lesson is that the other woman is you. If you look at other women and see beauty and positive energy, it's because that's what you are projecting and reflecting. If you look at other women and see hate, jealousy, and scorn, guess what? That's what you are also projecting and reflecting.

What's going on with the woman in the mirror? How are you being judgmental? How have you been hateful, jealous, and scornful? Who might you be betraying right now? Are you the terrible boss? Keeping it real forces me to admit that yes, I have been betrayed but I have also betrayed other women. I have publicly mocked and ridiculed other women for laughs. There are times I could have been a better friend or offered support but I did not. Sometimes it was because I didn't want to. Other times it was because I didn't care, but here's the real deal. Any time someone says, "I don't care," watch out! What she means is, "It hurts too much to care."

If there are unhealed rifts that trigger your primal wounds, communicate. So much can be fixed with a simple conversation.

Bombshell Challenge: Make living amends to a woman you may have wronged. Making amends is more than an apology. Amends is taking an action of restoration to make it right. There is no statute of limitations. If you are no longer able to make it up to her, or it would it would cause her disruption for you to do so, pay it forward. Amends means amending the way you live.

Stand Up, Stand Out, Stand in Love

This is an abundant universe with unlimited resources. You are not in competition for your blessings. Another woman's success in love, money, career, or family does not diminish the chances of yours. Instead, her success shows you what is possible. She is not leaving you behind. She is carving a path. Your gratitude for another sister's well-being creates the climate for your own.

Just as there are designated drivers, I have designated that I will have the courage to speak out and say, "Stop it, what you are saying is unacceptable, racist, sexist, homophobic, unsisterly, or just plain wrong." This means that I will not participate in low energy conversations that stereotype or belittle. I have designated myself to stand for who is not there and say, "This is not something we should be talking about." I am my sister's keeper.

I have not been your only guide on this journey. You have been blessed with the wise woman energy of our Historical Bombshell Mentors Josephine Baker, Tina Turner, Celia Cruz, Marilyn Monroe, Zora Neale Hurston, Pam Grier, Diana Ross, Maya Angelou, Jane Fonda, Elizabeth Taylor, and Rita Moreno. You have received countless gems from the inspiring Bombshell Dialogues – self-love classes with your bombshell sisters.

Be responsible for the love and the energy that you carry forward. If you want a friend, be a friend. If you want love, be loving.

When your life is stagnant, give. Giving is a part of the Ubuntu cycle. Remember that the converse also means learning how to ask for and receive support. These are the bombshell keys to community, friendship, sisterhood, and positive relationships.

Woman, first love thyself. Use the sacred secrets of this book to become the woman you were born to be. It's going to be exciting to witness the miracles in your life over the coming season: mentally, physically, emotionally, and spiritually!

Here is your delicious mandate: I am my sister's keeper and now so are you. You have been given the formerly forbidden secrets of feminine power. Now that you know, you can't pretend that you don't. You are obligated to share these femergetic lessons with your goddess sisters. Let us lift as we climb. "Each one, teach one" was the method employed by slaves to learn to read when it was illegal. No matter your background, I'm talking to you. Let each one, teach one. We are all in this together. I see you full and triumphant.

Rise and shine, my bombshell. Put on your crown. Step into your greatness. You have been initiated into your own power. Self-love looks beauteous on you. Return to this path as often as you need to. I'll be waiting with pleasure, passion, positivity, and play. We'll share a sunlit dance on fresh hibiscus petals. I've prepared a sparkling elixir of pomegranate champagne tea. There's a gold candle on my altar for you. Follow the scent of the rose oil...

You are now a sister of the Sacred Bombshell Club. Yes. We have just begun.

Blessings to you, Sacred Bombshell!

The Bombshell Sutras

1. The Sacred Bombshell knows that her creative femergy is a catalyst.

2. The Sacred Bombshell accepts that there is power in just being, in self-being, in newness.

3. The Sacred Bombshell acknowledges that she deserves to receive the sweetness of life.

4. The Sacred Bombshell gives herself permission to feel and express her feelings.

5. The Sacred Bombshell loves, honors, and cherishes herself unconditionally.

6. The Sacred Bombshell finds her fullness when she dares to stop shrinking.

7. The Sacred Bombshell believes that life loves her authentic uniqueness.

8. The Sacred Bombshell embraces beauty as a spiritual practice.

9. The Sacred Bombshell liberates herself by letting go.

10. The Sacred Bombshell accepts that she is worthy of abundance.

11. The Sacred Bombshell teaches that togetherness is the key to our evolution.

Bombshell Dialogue with Carolyn House Stewart: How to Be a Leader

When I wanted to have a conversation about sisterhood, community, and leadership, I knew that Carolyn House Stewart, International President of Alpha Kappa Alpha, Incorporated, was the one to speak with. AKA, my sorority, has a 106-year-old legacy of serving the global community with initiatives such as healthcare and education. Active members of all ages and backgrounds span the globe. Madame Stewart of Tampa, Florida, is the first lawyer to head the organization.

I interviewed Ms. Stewart for a column but the conversation was too inspiring not to share it with you.

The year I was born, AKA purchased Martin Luther King, Jr.'s birth home and donated it to the Martin Luther King, Jr. Center for Nonviolent Social Change. Coretta Scott King, a member of AKA, was president of the center. Therefore, when I was interested in becoming a Soror (sorority sister), there was only one place for me – the organization that has called women from Eleanor Roosevelt to Maya Angelou "sister."

From other wonderful sororities like the Deltas, Zetas, Sigmas and Lamda Ladies to groups at churches, synagogues, and mosques to organizations like the National Association of Women Business Owners, women gather together to change the world. I saw this firsthand at the Brearley School for girls where I was blessed to receive my middle school and high school education. I was taught that if I wanted to fly, I need only set my mind to do so.

Abiola: Madame Stewart, Alpha Kappa Alpha is a service organization and your successful term of leadership has been about global leadership through timeless service. What does service mean and why does it matter?

Carolyn: Well, we are all members of a global community. If you go back to the basic tenets of the Bible – "render unto the least of them," "love thy neighbor as thyself" — we're in a global community and service means giving of yourself to help someone else to lift. So this whole component of service is really giving of yourself to make the world better, inspiring young people to come up with new ideas for environmental sustainability, doctors for quality of life, scientists for quality of life. Service is basically living up to our existence as a human beings on this earth.

Abiola: Can you please tell us about your social justice and human rights initiative?

Carolyn: The civil rights and social justice initiative relates to human trafficking, it relates to children aging out of foster care, it relates to awareness of domestic violence, and voter empowerment. During the election year, we took over 12,000 people to the polls and registered over 60,000 new voters.

And also, of course, [it includes] equal pay for women. Women have cracked the glass ceiling in some instances, but we're still absent around the boardroom. And women still make 32 cents [on the dollar] less than men. We had a panel on cracking your glass ceiling in Canada. And we're having another one. But this time, instead of having the women who cracked the glass ceiling, we're having the men who control those decisions come to tell us, "What are you doing in your corporation to bring qualified women to the executive level in your community, in your company, and around the board table?"

Abiola: Brilliant! You are a bold and courageous leader and that can seem out of reach for some. How do you cope with feeling nervous, afraid, sad, or when difficult challenges come up?

Carolyn: I pray. I find peace and solace in prayer. I have strong religious convictions. We all have fears because we think, "If I go to pursue this dream, will I make it? Will I fall short?" But I always tell people, first, never be afraid of yourself. Never be afraid to pursue your dreams. Work on your shortcomings because none of us are perfect. We have to find this balance of, "I am not superwoman. I'm just a person that God has given some gifts."

Abiola: Thank you so much for sharing something so personal. What makes you a bombshell, Madame Supreme?

Carolyn: What makes me a bombshell is that I've been given the privilege to lead an organization of outstanding women. And women have accepted this mission of service and the mission possible. That was my theme when I ran for office, a possible mission. And they embraced global leadership through timeless service. That is what makes Alpha Kappa Alpha the bombshell. It is not Carolyn House Stewart.

As women, we have to understand that we have been given certain roles in society that we have accepted. Women are the largest class of wage earners when you look at people in under-developed countries. Women raise the future because we birth children. So the power of the future lies in women. The power of who we're going to be as a nation lies in how we raise our children and how we see ourselves.

But women, if I had to sum it up, we are it. We're the alpha and the omega of our existence as human beings because God gave us the power, the power to give birth.

Bombshell Takeaways:

- The power of the future is in your hands.
- Giving of yourself makes the world better for all of us.
- All missions are possible when we work together.

Secret of Ubuntu Resources

1. ***Goddesses in Everywoman*** by Jean Shinoda Bolen
2. ***Mother-Daughter Wisdom*** by Dr. Christiane Northrup
3. ***My 52 Weeks of Worship*** by Ekpedeme "Pamay" M. Bassey
4. Move the Crowd by Rha Goddess (program)
5. SereneSocial.com, run by Millana Snow and Erin Ralph

Ubuntu Affirmations

1. My world is my mirror.
2. I have a mighty tribe.
3. I surround myself with positive people.
4. It is easy for me to be generous with others and myself.
5. My life is a miraculous journey and we're all in this together.

Bombshell Leadership Agreement

Congratulations! This part of your Big Brave Bombshell Breakthrough journey is coming to an end, but you are just beginning. Taking responsibility for your life means taking ownership of yourself. This is what it means to be a Sacred Bombshell. This is the measure of a woman.

Consider this a binding, sacred agreement. Please read carefully, sign it, make a copy or rip it out, and keep it. You can may choose to add it to your Big Brave Bombshell Bliss Board or put it in your wallet.

I _____ am worthy and deserving of magnificence. I am no longer willing to play small. I now rise and shine.

Previously, I lived in the darkness of blame. I falsely believed that my life just happened to me due to the missteps of others. Today, as a tribal leader, I realize that this was a lie I told myself for false comfort. Never again will I blame chance, the stars, my parents, education, society, or foes for my present situation.

I realize that those I previously blamed did the best they could with what they knew. I cannot control anyone else's behavior but I am always in charge of my response. My past choices led to my present circumstances.

I forgive myself because I was only doing what I knew how to do. Now I will do better. I release all guilt.

I pledge that I will no longer sabotage myself as it is my duty to live my juiciest life. I no longer blame my circumstances, gender, ethnicity, class, geography, health, or other False Evidence Appearing Real. I am greater than earthly obstacles because I was created by the same One who created the sun. I forgive those I falsely blamed and release them.

I am thankful for the lessons of my past missteps as there are no mistakes. I am free. I pay close attention to the coincidences and the lessons that these miracles carry. It is my responsibility to hear the whisper of my Creator, not the Creator's responsibility to shout or translate for me.

I am responsible for my own well-being, moods, emotions, and actions. I cannot control others, nor do I wish to. Blame, guilt, and shame are the daughters of fear. I thank them for attempting to warn me and send them on their way. I am safe and it is safe to be safe. I am warmed and caressed by love.

There are no coincidences. Today I align myself with the stream of miracles. My world is a mirror and it is crystal clear. I attract love, wellness, and prosperity and I give them abundantly. Love in all forms is my birthright.

I love myself unconditionally.

_____

Signature

_____

Date

My Dearest Bombshell,

Thanks so much for reading. So that we can continue this conversation I am building a new site at SacredBombshell.com and a powerful community on Facebook.com/abiolatv. If you want to delve even deeper, find "The Sacred Bombshell Handbook" e-courses on the site – and let's go for it together. There are many interviews that didn't make it into the book. You can find those in an upcoming e-book called *The Sacred Bombshell Dialogues*. You can also find the full dialogues from this book on the site. The *Sacred Bombshell* books will be a series.

To inquire about me speaking at your organization, Skypeing your book club or reading group, or one-on-one coaching, email business@abiolaabrams.com. Let me know what you think, bombshell to bombshell, on Twitter, YouTube, Tumblr, Instagram, Pinterest, Google+, and across the web @abiolatv. My main hub is still AbiolaTV.com. Let the TV stand for transformation and victory!

Remember that you can take some of the wisdom with you with my affirmation cards, self-love journal, and your very own place to do homework – the downloadable Bombshell Playbook. Subscribe on my site and you'll be the first to know of these goodies as soon as they become available.

Passionately yours,

Thanks Giving

I thought that this book took far too long to write, but now I see that it was right on time. To everyone who loved me through this process, I thank you. Thank you for accepting the many times when I needed to be alone with my laptop. Thank you for accepting *me*. I am grateful.

I love the men in my life – like the brilliant one who fathered me, the supportive one who grew up beside me, the first one to call me Auntie – but this one is for the women. Thank you to my mom, the classiest woman I know. Lady Norma, I am grateful for the caring notes and generous hugs. Thank you to my beauty-full faerie artist sister Damali for the teas, guidance, and experimental recipes that always turn out just right. Thank you for being my sounding board, advisors, and best buddies.

Thank you to Miss Kristal Mosley for being the most sacred sister-friend and confidante a bombshell could ever want. Without your company, ICreateTV.com, I wouldn't have been able to capture many of the Bombshell Dialogues here. Thank you to Patranila Jefferson and Shelley Nicole for being my sing-out sister circle for this process. I have 108 beads just for you. PJ, we are living in "ultimately"! Thank you to my entire family: Adana Collins for being my yoga partner and bearer of Lovable Treasures and Michelle and Imani for being the only true divas. I am already in awe of future sacred women like my brother's unborn daughter "Baby Girl Abrams" (Thank you, Tammi) and my "great-niece" Zamaya. Thank you Diana and Ariella for always being hot pink, and Keisha and Mya for being adorable. Thank you Leslie Lewis Sword for being my bridge in this journey although you had no idea!

Thank you Aunt Sylvie for believing in me with your whole heart. Thank you to my greatest grandmothers – Eve and Beryl, Ma and Aunt Tamar, Matilda and Aunt Irene – for your wisdom that I am just beginning to learn. Thank you Aunt Wendy for being you.

Thank you to my "editrix" Alissa McGowan – Senior Editor at Red Pen for Rent (www.redpenforrent.com) – for being a true goddess-send. Your "red pen" is like Wonder Woman's bracelets, able to obliterate what isn't working in a single bound. I never want to write another book without you editing it!

Thanks for giving women a channel to reach me: my editors, Charli "I Love It" Penn-Watkins of ESSENCE.com and Karen "Let's Do It" Hudson with Kweli "Great" Wright of MommyNoire.com; incredible producers Kim Brechka and Joyce Sampson of *The Bill Cunningham Show*. My Passion Posse, Tinzley Bradford, Grear "Yaddie" Turnbull, and Coye LeRocke – thanks for keeping my blog "bombshell hot." Thanks to DeeArah Wright of Freebrook Spaces, Amy McCloskey of Madame X, and Carmen Victorino of Le Femme Suite.

I am grateful for the tireless support of my assistants and transcribers, Head Bombshell Davisha Davis, Elizabeth Amani, Nadine Goggins of Libelle Co., and Debbie Rojonan of DB Transcription Services. #IAmGrateful for Gressene Watson, co-host of my Twitter thankfulness tweetups. Much gratitude for my publicist Dawn Michelle Hardy of Dream Relations PR and Literacy Consulting Agency. Thank you to my sister Cherise Fisher of Scribe's Window for your zephyr-powered wisdom.

I am extremely appreciative of my mentors and big sisters Cheryl Hill, E. Jean Carroll, Vivian Kurutz, Bevy Smith, Lisa Sasevich, and Rha Goddess for being my kick-ass bombshell inspirations; and Carol Martin for sharing "healthy living by holistic methods" with me almost 20 years ago as your "Alive and Wellness" intern.

I am grateful for the blessing of being in service to my coaching clients, who allow me the humbling honor of being a catalyst for your dreams whether we're one-on-one, in groups, or online. You inspire me to be greater. I thank you, my vast and splendiferous family and network of supporters who would need a whole other book for me to mention each of you. Thank you to the women and men interviewed and quoted in this book. Much thanks for the best landlady in the world, Jeanette Fuller. And for my Sacred Bombshell tribe of "coachees," readers, subscribers, viewers, and friends – this is for you.

I salute you with the words of St. Catherine of Siena: "Be who

God meant you to be and you will set the world on fire." Let the Sacred Bombshells say amen!

A Laying On of Hands

My hands are open, palms up. This is my prayer. There is an awakening happening and you are a part of it. You have always known that there is more. You were waiting for the light bulb moment, hoping for the leader. Well, the time has come for you to step into yourself. Take a breath.

You know what it's like to be a scared woman. Now you know how to rearrange the words and become a sacred woman instead. This is my prayer. Sacred Bombshell, this is a calling to rise and shine. You are here at this moment because you are needed.

Let the bombed shell become a Sacred Bombshell. Lift the veil; remove the mask. Show your true face so that we may all be healed together. There is only one story and one lesson. This is a laying on of hands. I see a world where we no longer believe lies about ourselves nor tell them about each other. You are not broken. You are not the weaker sex. Because you are I am. Because I am you are. This is a rebirth and we are one.

There's stuff we know, stuff we don't know, and stuff we don't know that we don't know, but there's yet another category. There's the stuff that we don't know that we do know. Much of our wisdom lives in this category. What do you deny to yourself that you really know? These teachings were always there and always will be. It is we who have forgotten. What forbidden secrets can lift you from your current illusions? Once you remember that you know, you can't pretend you don't.

Some say that these teachings have been hidden. Some say that these teachings have been lost. Others say that these teachings are fantasy. This is not about patriarchy or matriarchy; I urge our divine brothers to share their own sacred stories and secrets. This is about you and your personal power.

When my Kindergarten teacher reminded me to color in the lines, I have a clear memory of asking why. I dare you to join me. Why? Take a breath. You are returning to yourself. Open your eyes and see the divine you. Respect your body as a vessel for magic.

Be unapologetic. You are not sorry. You are a Sacred Bombshell.

Melissa Staiger has given healing polarity therapy – a life-energy laying on of hands practice like reiki or massage – to members of my family and me. An intergenerational art wall stands guard opposite her healing studio. The wall features Melissa's colorful geometric paintings along with those of her mother and grandmother. Melissa is of Cherokee descent. In her guided visualizations, she tells me what I tell my clients: to see myself as large and expansive.

Let the art of your life stand metaphorically with the Great Ones that came before you. Let us be united by our hands rather than divided by our flags and our prayer books. Loving, positive, healing energy is flowing toward you, from you, and through you. Receive it.

In 1972, Shirley Chisolm became the first black woman to run for president. *Ms Magazine* also put out its first regular issue in the month I was born – with Wonder Woman on the cover. Title IX empowered girls to compete equally in sports, Maya Angelou produced her first film *Georgia*, the Equal Employment Opportunity Act was passed, the first Rainbow Gathering took place, Native American activists marched and took over the Bureau of Indian Affairs, and a DC Comics super-villain named Granny Goodness trained the Female Furies.

However, one of the events of my birth year that stands out most is that Japanese soldier Shoichi Yokoi was discovered hiding in the jungles of Guam. He'd been there for 28 years. The war was over but he didn't know it. What wars are you still fighting or hiding from that have ceased? What enemies are you still battling that are only raging in your mind?

This is a laying on of hands. Babies need touch and so do we. On the day I was born, my Aunt Bobsie took my mom to the hospital. Aunt B had to go to work so she left my mom, with me ready to be born. For the next 24 hours, my mom didn't know that the hospital wouldn't allow calls or visitors – not my dad, my aunts, or anyone. So my mom felt abandoned and rejected as she went into labor in a foreign land and bore her first child. I imagine her crying softly, "It's you and me baby girl." I took up those tears but now I let them go. Whose tears and fears must you release?

We are here to evolve. Let's take a collective breath.

Let this book be a source of healing, a source of fun, a source of pleasure. Sing your song, my sister. Dance your dance. Paint your "pain-ting." Roll your boo-tay. Scream your scream and cry your cries just a little bit too loud for everyone else's comfort. Dream your dream and be your own Sacred Bombshell best. Turn a hip and your head while eating too much raw chocolate and wearing too-high heels. Join me in a table dance of a thousand clapping hands. Yes!

Let us not lose our stories, lessons, eccentricities, and histories. There are an infinite number of ways to communicate on platforms never before imagined. Use them all to share your story – again and again until you no longer need it. Let us use these channels to empower each other and embody our best selves.

In certain areas of Guyana, the bride is bathed by her maid of honor the night before the wedding. This is a ritual of sisterhood, respect, and honor that says, "We are in this together." Consider these words as drops in the mighty ocean of knowledge available to us when we share.

Take my hand. Let's go…

Bombshell Dialogue Index

I have interviewed hundreds of people throughout the years. It was important for me to share lessons with you from some of the most uplifting and inspiring women I've met. Here's where to find your phenomenal guest teachers from the featured empowerment dialogues:

Bershan Shaw: Interview took place on January 30, 2014 via phone. Find her at URAWarrior.com.

Viola Davis: Interview took place on June 22, 2012 in New Orleans, Louisiana. Find her at JuVeeProductions.com.

Rha Goddess: Interview took place on March 12, 2014 via phone. Find her at MoveTheCrowd.me.

Gabrielle Bernstein: Interview took place on December 13, 2011 in New York City. Find her at GabbyB.tv.

Donna D'Cruz: Interview took place on March 27, 2013 in New York City. Find her at RasaLiving.com.

Cheryl Richardson: Interview took place on September 13, 2011 via phone. Find her at CherylRichardson.com.

Demetria Lucas: Interview took place on January 14, 2014 via phone. Find her at ABelleInBrooklyn.com.

Christelyn Karazin: Interview took place on February 24, 2014 via phone. Find her at BeyondBlackWhite.com.

Alexyss K. Tylor: Interview took place on December 7, 2013 via phone. Find her at AlexyssKTylor.net.

Kia Granberry: Interview took place on March 3, 2014 via phone. Find her at LiveLoveKia.com.

Tracey Bryant: Interview took place on February 24, 2014 via phone. Find her at HoneyLuvRomance.com.

Issa Rae: Interview took place on October 13, 2014 in Brooklyn, New York. Find her at IssaRae.com.

Essence Revealed: Interview took place on July 18, 2013 via email. Find her at TheEssenceRevealed.com.

Tamar Braxton: Interview took place on December 12, 2012 in New York City. Find her at TamarBraxton.com.

Jackie Collins: Interview took place on September 12, 2011 in New York City. Find her at JackieCollins.com.

Amel Larrieux: Interview took place on August 14, 2013 in New York City. Find her at BlissLife.com.

Sheena LaShay: Interview took place on February 21, 2014 via phone. Find her at SheenaLaShay.com.

Jill Scott: Interview took place on May 17, 2011 via phone. Find her at MissJillScott.com.

Meg Batterson: Interview took place on January 5, 2014 via phone. Find her on LinkedIn.com.

Kimora Lee Simmons: Interview took place on January 24, 2011 via phone. Find her at LifeWithKimora.com.

Kara Stevens: Interview took place on June 13, 2013 via email. Find her at TheFrugalFeminista.com.

Carolyn House Stewart: Interview took place on March 3, 2014 via phone. Find her at AKA1908.com.

Lightning Source UK Ltd.
Milton Keynes UK
UKOW04f2036130115

244443UK00004B/276/P